DEC 1 7 2018

 P9-CJM-589

ROCK -AND- ROLL WOMAN

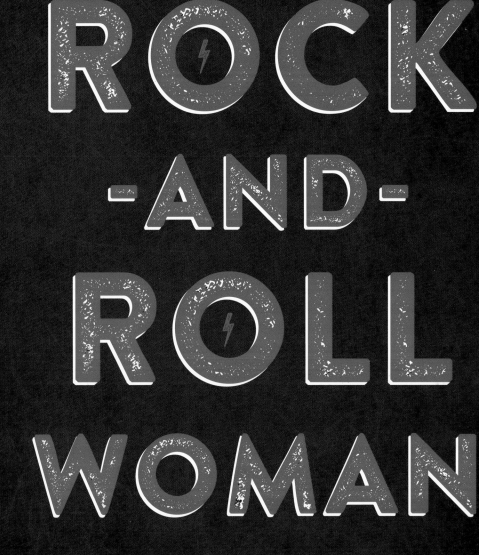

ROCK
-AND-
ROLL
WOMAN

THE 50 FIERCEST FEMALE ROCKE

MEREDITH OCHS

STERLING

STERLING
New York

An Imprint of Sterling Publishing Co., Inc.
1166 Avenue of the Americas
New York, NY 10036

ISBN 978-1-4549-3062-4

Distributed in Canada by Sterling Publishing Co., Inc.
c/o Canadian Manda Group, 664 Annette Street
Toronto, Ontario M6S 2C8, Canada
Distributed in the United Kingdom by GMC Distribution Services
Castle Place, 166 High Street, Lewes, East Sussex BN7 1XU, England
Distributed in Australia by NewSouth Books
45 Beach Street, Coogee, NSW 2034, Australia

For information about custom editions, special sales, and premium and corporate purchases,
please contact Sterling Special Sales at 800-805-5489 or specialsales@sterlingpublishing.com.

Manufactured in China

2 4 6 8 10 9 7 5 3 1

sterlingpublishing.com

Interior design by Shannon Nicole Plunkett
Cover design by Elizabeth Mihaltse Lindy
Photo credits—see page 216.

FOR LAWRENCE,
MY ROCK AND MY ROLL

CONTENTS

INTRODUCTION

Rock 'n' roll is built of fierce women. Blues, jazz, R&B, and country artists who laid its groundwork. Girl groups who projected a flashy, united front. Counterculture singers who protested the establishment. Punk rockers who democratized music-making. Riot grrrls who politicized it. And so many more. They all subverted stereotypes and challenged expectations, whether they set out to or not. Their rebellion is empowering and exponential.

So how does one choose the 50 fiercest? If I covered all the consequential female musicians I wanted to include, I'd still be writing this book, and you wouldn't be holding it.

Every woman on the pages that follow made an original, influential, and indelible mark on music and culture. Some are famous and sold millions of albums. Others are less well-known, their impact much like what's often said of the Velvet Underground: Only a few bought their records, but everyone who did started a band. Each of these women steadfastly carved out a place for herself as an artist. They made it look easy, but, as you'll soon read, it wasn't. Some battled those who told them it couldn't be done. Others fought addiction and abuse. The challenges each faced are inexorably linked with her achievements. Their stories are inspirational, and their art is timeless.

As it was impossible to condense these women's lives and careers into single chapters, I aimed instead to tell you some stories you may not have heard and introduce you to some artists you might not have met. I sought to celebrate the accomplishments of these extraordinary musicians and find the connective threads between them — the common experiences they share as women in music and the effect they've had on one another.

To expand on that, in each chapter you'll see other artists named who either influenced or were influenced by the "fierce 50." I wasn't able to devote more space to them in this book, but they still deserve a place in the canon. You'll also find a selection of "Deep Cuts"—suggested listening beyond the hits you already know (though for the more obscure artists, even their hits qualify).

Rock-and-Roll Woman is written in the spirit of exploration. It's arranged chronologically but can be read randomly; it will still make sense if you open up to any particular musician and see where that takes you. I hope you enjoy spending time with these phenomenal women as much as I did.

PAGE VI: Talent, attitude, and chutzpah comingle in this unofficial gathering of women who rock in London, 1980: [top, L–R] Chrissie Hynde (the Pretenders), Debbie Harry (Blondie), Viv Albertine (the Slits), Siouxsie Sioux; [bottom, L–R] Poly Styrene (X-Ray Spex), Pauline Black (the Selecter). OPPOSITE [L–R]: Joan Jett duets with frequent collaborator Kathleen Hanna in New York, 1994.

SISTER ROSETTA THARPE

BORN: Rosetta Nubin / March 20, 1915 / Cotton Plant, Arkansas   **DIED:** October 9, 1973 / Philadelphia

When the Rock and Roll Hall of Fame announced that the class of 2018 would include Sister Rosetta Tharpe, it had been a staggering eighty years since she made her first record. A one-woman ministry of American music, Tharpe brought gospel into the secular world with an ecstatic voice and canny allusion, and she wielded an electric guitar in consecrated halls. She was sanctified, amplified, and gratified. Tharpe's wild style and rebellious nature influenced the earliest rock 'n' rollers. If Elvis Presley, Chuck Berry, Little Richard, and Jerry Lee Lewis are cornerstones of rock, Tharpe is its foundation.

"Little Rosetta" was still in her single digits when she started performing in church, a tiny phenom with indelible power. Her mother, Katie Bell Nubin, was an evangelist for the Church of God in Christ, a Holiness-Pentecostal denomination that encouraged music as a form of spiritual expression and proselytizing. Founded by Charles Price Jones, credited with writing more than a thousand hymns, and Charles Harrison Mason, a son of former slaves who recognized the need to minister to African Americans moving around the country before World War II, the church created holy-rolling road shows that would give Tharpe her first taste of touring.

With her six-year-old daughter in tow, Katie Nubin left Arkansas for Chicago, part of the Great Migration.

Rosetta soaked up the urban noise of her environs. In the '30s, she became one of the first to adopt a then-new electric guitar, which she played loud enough to cut through any clamor and distorted enough to heavily influence the sound of rock 'n' roll. As a teenager, Rosetta went on a mission with her mother, traveling the country to play black churches and uplift worshipers with her bold voice and stage presence. At nineteen, she married Tommy Thorpe, an imperious Church of God in Christ pastor who'd been part of their evangelical tour, but Sister Rosetta, as she was now called, was indomitable. The marriage didn't last, but she kept his name, with a slight change.

Tharpe moved to New York City with her mother and landed a job singing at the Cotton Club. She found herself embraced by the all-white audience and loved by artists like Duke Ellington and Cab Calloway. Applying the jubilant tone and technique she'd honed in church to sing R&B, jazz, and pop, she became a star, casting her eyes toward the sky in performance as if she were having an epiphany and was taking the crowd along. She was signed to Decca Records in 1938 and recorded the label's first gospel hits, "Rock Me," "That's All," "The Man and I," and "The Lonesome Road." But she also set a template for generations of performers, like Aretha Franklin, Sam Cooke, Dionne Warwick, Whitney Houston, and countless others, for finding success crossing over from gospel to pop and contemporary R&B. Tharpe's shift between the ecumenical world and nightclubs was revolutionary, and

> Tharpe's wild style and rebellious nature influenced the earliest rock 'n' rollers.

> Sister Rosetta, as she was now called, was indomitable.

INFLUENCES: Memphis Minnie, Bessie Smith, Ma Rainey, Jesus Christ

INFLUENCED: All of rock 'n' roll

DEEP CUTS: "The Devil Has Thrown Him Down" / "Strange Things Happening Every Day" / "Ninety-Nine and a Half Won't Do" (with Katie Bell Nubin)

recording songs like "Rock Me," rich in the double-entendre of R&B, was downright sensational. There aren't many photos of her mother during this time, but, in the ones that still exist, Nubin's face mirrors the disapproval of their spiritual community.

This didn't stop Tharpe. She continued to bring gospel into mainstream music and perform electrifying church services. She was just as much at home at a jazz club as she was at Carnegie Hall or leading a choir, singing and reeling off riffs with the ease of a well-worn invocation. Her playing style was emphatic and instinctive, classic blues pentatonic 1-4-5 patterns punctuated by half-note bends and double-note slides up the neck of her Gibson SG. She bopped around the stage in a long skirt, her moves presaging Chuck Berry's "duck walk," Pete Townshend's "windmill arm," and so much more that would become standard in rock performance.

In a custom bus with her name emblazoned on the sides, Tharpe gigged around the country with her band the Rosettes, the Dixie Hummingbirds, and Marie Knight, her duet partner (and some say more); with Knight, she recorded songs like "Up Above My Head" and "Didn't It Rain." She also toured with the Jordanaires, who backed Elvis Presley for years. Traveling in the Jim Crow South, the all-white band would bring food out to the bus when they passed through towns that had only segregated restaurants. Tharpe handled discrimination with grace and street smarts. She had her bus outfitted with sleeper bunks for the regions where few motels accommodated African Americans.

In the late '40s, Tharpe met music promoters Irvin and Izzy Feld, two brothers who'd expanded their chain of

drug stores into record stores and who would later buy the Ringling Brothers Circus. They conceived of a concert that was also a wedding, but the twice-divorced Tharpe would have to find a groom, which she quickly did—Russell Morrison, an industry novice who would unfortunately also become her manager. On July 3, 1951, the two were married at Griffith Stadium in Washington, D.C. The wedding party was a virtual *This Is Your Life* for Tharpe. Marie Knight was the maid of honor, the Rosettes were bridesmaids, and the officiant was Samuel Kelsey, a friend and well-known local Church of God in Christ reverend (and later bishop). Lucky Millinder, the bandleader with whom she'd first signed in New York, was best man. After the ceremony, Tharpe performed in her wedding dress. Her label, Decca, released a "wedding album" of the ceremony and performance, with photos from the event on the cover. It was a publicity stunt worthy of megachurch pioneer Aimee Semple McPherson, but more than 20,000 fans showed up in earnest, dressed in their Sunday best with wedding gifts for the bride, filling the stadium on that hot summer night.

Like many American artists, Tharpe enjoyed even more success and a warm welcome in Europe, where she toured with Muddy Waters, among others. In 1964, she was part of a tour with Sonny Terry & Brownie McGhee, Reverend Gary Davis, and Otis Spann that included the "Blues and Gospel Train" gig in Manchester, England, at the disused Wilbraham Road Station in Whalley Range. The "stage" was just a platform decked out like a rural general store, with rocking chairs, wooden barrels, and even live goats and chickens wandering around. It was a bit farcical to have the urbane Tharpe dropped into such a setting, but the concert was being filmed for British television, and that was the visual context the producer felt was appropriate for American blues. Immediately following a downpour, Tharpe arrived in a horse-drawn carriage. She stepped onto the storm-drenched platform and extemporaneously changed her first song to "Didn't It Rain," much to the rapture of the small audience watching from across the tracks. Young British Invasion musicians had already fallen in love with blues

> Tharpe gave rock 'n' rock its rhythm, its soul, its feel, its power.

records during the first half of the decade, but when this concert was televised, it brought what hipsters in Manchester and London knew to the rest of the UK.

Tharpe continued to perform, even after her health deteriorated from strokes and diabetes. She died in relative anonymity in 1973, which seems incomprehensible for such an influential and hardworking artist. Though "rediscovered" every few years via magazine articles, books, documentaries, tribute recordings, and her own postage stamp in 1998, she didn't even have a grave marker until 2009. Tharpe gave rock 'n' roll its rhythm, its soul, its feel, its power, and even its rebellion. That she is finally in its Hall of Fame is only right.

PAGE 2: Sister Rosetta Tharpe playing with the Lucky Millinder Orchestra, c. 1938.
OPPOSITE: Publicity still, c. 1940. ABOVE: Brownie McGhee and Tharpe on their faux-country stage in Manchester, England, 1964.

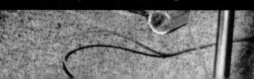

BIG MAMA THORNTON

BORN: Willie Mae Thornton / December 11, 1926 / Ariton, Alabama   **DIED:** July 25, 1984 / Los Angeles

Among the powerhouse blues belters, Willie Mae "Big Mama" Thornton was supreme. She sang, moaned, shouted, and growled, the latter inspiring songwriters Jerry Leiber and Mike Stoller to pen "Hound Dog" especially for her. She wrote her own songs, too, including "Ball and Chain," which Janis Joplin chose to close her chart-topping 1968 album *Cheap Thrills*. A gifted, self-taught multi-instrumentalist, Thornton was a dexterous harmonica player and drummer. She learned by watching musicians, and perhaps that's how she learned to be a bandleader as well, touring nationally with Johnny Otis, the "Godfather of R&B."

In performance, Thornton was unassailable. At around six feet, even taller when she wore a hat, she frequently towered over her male counterparts. She dressed mainly in men's clothing, sometimes accessorizing with sparkly earrings. Thornton projected strength, dignity, and self-possession, dominating whatever stage she was on, whether she was playing with the Muddy Waters Band or a random longhaired pickup band. She'd walk in front of an audience with a wide, knowing smile. Her eyes swept the room, then closed as she channeled her mojo, then opened again. Before launching into a song, she'd share a brief, sometimes dubious, origin story or a reflection on the music of "old times." When she'd open by singing, "I just want to tell everybody aaaaall aboooout it," Thornton expressed the fundamentals of the blues. It could be a way to exorcise misery, but it was also a way to communicate what was going on, first locally, then regionally, and beyond.

Thornton often gave her birthplace as Montgomery, Alabama, perhaps because her hometown of Ariton was so obscure it would require exposition, and she was not big on that. A tiny speck on the map seventy-five miles southeast of Montgomery, Ariton had been incorporated for just two decades when she was born in 1926. Her father was a minister, and though she says she didn't sing much in church, it clearly made a deep impression. She was discovered by Atlanta music promoter Sammy Green at fourteen, the same year her mother died. By some accounts, she won a singing contest, though she told Arhoolie Records' Chris Strachwitz that it was an audition at "a little theater there in the hometown." Thornton spent seven years on the road with Sammy Green's Hot Harlem Review, touring regional theaters with a show that included dancers, comedy, and music.

After the war, Thornton landed in Houston, a city rich in blues, rhythm, jazz, zydeco, country, and rock history. She was there at its musical ascent and became an integral part of its legacy. Thornton performed at local theaters, including the El Dorado Ballroom, a pre-war art deco building on Elgin and Dowling in Houston's Third Ward, a mid-century haven for black-owned businesses. The prestigious venue was owned by Anna and Clarence Dupree, self-made entrepreneurs, philanthropists, and Third Ward pioneers. It was the jewel in a stretch of the neighborhood called "Black Vegas."

> In performance, Thornton was unassailable.

INFLUENCES: Ma Rainey, Memphis Minnie, Victoria Spivey, Bessie Smith, Lowell Fulson, Sippie Wallace, Big Maceo

INFLUENCED: Janis Joplin, Ann Wilson, Shemekia Copeland, Susan Tedeschi, Annie Lennox, Melissa Etheridge

DEEP CUTS: "You Did Me Wrong" / "Down Home Shakedown" / "Willie Mae's Blues"

"The 'rado" hosted national and local acts, and it was here that notorious Houston record man Don Robey found Thornton and signed her to his Peacock Records label. She told Strachwitz that she made Robey wait before she agreed, a nod both to her fortitude and Robey's renowned strong-arm tactics. He'd come to own several more labels, along with a stable of pivotal artists including Thornton cohort Clarence "Gatemouth" Brown, Johnny Ace, and Johnny Otis.

It was via Otis that Thornton met two nineteen-year-old songwriters, Jerry Leiber and Mike Stoller. Though she was just twenty-six at the time, they were awed by her tough demeanor and imposing physical presence. Within hours, they'd written "Hound Dog," which she recorded for Robey's label. The song spent several weeks at number one on the R&B chart. It became a vital conduit between blues and rock when Elvis Presley recorded it three years later, with slightly different lyrics and a vastly different beat. Where Thornton's was corporeal, Presley's was brisk, replacing Thornton's snaky rhythm with a rockabilly slap. Presley's version helped to hurtle him and Leiber and Stoller into rock 'n' roll infamy. Thornton reportedly earned $500 for "Hound Dog."

In the late '50s, Thornton relocated to San Francisco, but it wasn't until well into the '60s that a new generation discovered blues and created a demand for her. She was one of the few female artists to tour Europe with the American Folk Blues Festival, playing with Buddy Guy, John Lee Hooker, and others in 1965. Thornton was on the bill at the 1968 Sky River Rock Fest, near the Skykomish River outside Seattle, along with the Grateful Dead, Carlos Santana, and Richard Pryor. She appeared at the Monterey Jazz Festival in 1966 and 1968, but it was her fan Janis Joplin who'd help kick off the Summer of Love at Monterey in 1967 and introduce Thornton's "Ball and Chain" to the rock world.

Throughout the '60s and '70s, Thornton made records for a number of labels, including Arhoolie and Vanguard, and she continued to perform live at festivals and theaters. By the 1980s, however, her health had deteriorated and she appeared gaunt, the big men's suit hanging off her emaciated frame. She smoked until the end of her life, which came by heart attack at age fifty-seven, though she looked decades older. Her last residence was a Los Angeles boarding house. She is buried in a section of Inglewood Park Cemetery reserved for the poor and shares a grave marker with two unrelated souls.

So much of Thornton's personal life is unknown. In interviews, she was guarded about even fundamentals. Her gender orientation is undetermined, and she doesn't appear to have had close relationships. She may have favored men's clothes for any number of reasons—at her size, they were easier to find, or she was more comfortable in them, or less likely to be hassled on the street if she

Thornton reportedly earned $500 for "Hound Dog."

was thought of as male, or she just liked the way they looked on her.

What is evident is that Thornton was revolutionary and defiantly herself. When asked about her musical influences, she'd name a few but add that she could only sing like herself. Since 2004, her given name has been cited by thousands of aspiring musicians at Willie Mae's Rock Camp for Girls in Brooklyn, New York. But Thornton, like many rock 'n' roll pioneers, remains largely unacknowledged and unrewarded. Her male blues contemporaries are lauded, yet she is overlooked. Her song "Ball and Chain" was essential for Janis Joplin, but Thornton's version is barely known—not the first time a white performer enjoyed mainstream success with her material and style while she walked away with so little. So many of the people who worked with her—Joplin, Buddy Guy, John Lee Hooker, Muddy Waters, Johnny Otis, Leiber & Stoller, and Elvis Presley—are in the Rock and Roll Hall of Fame, while Big Mama Thornton waits.

Thornton was revolutionary.

PAGE 6: Big Mama Thornton lights up the stage, c. 1970. OPPOSITE, TOP: Thornton at The Colonial, October 27, 1969. OPPOSITE, BOTTOM: Thornton's 45 rpm single of "Hound Dog," which launched a career; unfortunately, it was Elvis's. ABOVE: Thornton in 1978, the year her last album, *Mama's Pride*, was released.

WANDA JACKSON

BORN: Wanda Lavonne Jackson / October 20, 1937 / Maud, Oklahoma

Her voice is the fuse that lit the bomb. Bob Dylan called her a "hurricane in lipstick." She sang about love as lunacy, likening hers to a nuclear explosion, and tormenting suitors who mistreated her. Offstage, Wanda Jackson was a petite teenager from a good Okie family who picked up a guitar at six and had a radio show and a record deal by the time she was in high school. But she had ideas about shaking up the music business, and she had the fiery, untamed sound with which to do it. Her girl-growl became a template for future performers from Suzi Quatro to Tanya Tucker and Melissa Etheridge. She started as a country artist and for many years sang gospel exclusively, but Jackson is a rock 'n' roll innovator and legend.

She learned from the King himself. Jackson met Elvis Presley in 1955 when they were both young artists and toured together. He loved the grit in her voice and convinced her that she had the goods to sing this new kind of music that, for many folks, didn't yet have a name. Rock 'n' roll was relatively new, or at least it was to white performers. She and Elvis, along with others such as Johnny Cash, Carl Perkins, and Jerry Lee Lewis, were mixing an unholy concoction of country, western swing, blues, R&B, and gospel, and coming up with rockabilly.

She and Elvis bonded. Both only children, both spiritual and open-minded, they had a lot in common. They were an item, though she has intimated that it never got too intimate, and couldn't have done that anyway,

not with her father on the tour, keeping an eye on his teenage daughter. Her dad liked Presley, though, and let Jackson ride around with him in his big pink Cadillac. Not only did Elvis teach her his music and moves, he gave her a ring, which she wore for a year and still has to this day.

Jackson changed the sound of American roots music, and she also changed the way it was presented. Female country artists were often clad in gingham prairie frocks or Western shirts, long leather skirts, cowgirl hats, and high boots. Jackson, a fan of Elizabeth Taylor and Marilyn Monroe, wanted to bring glamour into her act, dreaming up designs that her seamstress mother turned into stage outfits. She wore snug dresses with rhinestone-dotted spaghetti straps, covered in rows of silky fringe that shimmied when she shook, drop earrings that glittered against her long dark hair, and high heels. It was all fun until she made her debut at the Grand Ole Opry in 1954, then held at the Ryman Auditorium in Nashville, Tennessee. In a dress custom-made for that night, Jackson was told to cover up—women were not allowed to perform bare-shouldered. Her friend Elvis had also shaken up the Opry that year, and management asked that he never return. She put on a jacket, did the gig, and left with no intention of ever playing the Opry again.

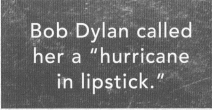

> Bob Dylan called her a "hurricane in lipstick."

> Jackson changed the sound of American roots music.

INFLUENCES: Kitty Wells, Rose Maddox, Elvis Presley, the Collins Kids, Jimmie Rodgers

INFLUENCED: Rosie Flores, the Cramps, Southern Culture on the Skids, Cyndi Lauper, Adele, the White Stripes

DEEP CUTS: "I Gotta Know" / "Tears at the Grand Ole Opry" / "Dust on the Bible"

The Queen of Rockabilly, though, was creating a legacy one song at a time. Signed to Capitol Records at eighteen, she was almost done making her eponymous debut album but needed one more song. Jackson brought in "Let's Have a Party," written by another prolific female music pioneer, composer Jessie Mae Robinson. Elvis sang it in his second film, *Loving You*, and Jackson liked the version done by her fellow Okies, the Collins Kids. It was a hit and became her signature tune, with a frantic rhythm, Jerry Lee Lewis-style rock 'n' roll eighth notes on piano, quarter note rests, and her repeated high-pitched "Woooo!" that rivaled Little Richard's.

Jackson was sassy and suggestive, and she was funny, too. She'd introduce "Hard Headed Woman" as "one of the most beautiful love songs ever written," rip into "Hot Dog! That Made Him Mad," a revved-up tale of revenge through dating a boyfriend's best friend, and blast off with "Fujiyama Mama," an atom-bomb metaphor that somehow was a huge hit in Japan. But her most striking tune is the haunting, proto-psychobilly number

Jackson was sassy and suggestive, and she was funny, too.

"Funnel of Love." Over an undulant backdrop of fuzz guitar and tinges of exotica, Jackson pulls you into the core-shaking, mind-altering effects of being hopelessly besotted.

Jackson wrote songs, and she also recorded many of the same cuts as her rockabilly brethren, but the movement faded by the mid-'60s. Ironically, the genre had a huge impact on the British Invasion bands who repaid the favor by putting a great dent in the careers of their heroes. Jackson went back to singing country music, and in the '70s became a born-again Christian, using her vocation as a ministry with Wendell Goodman, her husband and manager for fifty-five years (until his death in 2017), singing and spreading the gospel. She would not return to rock 'n' roll until it sought her out nearly fifteen years later, when a new generation fell in love with her old sound.

Since the mid-'80s, Jackson has recorded and toured with some of the rock artists she influenced, including Rosie Flores, the Cramps, and Justin Townes Earle, and she was inducted into the Rock and Roll Hall of Fame in 2009. But it was her 2011 collaboration with Jack White that brought her full circle when they performed "Shakin' All Over" together—at the Grand Ole Opry. After nearly six decades, Jackson finally got to rock the temple of country music, wearing whatever she liked.

PAGE 10: Jackson as a glam rockabilly teenager, 1950s.
OPPOSITE: With her backing band, the Party Timers, undated.
ABOVE: Wanda Jackson with one of her signature guitars, undated.

ARETHA FRANKLIN

BORN: Aretha Louise Franklin / March 25, 1942 / Memphis

When Aretha Franklin announced in 2017 that she would no longer perform in concert, she didn't hold a press conference or book a high-profile television appearance. Franklin doesn't do many of those; a notoriously thorny interview, she's known for plying clipped, cagey responses that make even veteran journalists uneasy. Instead, she mentioned it during a phoner with Evrod Cassimy, a local television anchor whose morning show she regularly watched from her home in the Detroit suburb of Bloomfield Hills. Cassimy had interviewed Franklin in the past, and she was sufficiently impressed to invite him to her star-studded seventy-second birthday party in New York City. It made sense that she'd want to give the scoop to someone she was fond of.

Retirement for the Queen of Soul, however, doesn't mean shuffling off to Florida. Franklin would have to take her bus there anyway—her extreme fear of flying has kept her ground-bound since the '80s. She said her plans included opening up a live music club in Detroit, where she would occasionally perform; and continuing to make records. She also scheduled gigs well into 2018, including a headlining spot at the New Orleans Jazz and Heritage Festival, and a show at the New Jersey Performing Arts Center in Newark on her seventy-sixth birthday, though they'd later be cancelled on orders from her doctor.

Franklin continues to fascinate. Her legendary voice is a colossus: deeply rooted in gospel, and versatile enough to purvey R&B, rock, soul, pop, jazz, standards, and more over her six-decade career. Her family was enmeshed in the civil rights movement; between their legacy and the power of her voice, even her relationship songs during the late '60s and early '70s were imbued with social consciousness. Franklin's highly guarded demeanor about her family's complicated history, her own complicated history, and more recently speculation about her health, only adds to the conjecture.

But Franklin also still thrills because when she's on, there's no one better. Her 2014 album, *Aretha Franklin Sings the Great Diva Classics*, was her highest-charting effort since her lite-R&B

> Franklin continues to fascinate.

'80s heyday, when *Who's Zoomin' Who* (1985) powered to number thirteen via the hit "Freeway of Love." *Diva Classics'* lead single, a cover of Adele's "Rollin' in the Deep," made Franklin the first woman to land one hundred songs on *Billboard*'s Hot R&B/Hip-Hop chart. In 2015, she appeared in fine form and fine voice at the Kennedy Center Honors for Carole King. Franklin played piano and sang "(You Make Me Feel Like) A Natural Woman," which King co-wrote especially for her. She stepped to center stage as she hit the song's concluding high notes with complete vocal power and a dramatic "fur drop," letting her full-length mink fall to the floor (a move she learned from her mentor, gospel singer Clara Ward). King freaked out for the full four minutes, the normally cool President Obama wiped a tear from his eye, and the Internet nearly broke. Franklin herself has referred to it as "one of the three or four greatest nights" of her life.

Franklin received her own Kennedy Center honor in 1994. There are few honors she hasn't received, and her

INFLUENCES: Clara Ward, Sister Rosetta Tharpe, Sarah Vaughan, Mahalia Jackson

INFLUENCED: Janis Joplin, Amy Winehouse, Bonnie Raitt, Susan Tedeschi, Annie Lennox, Joss Stone

DEEP CUTS: "Rough Lover" / "Sweetest Smile and the Funkiest Style" / "When the Battle Is Over"

accolades include eighteen Grammys and being the first woman inducted into the Rock and Roll Hall of Fame. She has performed for presidents, Prince, and even the Pope. She inspires a reverence that goes beyond her prodigious talents and delves into her gospel origins. It's in her DNA. Her father, Reverend C. L. Franklin, was a charismatic and renowned minister whose fervent preaching often crossed into singing when he got especially emotive. He was drawn to brilliant, complex people, and Aretha grew up around his circle of friends, including civil rights leader Martin Luther King Jr., jazz piano legend Art Tatum, and crossover soul singer Sam Cooke.

When the Reverend toured the country, he brought Aretha along and had her sing before he took the pulpit. Though her parents separated, and her mother died, before she turned ten, she had two powerful female role models in gospel singers Mahalia Jackson and Clara Ward; both were close with Reverend Franklin, and both encouraged her to perform.

After being scouted by John Hammond, who'd also found Billie Holiday, she had a deal with Columbia Records by the age of eighteen. She gained tremendous experience playing standards with an array of musicians; but after nine albums and not a lot of notoriety, she moved to Atlantic Records in 1967. Signed by Jerry Wexler (who wrangled Carole King and Gerry Goffin to write "(You Make Me Feel Like) A Natural Woman" for her), the plan was to get Franklin closer to her roots. Backed by various Swampers—the venerable R&B session players from Muscle Shoals, Alabama—Franklin's sisters Erma and Carolyn, and others, it marked a period of turbulent creativity that yielded her most enduring work.

Franklin's vocal wallop was a mix of preaching, rebuke, and elation that soared over her gospel-steeped piano, the boggy-bottomed rhythm of the Swampers, and Erma and Carolyn's unconsecrated tabernacle whooping. From the languorous "I Never Loved a Man (the Way That I Love You)," to the tremoloed, funky "Chain of Fools," to the fiercely feminist "Think," to the definitive, demanding version of Otis Redding's "Respect," Franklin's songs played out against the tumultuous sociopolitical backdrop of the late '60s like a soundtrack meant to set things right.

Years later, she'd return to Columbia via Arista Records and enjoy a rock 'n' roll comeback, making cameos in *The Blues Brothers* movies, playing with the Rolling Stones, and collaborating with Eurythmics and George Michael. In 1998 she appeared in the first annual *VH1 Divas Live*, proving that no one could out-diva Franklin, as if that wasn't already known. She remains one of the most spectacular conduits between gospel and rock, between the sacred and the profane.

PAGE 14: Aretha Franklin dominates the stage, undated. ABOVE: Performing in front of the Lincoln Memorial at President Bill Clinton's 1993 inauguration. OPPOSITE: At New York's Radio City Music Hall, 1991.

Franklin's vocal wallop was a mix of preaching, rebuke, and elation.

RONNIE SPECTOR

BORN: Veronica Yvette Bennett / August 10, 1943 / New York City

She made Joey Ramone and Johnny Thunders cry. Ronnie Spector has that effect on people when she sings, because she is absolutely believable. It's her voice, tender and tough, teenaged and classic, a high-heeled strut with a teardrop of its own that makes listeners feel her pleas in "Be My Baby"—rebellious for its time, when men were supposed to do the asking of such things—"Baby I Love You," and many others. Even decades of smoking couldn't obscure Spector's emotive lilt and aching vibrato.

She crafted her own style and sound while still a teenager, but received no credit for her contributions to the records and performances that made her a star. She survived an abusive marriage to legendary producer Phil Spector, who confined her to their house for five years and many years thereafter in court battling over royalties. Almost half a century later, she's the one performing for adoring audiences, and her ex-husband is in prison.

Spector's influence is heard and seen in R&B, neo-soul, pop, garage rock, even punk. She was called the "original bad girl of rock 'n' roll," though she grew up in a strict household. Her mother helped her dress up to go clubbing, but she made Spector graduate from high school before continuing her career with sister Estelle Bennett and cousin Nedra Talley—the Ronettes. It was Ronnie who had the gift of the voice. She knew it at eight years old, thanks to New York City's grand old apartment buildings with lofted ceilings that made a fantastic echo when she sang out loud, strangely prescient of Phil Spector's "Wall of Sound" that would characterize the Ronettes' most celebrated recordings.

The group's distinguishing getup—beehive hairdo, sable eyeliner, slinky dresses—was inspired by the tough girls in their Spanish Harlem neighborhood. Spector wasn't one of them, but she loved the way they looked. It was the streetwise opposite of the way demure girl groups dressed at the time, which made the trio stand out. It also made the teenage Ronettes look older, so they could catch the eye of the doorman at New York's Peppermint Lounge nightclub. They were eventually hired to dance at the club, and within a year became backup singers, and then recording artists.

Meeting Phil Spector and making "Be My Baby" in 1963, however, changed not only the Ronettes' lives but pop music history. That tune is considered not just the apotheosis of Spector's complex, deeply nuanced production style but one of the greatest songs of all time. It inspired the Beatles, and drove Brian Wilson to create his own magnum opus. Co-written by Brill Building songwriters Ellie Greenwich, Jeff Barry, and Spector, it has been covered on dozens of recordings, but none compares with the ardor and longing of the Ronettes' version. The band traveled to the UK, where the Rolling Stones opened for them, and they hung out with the Beatles. Everyone fell in love with Ronnie Spector.

INFLUENCES: Frankie Lymon, Hank Ballard, Ellie Greenwich

INFLUENCED: Debbie Harry, Amy Winehouse, Tina Turner, the Crystals

DEEP CUTS: "Hot Pastrami" (the Ronettes; credited to the Crystals) / "Baby Please Don't Go" (with the E Street Band) / "Darlin'"

Two albums and numerous singles later, her life became hell. Spector refused to let her go on tour with the Beatles, substituting her cousin. The British Invasion's impact on American rock music led to the end of girl groups, who faded in favor of singers like Janis Joplin and Grace Slick. Ronnie Spector endured her husband's jealous rage and other abusive behavior until her mother helped bust her out of their California mansion in 1972. Barefoot and broke, she spent several years drinking off the nightmare, believing her career to be finished.

It wasn't. Spector was still loved. Her 1980 solo debut was produced by pioneering musician Genya Ravan, who'd been in Goldie and the Gingerbreads, one of the first all-female rock bands signed by a major label. She worked with Little Steven Van Zandt, recording "Say Goodbye to Hollywood" (written for her by Billy Joel) with the E Street Band, and sang with Southside Johnny. She lent her iconic "Be My Little Baby" to a *Billboard* Top Five hit, "Take Me Home Tonight," with Eddie Money, and she collaborated with Joey Ramone on *She Talks to Rainbows*. Spector still tours, including her legendary Christmas shows. She published a memoir in 2004, named after her biggest hit, an unflinching, funny, and poignant account of her life and career.

Spector doesn't like to talk about her marriage to the domineering genius whose name she bears, but she will. She's forthright, once calling Kanye West a "dick" in an interview, and chiding young artists for changing their looks too much. She never changed hers and is still instantly recognizable, with her long brown hair, bangs, and red lipstick. Her giant beehive, once consigned to the dustbin of fashion history, was resurrected by Amy Winehouse, who borrowed elements of the Ronettes' girl-group sound to create her twenty-first-century soul music. Spector adored her. She felt honored by Winehouse's tribute. She also saw a troubled soul who reminded her of her younger self. When Winehouse died in 2011, it broke Spector's heart; she recorded the singer's "Back to Black" and donated the proceeds to the Daytop Village drug-addiction treatment center. But Ronnie Spector is a survivor. The resilience is right there in her voice, from "Be My Baby" all the way through the next time you hear her sing.

Ronnie Spector is a survivor.

PAGE 18: Ronnie Spector showcasing her signature beehive hairdo, c. 1968. OPPOSITE: Performing at New York's popular gay bathhouse, Continental Baths, 1974; according to Spector's memoir, *Be My Baby*, "The Baths was one place where I knew I could really cut loose." ABOVE: The Ronettes, c. late 1960s.

TINA TURNER

BORN: Anna Mae Bullock / November 26, 1939 / Nutbush, Tennessee

The voice smolders, growls, and shouts. The dance moves—the ones Mick Jagger famously lifted—are a full-body frenzy that even the synchronized routines she shares with her backup singers can't contain. It starts with her feet, in punishing heels—Christian Louboutin, lit by the fiery flashes of their red soles, and Manolo Blahnik. Advance, retreat, advance, sideways shimmy, Tina Turner churns out and channels energy. It ripples up through her long, eminent legs, convulsing her torso and flailing arms, filling up her face and contorting her lips as she sings. It's similar to the way she describes how the chanting of her Buddhist faith resonates through chakras, considered the seven centers of power in the human body, connecting with the subconscious mind.

Turner's faith carried her through a brutal marriage and musical partnership with Ike Turner and the poverty she lived in when she finally left him. It also gave her conviction in making career choices, like what songs to sing and how to style herself. It led her to sell an estimated 200 million records, embark on top-grossing worldwide tours, and receive numerous honors and awards, including eight Grammys. Her faith also helped her find a more harmonious private life, a three-plus-decade relationship with record executive Erwin Bach, who she married in 2013, the same year she became a citizen of her longtime home of Switzerland.

Long before Turner found Buddhism in the early '70s, she had located an inner strength that sustained her when she felt unloved by her parents or suffered the sting of racism. She grew up in rural Tennessee, outside Memphis, in a town she'd commemorate on 1973's booty-shaking "Nutbush City Limits," and moved to St. Louis as a teenager. Turner struggled with feelings of being "less than" for decades, looking outward for inspiration and aiming to better herself. In high school, observing classmates who dressed well and made good grades, she tried her best at both. She worked as a babysitter for a couple who she saw as kind and loving, emulating the refined moves and manners of her female employer. While "rough" became her singing style, a defining descriptor on and off stage, and the title of her second album, at times she'd express conflicted feelings about it. "I always wanted to make myself a better person, because I was not educated. But that was my dream—to have class. Now it's too late for that," she told *Rolling Stone* in 1986, at the height of her fame. "You can't read a book like my autobiography and say, 'She's classy.' You can say, 'She's a respectable woman,' but you can't say 'classy.'" She acknowledges, though, that without her hardscrabble childhood, she wouldn't have one of her greatest gifts—her voice.

Hearing Turner discuss her class and race consciousness is poignant, but hearing her sing is emboldening. As a solo artist, she's an icon of empowerment with songs like "Better Be Good to Me," "We Don't Need Another Hero (Thunderdome)" (from her starring role as antihero Aunty Entity in *Mad Max Beyond the Thunderdome*), and her biggest hit, "What's Love Got to Do with It?" She's carnal and terrifying as the drug-pushing Acid Queen in the Who's 1975 film *Tommy*. She makes John Fogerty's "Proud Mary" sound semi-autobiographical. Long part of her solo act,

> "Rough" became her singing style.

INFLUENCES: Ruth Brown, Etta James, Big Mama Thornton, Koko Taylor, Big Maybelle

INFLUENCED: Annie Lennox, Janis Joplin, Ann Wilson, Grace Potter, Macy Gray

DEEP CUTS: "Too Hot to Hold" (with Ike Turner) / "Rockin' and Rollin'" / "Bayou Song"

that song dates back to her days in the Ike and Tina Turner Revue; the duo won a Grammy for their version. Turner was still in her teens and going by Anna Mae when she first saw Ike Turner and the Kings of Rhythm perform. Eight years older than her, Ike was already a rock 'n' soul pioneer who'd played guitar and led his band on one of the earliest rock records, "Rocket 88."

Even under the control of Ike, Turner's power as a performer was unbounded. The couple's rocking R&B was vastly influential, especially on British Invasion artists like the Rolling Stones, Rod Stewart, David Bowie, and Eric Clapton. Throughout the '60s, Ike and Tina churned out hits: the soul-shouting pop of "A Fool in Love," the call-and-response duet "It's Gonna Work Out Fine," the fierce funk of "Bold Soul Sister," and "River Deep—Mountain High," the Wall of Sound–soaked UK smash that made producer Phil Spector nearly quit the music business.

Tina found her voice and her name with Ike, but she lost herself in nearly two decades of his violent physical and psychological abuse. After she broke free, Turner thought she was forgotten, but the English musicians who'd loved Ike and Tina helped her relaunch her career. Her 1984 album *Private Dancer* was her solo commercial breakthrough. Though it introduced pop and smooth jazz elements to Turner's raw R&B, she never lost her edge. She saw herself as a rock 'n' roller, kept songs from her rollicking past in her repertoire, and dressed like a rocker in denim, leather, and fishnet stockings.

As wild as Turner appeared on stage, she says everything she did was born of practicality. She wore fishnets because they didn't run, short skirts because she couldn't dance in long ones, and leather because it didn't show sweat or dirt and didn't wrinkle when she traveled, which was all the time. In concert, she sang to the women in the audience, thinking if she won them over first, she'd win the guys, too. Her gargantuan touring stage sets included an enormous robotic arm that swept her out over the crowd; she lithely pranced back and forth on it, bending over the railing to look in the faces of her fans, feeding off their energy. Turner attempted retirement a few times but it didn't stick until 2009, when at age sixty-nine she did her fiftieth-anniversary tour. She continued to record, though, and in 2017 returned to public life to work on and promote *TINA the Musical*, which opened the following year in London.

She wore fishnets because they didn't run, short skirts because she couldn't dance in long ones, and leather because it didn't show sweat or dirt.

PAGE 22: Tina Turner backstage at Jones Beach on Long Island during her 1987 *Break Every Rule* world tour, the largest by attendance (over 4 million) for any female artist. LEFT: Performing, undated. OPPOSITE: Ike and Tina at New York's Waldorf Astoria, 1976.

Turner's power as a performer was unbounded.

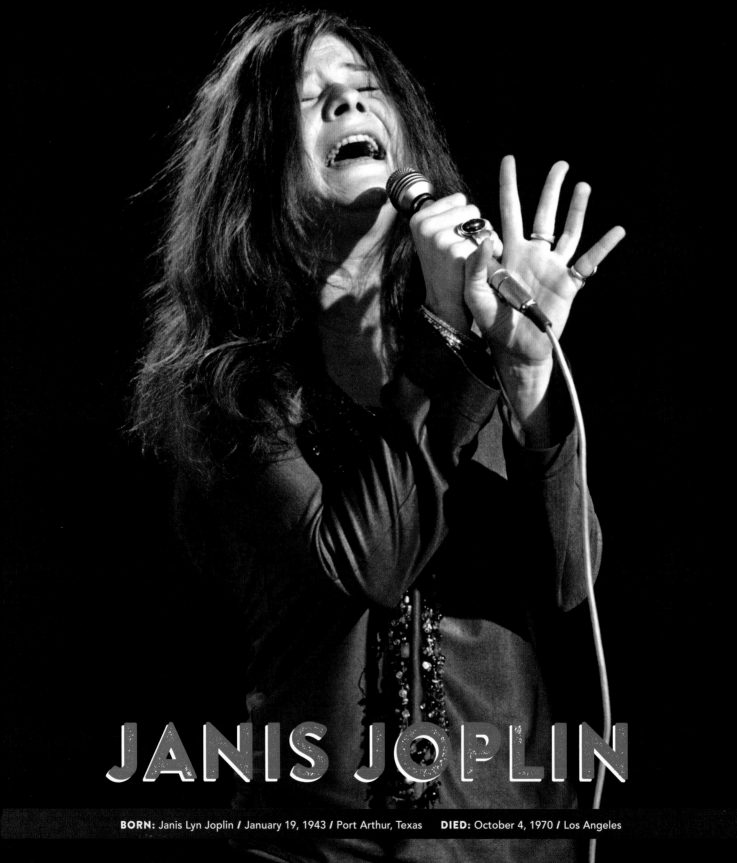

JANIS JOPLIN

BORN: Janis Lyn Joplin / January 19, 1943 / Port Arthur, Texas   **DIED:** October 4, 1970 / Los Angeles

Janis Joplin didn't spiral down toward the end of her life. In 1970, things were on the upswing for the twenty-seven-year-old singer. She had a new band—the muscular, improvisational Full Tilt Boogie—that gave her more creative recoil than her prior backing musicians, the expansive, brass-heavy Kozmic Blues Band. Not long before, Joplin had joined up with the loose-limbed hippie outfit Big Brother and the Holding Company to reinvent herself from autoharp-strumming coffeehouse singer to unfettered, psychedelic blues screamer. It had been a profound evolution in a short time—three albums in three years—as well as performing at the two most significant concerts of the era: the 1967 Monterey Pop Festival and Woodstock in 1969.

Joplin also had a new producer, Paul Rothchild, who'd guided her through the recording of a fourth album, *Pearl*, which was an artistic leap forward for her. He'd helped her voice become a more finely tuned instrument. Singers know where to hide notes in plain sight when they can't quite access them—some push themselves into vibrato, for instance, but Joplin, who smoked and drank, rasped through hers. Now she was finding vocal nuance she didn't know she had and developing techniques for not destroying her voice—techniques that would set her up for a lifelong singing career. A letter to her family in which she expressed hope not to "blow it this time" was obliquely optimistic, but she'd kicked heroin and was looking and sounding healthy.

In her last few weeks, however, dark signposts emerged. She was sinking deeper into alcoholism and had quietly started using drugs again. Her final recordings were the a capella request to God for a "Mercedes Benz," and an offhand birthday message to John Lennon—Dale Evans's "Happy Trails," a farewell song that hints at an afterlife.

In August, she'd gone to her tenth high school reunion in Port Arthur, Texas, somehow expecting a triumphant homecoming from the people who'd tormented her and the place that disavowed itself of her even as her star rose. Instead, it dredged up bad memories for Joplin, which she did her best not to react to. The most the organizers could bring themselves to do for her was present her with a tire for having traveled the longest distance to be there. The gesture of her making the journey from her adopted home in San Francisco was more symbolic than they realized.

Joplin had become a central figure in the counterculture for more than just her remarkable voice—a blistering blues shout that channeled the deepest roots of rock 'n' roll. Rebellious and uncompromising, funny and articulate, she defiantly smashed every expectation and stereotype that women were subjected to. She was loud and uninhibited, proselytizing for social change through sex, drugs, and music. She had numerous relationships and flings with men and women. She rarely wore makeup and dressed garishly, even for the era,

> She was finding vocal nuance she didn't know she had.

INFLUENCES: Bessie Smith, Ma Rainey, Big Mama Thornton, Aretha Franklin, Tina Turner, Koko Taylor

INFLUENCED: Heart, Melissa Etheridge, Susan Tedeschi, Linda Ronstadt, Stevie Nicks, Joss Stone, Courtney Love

DEEP CUTS: "One Night Stand" / "Ego Rock" / "It's a Deal"

far from the conservative Texas oil town as she could get in every way, but returning rich and famous did nothing to heal the psychic wounds that growing up there had left on her. Journalists at the event tossed a barrage of idiotic questions at her, including what she thought made her different from her classmates. "I don't know," she answered glumly. "Why don't you ask them?" Though she was able to deflect some of the experience with her easy humor and crackling cackle, even her oversize, tinted round glasses could not obscure her pain.

Death and legacy were on her mind in those final weeks. She co-paid for a headstone for Bessie Smith, the legendary blues and jazz singer who she loved so madly that she liked to say she was Smith reincarnated (Smith's funeral had been held on October 4, 1937—the same month and day Joplin would die). She also updated her last will and testament on October 1, leaving $2,500 to throw her friends a party, "as a final gesture of appreciation and farewell to such friends and acquaintances."

Three days later, Joplin overdosed on heroin and was found on the floor of room 105 at the Landmark Motor Hotel in Hollywood, between the bed and a nightstand, her face bloodied on her way to the ground, fresh track marks in her arm and clutching $4.50 in her hand (apparently change from the cigarette machine). Her wildly painted Porsche was parked outside. Her friends got their party, at the Lion's Share in San Anselmo. The Grateful Dead played. The invitations read "Drinks are on Pearl"—one of Joplin's nicknames.

Pearl was released posthumously and spent nine weeks at number one on *Billboard*'s Top 200. From the rowdy "Move Over," which Joplin wrote herself, to the heavy soul of Howard Tate's "Get It While You Can," and "Trust Me," which Bobby Womack wrote for her, the album was hailed as her best work. Joplin's recording of

Joplin had become a central figure in the counterculture.

in bellbottoms and kitten heels; flowing, jewel-toned blouses and vests; long strands of beads and an arm full of bangles; colorful feather boas in her hair; velvet, satin, and always something glittering. She was as

"Me and Bobby McGee" became its definitive version and was her first and only number-one song. Penned by fellow Texan and former flame Kris Kristofferson, its rambling country-blues was a soul-soothing visitation of her teen years, when she sang along with Lead Belly records and came to realize that this music was her calling. Unlike her ill-fated return to Port Arthur, Joplin's swansong really brought her home.

Death and legacy were on her mind in those final weeks.

PAGE 26: Janis Joplin preaches, undated. OPPOSITE: Joplin at Woodstock, 1969; she finished her encore with Big Mama Thornton's "Ball 'n' Chain." ABOVE: Partying in London, 1969.

GRACE SLICK

BORN: Grace Barnett Slick / October 30, 1939 / Highland Park, Illinois

Grace Slick didn't demand equality. She behaved as if it was already hers—and it was. In 1966, Slick walked into the job of singer in Jefferson Airplane on equal footing with the guys in the band, bringing two songs with her that would become their first and most enduring hits: "Somebody to Love" and "White Rabbit."

The latter was her own, composed after an LSD trip on a busted piano in the house she shared with her first husband Jerry Slick. The music was inspired by Miles Davis's use of bolero on his 1960 album with Gil Evans, *Sketches of Spain*. The lyrics plundered Lewis Carroll's exercises in literary nonsense—*Alice's Adventures in Wonderland* and *Through the Looking-Glass*. The combination was as vital as the Airplane's recorded version of the song, a seductive rhythm twining beneath the icy timbre of Slick's voice. Written in 1965 as the counterculture simmered, and released as it was igniting in 1967, "White Rabbit" is a rumination on hallucinogenic drugs that summons the listener to experiment, not just with substances but with everything. It underscores the subversive adult subtext of certain children's books, and it's metaphoric of Slick's journey from a patrician Palo Alto, California childhood to the vortex of the psychedelic '60s.

Raised by an investment-banker father and a mother descended from Mayflower Puritans, Slick attended the all-girl Finch College in New York and studied art at the University of Miami before returning to San Francisco and getting married. She found modeling work at I. Magnin, a West Coast luxury department store, where she walked the floor in couture to entice moneyed shoppers into buying the outfits she wore. Drawn to the freedom of an artist's life, she started composing music for a film that her husband Jerry Slick, a film student and later a cinematographer, was working on. After seeing Jefferson Airplane perform in San Francisco at the Matrix, a club co-owned by band founder Marty Balin, the couple started playing music and called themselves the Great Society.

Though quickly signed to a record deal and recording sessions with Sly Stone, both the Great Society and the marriage fell apart. When the Airplane's folky, pig-tailed singer Signe Toly Anderson left to raise a child, the remaining band members invited Slick to join as a co-lead singer with Balin. The job was sometimes divided further when guitarists Paul Kantner and occasionally Jorma Kaukonen took the mic, but Slick's arrival gave the group a tough new dimension. Their first album with her, *Surrealistic Pillow*, was acid-etched folk rock powered by Slick's unyielding vocals. It reached number three on the *Billboard* albums chart, and the two songs she carried over from the Great Society became the Airplane's only Top 10 singles. Along with a flurry of press coverage, including the band on the cover of *Life* magazine, and a few trippy television appearances, the success of the album helped turn the nation's collective head toward

> Slick believed in peace, love, and LSD, but she also believed in art as a means to confront and incite.

INFLUENCES: Odetta, Jefferson Airplane, Grateful Dead, Bessie Smith

INFLUENCED: Grace Potter, Debbie Harry, Courtney Love, P!nk, Linda Perry, Heart, Patti Smith, the Bangles, Karen O

DEEP CUTS: "Greasy Heart" (with Jefferson Airplane) / "Out of Control" (with Jefferson Starship) / "Ballad of the Chrome Nun" (with David Freiberg and Paul Kantner)

San Francisco just as the Summer of Love was about to commence.

Slick believed in peace, love, and LSD, but she also believed in art as a means to confront and incite. She relished her role as an artist and her place in the culture that allowed her to do and say as she pleased. Already forthright, opinionated, and quick-witted, her personality was amplified by drugs and alcohol. Beyond her provocative statements and middle-finger photos, her antics on- and offstage set outrageous rock 'n' roll precedent. She performed in blackface on the Smothers Brothers' television show in 1968, dressed entirely in white except for long black gloves, and gave a raised-fist black-power salute at the end (several months later, a photo of her in that guise appeared on the cover of *Teenset* magazine). In August 1969, she and the Airplane were the first to deploy the word "motherfucker" on national television while singing "We Can Be Together" for Dick Cavett's post-Woodstock episode. The following year, the "Acid Queen" was invited to an actual tea party at the White House given by First Daughter and Finch college alum Tricia Nixon. Slick arrived with a flag-draped Abbie Hoffman and a pocketful of powdered LSD meant to dose someone, perhaps the President (Secret Service turned them away). It was an even more subversive stunt than the pill-addicted, strapped Elvis dropping in on President Nixon a few months later to gift him a gun and collect a Department of Justice badge.

Slick's deep disdain of authority played out repeatedly in her numerous arrests, most of them in conjunction with her love of sports cars and speeding, almost all of them fueled by alcohol. A spectacular crash (from which she emerged relatively unscathed) while street-racing with Kaukonen in 1971 did little to slow her down, although she quit hallucinogens when China, her daughter with Paul Kantner, was born earlier that year. As Jefferson Airplane became Jefferson Starship in the mid-'70s, her creative role receded and her substance abuse

increased. In 1978, it led to her taking a lengthy hiatus from the band after two extremely bad nights on a German tour—a riot erupting when Slick was too sick to sing, followed by a now-legendary World War II–related drunken rant at a Hamburg audience.

She returned to Jefferson Starship during the '80s, a period of explosive success for the group.

Slick survived it all. She made four solo albums and returned to Jefferson Starship during the '80s, a period of explosive success for the group. A decade heavy in electronic sounds, angular fashions, and unabashed commercialism suited the singer who David Crosby had nicknamed the Chrome Nun. Her long hair cropped and swept into an updo, she donned the jarringly bright patterns of the times and sang songs written by pop-crafting professionals. After half the group, including Kantner, left and took the name Jefferson with them, the newly christened Starship reached its commercial apogee and critical low point with "We Built This City," a synthesizer-driven, barbed number-one hit considered so bad that an oral history dedicated to its awfulness has been published. It was followed by "Nothing's Gonna Stop Us Now," the Oscar-nominated theme to the film *Mannequin*, a critically panned box office smash. With the Woodstock generation reaching middle age, former hippies like Jerry Rubin working on Wall Street, and MTV videos driving album sales, Slick got her last hurrah as a rock star and quit performing as the decade ended.

Even at thirty, Slick was already planning her own obsolescence. She frequently reasoned why no rock 'n' roller should continue after fifty, and unlike artists who made similar proclamations, she has stayed true to her word. Rare appearances notwithstanding, such as the 9/11 firemen's benefit where she walked onstage in a burqa, yanking it off to reveal a homemade top with stars and stripes on the front and the words FUCK FEAR on the back, she is primarily a painter. She draws from surrealism, post-expressionism,

> She draws from surrealism, post-expressionism, realism, and whatever else she feels like exploring.

realism, and whatever else she feels like exploring, painting old friends like Jerry Garcia, Janis Joplin, Jimi Hendrix, and sometimes herself, and always white rabbits. Retiring from rock, however, hasn't assuaged Slick at all. In 2017, she sold the rights to "Nothing's Gonna Stop Us Now" to be used in a commercial for Chick-fil-A, known for their stance against marriage equality. She promised to donate all the proceeds to Lambda Legal, an organization dedicated to LGBTQ civil rights, and called on artists to manipulate the system rather than drop out of the fight. Her generation never fully realized its idealism, but Slick continues to live hers.

PAGE 30: Grace Slick as a 1980s pop star. OPPOSITE: With Jefferson Airplane, opening for the Rolling Stones at the disastrous Altamont Speedway concert on December 6, 1969. ABOVE: With Jefferson Airplane in San Francisco, 1968.

FANNY

FORMED: 1969 / Los Angles

Fanny was the first. There were women singers, musicians, and "girl groups" backed by men, but no all-female rock band had released an album on a major label before their 1970 eponymous debut. Their sinewy rock was exultant, psychedelia-kissed, funky, tough, and tender. Their multi-part harmonies had a familial core—sisters June and Jean Millington, who'd been playing together since they were kids in the Philippines—so to say they sounded sisterly is not just a reflection of their era or a feminist statement; it's a fact. And they were exciting, versatile players. Keyboardist Nickey Barclay's barrelhouse boogie swagger could give way at any moment to descending raindrop-like notes or opalescent waves of Hammond organ shimmer. Drummer Alice de Buhr was serious and solid, matching her percussive flourish to the mood of each song, and locking in with bassist Jean Millington's loping groove. June Millington's lyrical lead guitar gave the band a fifth voice, but she could also shred, slide, and play crunching rhythm, her notes sparingly accented with fuzztone or wah-wah pedals.

The roots of Fanny run deep, even beyond 1950s Manila, where the Millington sisters grew up, the daughters of a US Navy officer dad and a Filipina mom. Their paternal grandmother, Marjorie Lansing Porter, was a journalist and songcatcher who'd spent decades traveling around the Adirondack region of northern New York and Vermont, interviewing locals about their family histories and recording songs handed down through generations on rudimentary equipment. A friend of folksinger/activist Pete Seeger, Porter gave him the material that became his *Champlain Valley Songs* album. Seeger remembered her fondly as "an early women's libber" who once told him "Everything I need a man for, I can pay him to do."

Jean and June wouldn't learn this until years later. They grew up mastering folk and pop songs on ukulele, and moved to guitar shortly before the family moved to Sacramento, California in 1961. It was a culture shock, far more lax and loose than what they were accustomed to, and they felt like outsiders. Part of the impetus to play music was to make friends. The other part was the sheer excitement of discovering Motown and British Invasion bands on *The Ed Sullivan Show* and *Hootenanny*, and hearing singles on the radio. Bands like the Shirelles and the Chiffons had a huge impact on them, according to June Millington. "They sang out as if their lives depended on it," she says. "They didn't appear shy. That was so important to us, who desperately needed role models—which they most certainly were. There simply wasn't anyone else. We never saw women playing instruments. Not one, ever." By 1965, they'd formed their first band, the Svelts; the name came from their younger brother, who'd learned the word at school, and it sounded alluring to them. Still in high school, the Millingtons were mastering not just the rock but also the roll—how to book gigs, buy and work a PA, and haul gear from venue

> Part of the impetus to play music was to make friends.

INFLUENCES: The Supremes, Sister Rosetta Tharpe, Cream, Staples Singers

INFLUENCED: Indigo Girls, the Runaways, the Bangles, Jill Sobule, Bonnie Raitt, Birtha

DEEP CUTS: "Soul Child" / "Place in the Country" / "Walk the Earth" (with Fanny Walked the Earth)

to venue. They traveled the West Coast in a converted bus, merging with another all-girl band, Wild Honey. By the time they landed in Los Angeles in 1969, they were polished pros, ready for their shot at fame.

And they got it, discovered playing an unsigned band night at the Troubadour. They were signed to Warner/Reprise via producer Richard Perry (Carly Simon, Ringo Starr), who'd shepherd them through three albums—*Fanny*, *Charity Ball*, and *Fanny Hill* (named after their house, not the film or the early British porn novel)—and hire them as session players on Barbra Streisand's album *Barbra Joan Streisand* in 1971. They became a songwriting force; even the

> They toured the world with major rock acts like Jethro Tull, Slade, and Humble Pie.

couple of well-chosen covers on each album, such as Cream's "Badge," the Beatles' "Hey Bulldog," and Buffalo Springfield's "Special Care," blended seamlessly with their originals. In late 1971, they headed to Apple Studios in London to work with Beatles engineer Geoff Emerick and emerged with *Fanny Hill*, their sound expanded with elements of baroque pop, glam rock, horn sections, and steel guitar. They performed on *The Tonight Show*, *The Sonny & Cher Show*, *The Midnight Special*, and others. They toured the world with major rock acts like Jethro Tull, Slade, and Humble Pie, bringing with them Leslie Ann Jones, the pioneering female sound engineer who'd go on to win multiple Grammys and other honors, as their sound mixer/road manager.

For their fourth album, they put themselves in the hands of producer Todd Rundgren, whose sonic stamp resonates throughout *Mother's Pride*. Amid the interplanetary synth blips and bowed backing vocal "aaaaaahs" is

PAGE 34: Fanny in London, 1973. ABOVE: Fanny on tour in 1972; *Mother's Pride* was the name of their fourth album. OPPOSITE: Fanny on stage, undated.

continued to work in music. June Millington, who loved to jam above all else, played R&B, jazz, funk, and rock with numerous artists including former members of Goldie and the Gingerbreads, a fellow early all-female band. She recorded and toured with Cris Williamson, playing on her feminist landmark *The Changer and the Changed*, and becoming involved in the women's music movement. Millington also established the Institute for the Musical Arts with partner Ann Hackler, a rock retreat for girls and women. Set on twenty-five acres in western Massachusetts, the IMA teaches everything from how to run a soundboard to how to tune out negative messages that stop women from pursuing music.

the Beatles-y "I'm Satisfied," used for a tea advertisement in the UK, complete with footage of the bandmembers performing and sipping tea. But it also contained June Millington's lamenting "Long Road Home," which all but announced her departure from the group, tired of the image-making side of the business and hungry to explore a spiritual path. Alice de Buhr soon followed. Fanny brought in their former drummer/singer Brie Howard and former Pleasure Seekers guitarist Patti Quatro, made one more album as a glammed-up version of themselves, and scored their highest charting hit when "Butter Boy" went to number 29. But the band was over shortly thereafter.

It would be decades before Fanny even began to be recognized as trailblazers, but most of the band

> It would be decades before Fanny even began to be recognized as trailblazers.

In 2011, June and Jean released *Play Like a Girl*, and in 2018 they regrouped as Fanny Walked the Earth with an album of the same name. This time, some of the women they inspired joined in, including Cherie Currie (the Runaways), Susanna Hoffs and Vicki and Debbi Peterson (the Bangles), Kathy Valentine (the Go-Go's), Genya Ravan (Goldie herself of Goldie and the Gingerbreads), and their old bandmate Patti Quatro. The songs are new, but the sounds and sense of joy are the same. No one can make up for the lost decades, but Fanny is now forever part of the rock 'n' roll canon.

CAROLE KING

At four, she was a literal wunderkind with perfect pitch and piano prowess, so smart and advanced that her parents enrolled her in school early and then had her skip a grade. By fifteen, she was riding the subway from her home in Brooklyn to Manhattan, pitching her songs to titans of the music industry. Before she turned twenty, Carole King had a publishing deal, a marriage, and a baby, and she'd co-written a number-one hit record—the first of many.

King's early career was enough to make her a legend, a teenaged pioneer who wanted to be a songwriter, not a star, in a completely male-dominated industry at the dawn of the '60s. Her work with husband/lyricist Gerry Goffin bridged Tin Pan Alley with rock 'n' roll and postwar morality with the sexual revolution. Their vast catalog was so influential that the Beatles studied it.

But that was just the beginning for King. She left the philandering Goffin in 1968 and moved across the country with her two young daughters. Falling in with singer/songwriters in the musically fertile Laurel Canyon, she found encouragement to build a solo career and in 1971 recorded *Tapestry*, one of the best-selling albums of the twentieth century. Once again, King articulated profound cultural shifts, from the not-so-subtle misogyny of hippie culture to the women's movement, from the fracturing family unit to a reevaluation of relationships and self-actualization, from clustered suburbs and increasingly violent cities to a desire to get back to nature. She created a language of independence and self-fulfillment, particularly for women, and she lived it, marrying and divorcing three more times (and having two more kids), with music being her life's constant.

Growing up in a loving and supportive Jewish family, King was surrounded by music. Her pianist mother took her to Broadway musicals, not far from the building at 1650 Broadway where she and Goffin would write enduring pop hits, and near the Stephen Sondheim Theatre where decades later the Tony-winning jukebox musical *Beautiful* would chronicle her life and work. From grade school until she enrolled in Queens College at sixteen, being two years younger than her classmates made King feel isolated, and playing piano was her safe haven. She also fell in love with rock 'n' roll via the man often credited with coining the term—legendary deejay and promoter Alan Freed, who tapped into his young, white audience's love of blues and R&B.

King developed a style of sweeping melodies, pop hooks, and dynamic rock 'n' roll piano riffs that powered the duo's collaboration. Goffin wrote the words, articulating respite from urban chaos in "Up on the Roof" for the Drifters, female confidence in "One Fine Day" for the Chiffons, and love, lust, and uncertainty in "Will You Love Me Tomorrow," which made the Shirelles the first black girl group to have a number-one song. He also wrote the lyrics to "(You Make Me Feel Like) A Natural Woman" for Aretha Franklin, who made it a classic. But King's spacious, soulful piano arrangements were a harbinger of what was next for her.

> She created a language of independence and self-fulfillment.

INFLUENCES: Ruth Brown, Joni Mitchell, Dinah Washington, Patti Page

INFLUENCED: Sheryl Crow, Rickie Lee Jones, Laura Nyro, John Lennon, the Bangles, Amy Winehouse

DEEP CUTS: "Pleasant Valley Sunday" / "There's a Space Between Us" / "Welcome Home"

PAGE 38: Carole King at the piano, c. 1970. LEFT: King performing at London's Hammersmith Odeon, 1973. BELOW: At New York's Beacon Theater, 1989. OPPOSITE: King's 1971 masterpiece, *Tapestry*, sold more than 10 million copies in the US.

With her marriage to Goffin falling apart, King found she had more to say, and friends in her new Los Angeles environs helped her say it. She collaborated with lyricist Toni Stern on "It's Too Late." Melancholy, considerate, and unrelenting all at once, it's one of the great breakup songs of all time. James Taylor encouraged her to step out from behind the scenes and perform; King gave him "You've Got a Friend," which became one of his defining songs, before releasing it on *Tapestry*. Her second solo album, it set a new singer/songwriter standard, winning four Grammys and remaining on the charts for several years. On it, King found her voice, earth-toned, soulful, weary but optimistic, from the rain-misted blue mood of "Far Away," to the sensual abandon of "I Feel the Earth Move," to the three-quarter-time new age dream of "Way Over Yonder," to stripped down Goffin/King standards recast as her own. As the '60s came to a turbulent end, King's gentle, sophisticated pop offered a sort of wistful comfort in which future generations would continue to take refuge, the sparse arrangements leaving room for every listener to fill in their own story.

As the '70s progressed, King's albums reflected the decade's "back-to-the-land" movement and growing environmental consciousness—1970 saw both the first Earth Day and the creation of the Environmental Protection Agency. At odds with the superficiality of life in Los Angeles, King made a lasting home base in rural Idaho.

King's gentle, sophisticated pop offered a sort of wistful comfort.

A New Yorker turned mountain mama, she learned to farm and live, for a time, without electricity, homeschooling her youngest child. The lifestyle led King to environmental activism, lobbying to protect the Northern Rockies and advocating for clean energy. In the '80s, she bought the 128-acre Robinson Bar Ranch in Stanley, Idaho, rehabbing the century-old house into a green space with a home studio, and moving in the Steinway that appeared on the cover of her album *Music*.

In the decades that followed, King worked with Mariah Carey and Celine Dion, toured with Mary J. Blige and the Black Eyed Peas' Fergie, and reunited with her old friend James Taylor in 2010 for their Troubadour Reunion Tour, named for the Sunset Boulevard club where they had played together in the early '70s. She won the Kennedy Center Honor in 2012, and the following year became the first woman awarded with the Gershwin Prize for Popular Song by the Library of Congress, joining Paul Simon, a colleague and friend from her New York songwriting days, and Paul McCartney, who was influenced by her early work. And in January 2017, King participated in the Women's March in her adopted hometown of Stanley, Idaho alongside twenty-nine others—about half its residents—carrying a small handwritten sign with the title of her 1983 song "One Small Voice." A week later, she released a free re-recorded version of the song, which honors the power of protest.

MARIANNE FAITHFULL

BORN: Marianne Evelyn Gabriel Faithfull **/** December 29, 1946 **/** London

By the early '70s, Marianne Faithfull had gone from teenaged songbird, film and stage actor, and half of rock 'n' roll's most glamorous couple to peripatetic junkie in less than two years. But during the decade between her lilting covers of contemporary pop, traditional English ballads, and folk songs, and her propulsive 1979 post-punk classic "Broken English," Faithfull never completely dropped out of sight. She remained irresistible tabloid fodder.

Faithfull was a former ingénue whose performance of "As Tears Go By," written expressly for her by Rolling Stones Mick Jagger and Keith Richards, made her a mid-'60s pop idol. She recorded several more albums and singles, playing off her fascinating, and often contradictory, personas: The sad-eyed, delicate-featured descendant of Austrian royalty, whose great-great uncle had penned the nineteenth-century S&M novella *Venus in Furs*. The daughter of an academic-turned-British-wartime-spy-turned-commune-dweller. The erudite, cultured former partner and muse of Jagger who attempted suicide and suffered a miscarriage during their turbulent romance. The convent-raised inno-cent who became *The Girl on the Motorcycle* (a film she starred in) and "The Girl in the Fur Rug" (a moniker she earned for her part in an infa-mous 1967 drug bust with Jagger and Richards), whose debauched life in rock had cost her everything,

> She remained irresistible tabloid fodder.

> The lost gem of her "lost" years wouldn't be uncovered until 1985.

including custody of her young son Nicholas (though they'd reunite in later years) with first husband John Dunbar. Through the '70s, she was the subject of "The Curse of Being Marianne"–type articles in England and the US, and posed for famous photographers, including Robert Mapplethorpe.

She also worked, playing the titular apparition in the 1974 film *Ghost Story* and acting in theater. She duet-ted with David Bowie in 1973 on his *1980 Floor Show* (pun intended) television project for *The Midnight Special*. It was his last-ever perfor-mance as Ziggy Stardust, and he cast Faithfull as a nun in full habit (multiple puns intended), with an allegedly body-revealing open back. She even made a country album in 1976, *Dreaming My Dreams*, a strange rendering of songs by Waylon Jennings, Jessi Colter, and other twang luminaries, her vocal warbling atop treacly string orchestration.

But the lost gem of her "lost" years wouldn't be uncov-ered until 1985, after her '79 comeback, and on the cusp of major rehab at the Hazelden Clinic in Minnesota. It was 1971, the lowest of low points for Faithfull, when producer Mike Leander pulled her into a studio to record *Masques*, later released as *Rich Kid Blues*. A collection of covers, they seemed handpicked to tell her story—her tumble from the stars to the streets in Phil Ochs's "Chords of Fame" and Bob Dylan's "It's All Over

INFLUENCES: Lotte Lenya, Marlene Dietrich, Edith Piaf

INFLUENCED: Courtney Love, PJ Harvey, Ute Lemper, Lady Gaga

DEEP CUTS: "That Was the Day (Coke Came to Nashville)" / "Witches' Song" / "Madame George"

Now Baby Blue," her sidewinding life on Sandy Denny's "Crazy Lady Blues," even "Corrina, Corrina," the name she'd chosen for her baby with Jagger, the one she'd lost seven months along. The music is muted, elegiac, and gray as a London sky, gently rambling British folk rock like that of Tim Hardin (whose "Southern Butterfly" is also on the album) or Nick Drake.

Given the devastating fallout of her breakup with Jagger, it would be cruel to call *Masques* Faithfull's "Stones" album, but it's redolent of the acoustic and steel guitars that color early-'70s Stones. "Baby Blue" in particular evokes "Dead Flowers" (with a bit of Marc Bolan electric power chords), and the Stones released "Sister Morphine," written by Faithfull and Jagger, on *Sticky Fingers* that year as well. Totally over as a couple, they were still tethered through music.

The most remarkable element of *Masques*, however, is Faithfull's voice, a mile marker mid-descent from airy and aloof to the savaged, macabre croak that would emerge on *Broken English*, her future explorations of German cabaret, and numerous other songs that she'd dramatically interpret. There's bleak beauty in the sound of Faithfull barely keeping it together in the studio as she recorded *Masques*, tremulously sliding off notes, trying to steady herself as she sings. The result is haunting, like capturing a living ghost caught between worlds, which she was at the time.

There's a harrowing sense of loneliness that runs through all of Faithfull's work. It's in her voice on "As Tears Go By," in her own compositions like

The result is haunting, like capturing a living ghost caught between worlds, which she was at the time.

"Broken English" and "Vagabond Ways," and in the covers that she crawls inside and inhabits, like "The Ballad of Lucy Jordan," Shel Silverstein's tragic bourgeois heroine, and "Why'd Ya Do It?," her dramatic reading of the Heathcote Williams poem, a violent, graphic confrontation of an unfaithful lover over a cacophonous backdrop. As a singer, she remains a great actor, though she periodically returns to the stage and screen as well if the role is to her liking. Highly prolific since her Hazelden stint, she's become a sought-after collaborator by a new generation of songwriters, including Beck, Nick Cave, and PJ Harvey.

Faithfull is often called a survivor, and indeed she has put herself through brutal physical and emotional paces. But she's just as much a survivor of the double standard that put a dent in her work and her life. The Stones emerged from drug busts as outlaw rock heroes, while Faithfull's image was tarnished, her career options narrowed, and she was subjected to piles of hate mail and threats that suggested she leave the country. Her story underscores the bogus side of the 1960s' sexual revolution, in which men were freed up to indulge their whims, while women were more openly pressured to decide which of only two options they were going to be: Madonna or whore. There's also the ego-bruising that some partners of famous women experience and can't tolerate; some of Faithfull's former lovers displayed theirs through physical violence, emotional abuse, or abandonment. After a lifetime of that, a pang of loneliness seems a small price to pay for independence.

Faithfull is often called a survivor.

PAGE 42: Marianne Faithfull at Heathrow Airport, en route to an Italian pop festival, 1967. OPPOSITE: Faithfull in her legendary performance at New York's underground mecca the Mudd Club in 1980. ABOVE: In San Francisco, 1990.

SUZI QUATRO

BORN: Susan Kay Quatrocchio / June 3, 1950 / Detroit

A five-foot dynamo brandishing a bass that looked almost as big as her, Suzi Quatro wanted only to be a musician, not a "girl" musician. Entrenched among '70s glam-rocking men who wore glitter and heels, she cultivated an almost gender-neutral look in leather jumpsuits, very little makeup, and a shag haircut. She was an early purveyor of gravelly garage rock, yet she hit the US Top 10 with a soft-rock ballad, and starred in a family-oriented prime time TV comedy. Her steely image belies her love and study of classical music, as well as her starring roles in London theater productions of *Annie Get Your Gun*, and a play she co-wrote about actress Tallulah Bankhead. Quatro is also a high school dropout with an honorary doctorate from Cambridge, which she received in 2016. Raised just outside Detroit in Grosse Pointe, Michigan in a big Catholic family, she chose to spend her adult life in England, most of it in a proper countryside manor. "I'm a lot of different people all in one," she said in an interview at her Essex home in 1996. "It's hard to pin me down."

Fans who bought the single of "Stumblin' In," her 1978 pop duet with Smokie's Chris Norman, might never have known that she was in a raucous all-girl '60s band called the Pleasure Seekers. Viewers of the '70s hit TV show *Happy Days* who fell in love with her as Leather Tuscadero might have wondered why Quatro disappeared, not realizing that she was living overseas, cranking out records, touring the world, working in musical theater, and becoming a radio personality with her own classic rock show on BBC 2 called *Rockin' with Suzi Q.* and, later on, *Quatrophonic.*

The Pleasure Seekers, the group she formed at fourteen, has long enjoyed a cult following among deejays and garage-rock aficionados. Their 1965 song "What a Way to Die" was a rudimentary, unruly proclamation of the joys of cheap beer and how it's better than sex, sung by Quatro in an irredeemable teenage sneer. Although the song appeared on a mysterious, unlicensed compilation in 1983, the original 45 went out of print and became highly prized among record nerds; in 2001, it was reissued by Norton Records. Just knowing about it was a mark of cool.

The other founding band members—her sister Patti (sister Arlene would later join), sisters Nancy and Marylou Ball, and Diane Baker—were first to claim their instruments. Quatro was left with the bass, but she went full-immersion. She'd studied classical piano and used that as a blueprint to teach herself. As a child, she'd wanted to be a beatnik and had taken up bongos, so she had a grasp of the four-stringed instrument's percussive nature and the way it connects the drums to the rest of the music. Quatro's father, a General Motors engineer by day and musician by night, gave her a 1957 sunburst Fender Precision, a model prized by many bassists. John Entwistle of the Who once tried to buy it from her, but it remains in her possession.

Mercury Records signed the Pleasure Seekers in 1968, putting them among the first all-girl rock bands on

> She was an early purveyor of gravelly garage rock, yet she hit the US Top 10 with a soft-rock ballad.

INFLUENCES: Elvis Presley, the Sweet, Slade

INFLUENCED: Joan Jett, Chrissie Hynde, the Runaways, Tina Weymouth, Gaye Advert, KT Tunstall

DEEP CUTS: "Lipstick" / "Little Bitch Blue" / "Glycerine Queen"

at a solo career in the UK by British producer Mickie Most, which meant the end of the family band.

Quatro moved to England in 1971 and ultimately found her sound as a lone female voice in male-dominated glam rock. She forged a pop-metal hybrid with stout power chords, heavy bottom, and a big, raspy vocal screech. Her singles competed with bands like the Sweet, Slade, Mud, and Roy Wood's Wizzard on the mercurial British pop charts, scoring two number-one hits: "Can the Can" and "Devil Gate Drive." She had a fan and advocate in Chrissie Hynde, a rock journalist at the time who'd go on to found the Pretenders (when the Pretenders had their first big hit, Quatro sent Hynde flowers and a kind note). Quatro toured with numerous bands, including Slade, Thin Lizzy, and Alice Cooper. Quatro also found her defining look after relocating to England—the leather jumpsuit—inspired by her childhood love of Elvis Presley. Leather became her trademark, employed as recently as her 2017 Leather Forever Tour.

Leather was also the name of her character on *Happy Days*, a role she won by fitting the casting agent's requirement of appearing both "hard and soft," which aptly describes Quatro. She is very much a combination of her father's extroverted personality and her mother's devotion to home and family. The rock 'n' roller with the tough image never stopped working and simultaneously built her own family, two long-term marriages and two kids, all in the same British country manse. And in 2014, she was back on prime-time family TV—sort of—when the NBC comedy *Parenthood* used her song "What a Way to Die" in an episode. It no longer seems incongruous, as the world has caught up to Quatro.

a major label. Gender made them a novelty but it also stymied them, which frustrated the ambitious Quatro. Performance footage from their few months on the label reveal a band trying to find itself, caught between expectations of the industry, the music-consuming public, and years of firsthand professional experience. A cover of the Four Tops' "(Reach Out) I'll Be There" comes off as stifled, the organ more church-like than soulful. Quatro had been moved to lead singer and without her bass seems lost, a diminutive figure in a billowing satin tunic and ribbons in her hair doing a sort of Hully Gully, whipping her head in circles and not realizing her artistic potential. As the decade came to a close, they tried to keep up with the times, changing their name to Cradle, adding the fourth Quatro sister Nancy on vocals and percussion, and developing a heavier, more jam-oriented sound, but it didn't work. Quatro was offered a chance

PAGE 46: Suzi Quatro playing at New York's Bottom Line, 1974. OPPOSITE: At London's Hammersmith Odeon in 1978, the year her hit album *If You Knew Suzi . . .* was released. ABOVE: Advertising herself backstage, 1974.

STEVIE NICKS & CHRISTINE McVIE

FORMED IN: 1967 / London

Before they were rock legends and before they spun adultery into adult rock, it was all up to Fleetwood Mac's Christine McVie.

Following the bizarre departures of founding members Peter Green and Jeremy Spencer, the group was flailing. They'd been through lineup changes and a lawsuit, and in 1974 they relocated from London to Los Angeles. Drummer Mick Fleetwood and bassist John McVie wanted to hire guitarist Lindsey Buckingham, but Buckingham wasn't joining without his musical partner and girlfriend Stevie Nicks. Christine McVie, married to John at the time, was Fleetwood Mac's lone female singer/songwriter, and as such her bandmates thought it prudent to hand her veto power.

Fortunately, the two women connected immediately despite their dissimilarities, forging a friendship that would span decades. Nicks was a West Coast–bred folk rocker turned music mystic—born May 26, 1948, in Phoenix, as Stephanie Lynn Nicks—who was hyper-feminine and hippie-ish, as well as ambitious and perceptive. Her songs tapped into mythos, nature, and consciousness, and she'd pen the band's sole number-one single: "Dreams." She and Buckingham had a turbulent personal and professional relationship that roiled at the heart of their music. McVie, part tomboy and part English rose, was peaceable and witty, born July 12, 1943, in Lancashire, England. Over the years

> **Nicks was a West Coast–bred folk rocker turned music mystic.**

she'd joke that her birth name, Christine Anne Perfect, was too much pressure on her. She released an eponymous solo album, the first of only three she'd make in her career, and played in a blues band called Chicken Shack before joining Fleetwood Mac. A studious classical pianist, her left hand was set free when she fell in love with American blues and rhythm-and-blues, which gave her the rhythmic foundation on which to build sanguine compositions. Her "Don't Stop" was invoked as a generational anthem by first-ever baby boomer President Bill Clinton at his inaugural ball.

The new Fleetwood Mac lineup would go on to sell more than 100 million albums and embody the fractured emotional culture of the '70s, as well as its rock-star excess. The chemistry between the three singers was remarkable, Nicks's honeyed husk and McVie's elegiac cool against Buckingham's pugnacious fire. Their first, self-titled effort together rode to number one on *Billboard*'s album chart, driven by McVie's wispy "Over My Head" and soft-boogying "Say You Love Me," and Nicks's Middle Welsh folklore-inspired "Rhiannon" and contemplative, ageless "Landslide."

But the follow-up, *Rumours*, spent a total of thirty-one weeks at the top spot and is widely considered one of the greatest rock albums of all time. By then, both band couples had imploded, with Fleetwood's marriage to Jenny Boyd (sister of Pattie Boyd, who was married to

> **McVie, part tomboy and part English rose, was peaceable and witty.**

INFLUENCES: Janis Joplin, Grace Slick, Sandy Denny

INFLUENCED: Haim, Sheryl Crow, Courtney Love, Sarah McLachlan, Tori Amos, Dixie Chicks, Jewel

DEEP CUTS: "Let Me Go (Leave Me Alone)" (Christine McVie) / "Spare Me a Little of Your Love" (with Fleetwood Mac) / "After the Glitter Fades" (Stevie Nicks)

As an opening act in late-'60s San Francisco, Nicks observed powerful female figures, including Janis Joplin and Grace Slick, absorbing the message that women in rock needed to project strength and grandeur. She imparted that knowledge to McVie, and they used it as a survival technique to navigate a world dominated by men. They were very aware of their status as they moved through the music industry and its periphery, where women were more often wives, girlfriends, or groupies than musicians. But Nicks was also fiercely feminine in a way that channeled something ancient, in the sweet sorcery of her voice and the flowing outfits for which she became famous. Stage wear was another takeaway she'd gotten from Joplin and Slick, the notion that clothes could be a dramatization of personality as well as something of a shield. She'd twirl in gossamer gowns, fringes flying, long blond hair and shawls winging about her, sometimes with hundreds or even thousands of women in the audience imitating her. At times lampooned for her fairy-like attire, she'd later be lauded by *Vogue* magazine for her boho-chic and inspire a mass-tribute in the "Night of 1,000 Stevies," an annual gathering of fans who dress up like their rock idol, along with generations of girls getting their Wicca on.

George Harrison and then Eric Clapton) not far behind. McVie was writing songs about her new relationship with the band's lighting director, and Nicks would soon begin an affair with Fleetwood. The shifting liaisons and the group's notorious rock-star excess made for an extraordinary creative landscape as each song was recorded. The personal drama behind *Rumours* mirrored the '70s' rising divorce rates among Fleetwood Mac's boomer fan base, and it gave them a breakup album over which to ruminate. Being the ones who ended their respective relationships, the women gravitated toward each other, functioning as each other's support system.

As Fleetwood Mac transitioned into the '80s, McVie's pop songs sparkled ("Hold Me" on *Mirage*, "Little Lies" from *Tango in the Night*), while Nicks's were dark and dreamy ("Sara" from *Tusk*, "Gypsy" from *Mirage*). All of the band members began to work on solo projects, but none was more successful than Nicks's 1981 album *Bella Donna*, with its hits "Edge of Seventeen" and "Stop Draggin' My Heart Around," her duet with Tom Petty and the Heartbreakers. Both Nicks and McVie would quit Fleetwood Mac and later return, but McVie completely opted out of the band and Los Angeles for sixteen years, retreating to the English countryside.

Nicks kept working, despite addictions that she kicked during two separate and increasingly grueling rehab stints, recording several more solo albums and collaborating with other artists. She continues to be rediscovered through many approaches, including her contribution to the soundtrack of modern-day fairytale *Practical Magic*, the Dixie Chicks reinventing "Landslide" as a country hit, heaps of love from influential blogger/actor Tavi Gevinson, and recording with Lana Del Rey. Writer/director Ryan Murphy's adoration for Nicks was so great that he devoted a 2011 episode of his show *Glee* to *Rumours*, causing the album to reenter the *Billboard* chart at number eleven, the highest second act ever. He also cast her in *American Horror Story: Coven*, where she made her acting debut as the hero of the young witches. Nicks, who said her own home resembled the haunted manse on the show, was a natural.

Though Nicks inspires cultish devotion, the more taciturn McVie is equally significant. She joined her husband's band, but she became the hit writer, an equable powerhouse who moved millions from behind her keyboard. Independent of heart, she loved and wrote about whoever she pleased, and along with Nicks lived an elevated life, commanding treatment as rock 'n' roll royalty. When she was done with the lifestyle, she simply left, and when she wanted back in, her space in the band was waiting for her. McVie helped mollify the friction between Nicks and Buckingham so their explosive creativity could yield many more hits for the band, and she even released an album of duets with Buckingham in 2017. Both McVie and Nicks have outshone their former partners while still making a case for ensemble works, and their relationship is a paragon of how collaboration between women is far greater than competition.

Though Nicks inspires cultish devotion, the more taciturn McVie is equally significant.

PAGE 50: Christine McVie and Stevie Nicks perform with Fleetwood Mac in Atlanta on the *Rumours* tour, 1977. OPPOSITE: A white-gossamer-clad Nicks and Lindsey Buckingham in concert with Fleetwood Mac at the Meadowlands in New Jersey, 1982. RIGHT: McVie at their 1977 Atlanta show.

ANN & NANCY WILSON

FORMED IN: 1967 / Seattle

Robert Plant, Jimmy Page, and John Paul Jones, the surviving members of Led Zeppelin, sat in the balcony at the 2012 Kennedy Center Honors wearing the medals that President Barack Obama had placed around their necks earlier in the evening. The President and First Lady sat nearby. Along with the other honorees and attendees, they watched in awe as Heart's Ann and Nancy Wilson paid tribute to the band by taking on their most daunting song: "Stairway to Heaven."

It was familiar territory for the Wilsons, who'd been performing Zeppelin covers since they moved from their childhood home of Seattle to Vancouver to take a shot at a career in music. It was familiar territory for Page, Plant, and Jones, too, even if they didn't know it; in 1975, the three men and drummer John Bonham went to a Vancouver club after a gig at the Pacific Coliseum, walking by as the band on stage happened to be performing "Stairway." It was Heart, just a few months before their debut album *Dreamboat Annie* unleashed the heavy pulse and mystic overtones of "Magic Man" and cadenced acoustic advance of "Crazy on You."

Bands don't often cover "Stairway to Heaven." At just over eight minutes, with several shifting time signatures, it's hard to sustain. Its lyrics are inscrutable and a challenge for any singer to embody, and even a trained vocalist would need to strategize before attempting a Plant-like wail. The difficult song, however, lends itself perfectly to the Wilson sisters' skills: Ann's preternaturally powerful voice, and Nancy's heartbeat rhythm guitar and acoustic fingerpicking. Nancy began the performance by roundly plucking through rock's most recognizable arpeggios on her acoustic guitar. And no artist could send "Stairway" heaven-bound like Ann Wilson.

The women were backed by drummer Jason Bonham, the late John Bonham's son, which heightened the reaction from Zep's living members. But even with Bonham, a string orchestra, and members of the Joyce Garrett Youth Choir expanding the arrangement, it was the Wilsons' moment. As the song stretched toward its crescendo, Plant's eyes welled up, Page's face beamed, and Jones looked astonished, mirroring the mix of emotions that the audience was feeling. It was a stunning performance that stripped gender, stature, and pomp from the prestigious event, distilling it to the pure power of rock 'n' roll.

It's hard to fathom that nearly four decades earlier, the pioneering female-led hard rock band Heart was once casually referred to as "Led Zeppelin with tits." Meant as a joke at the time, it still sounds derisive. Even more shocking was the preposterous print ad that Heart's first label ran upon the platinum success of their debut, implying that the sisters were incestuous. A similar remark inspired Ann Wilson to write "Barracuda," the ferocious, galloping rock monster that became the hit on their second album, *Little Queen*. Wilson channeled her fury and feelings of

> Wilson channeled her fury and feelings of humiliation into the song, and as a result its power is elemental.

INFLUENCES: Led Zeppelin, Joni Mitchell, the Beatles, Grace Slick, Fanny

INFLUENCED: Alanis Morissette, Soundgarden, Alice in Chains, Sheryl Crow, Courtney Love, L7, Vixen

DEEP CUTS: "Kick It Out" / "Heartless" / "Rockin' Heaven Down"

humiliation into the song, and as a result its power is elemental. It's a torrent of righteous rage, an ocean hurling a tsunami of vulgarity back from where it came.

Ann and Nancy Wilson resolutely navigated the music business. Though raised in a military family (their father was a career Marine), they were equally influenced by 1960s flower-child ethos. They fell in love with the Beatles on *The Ed Sullivan Show* and got to see them perform at the Seattle Coliseum on August 25, 1966. But the sisters wanted to *be* the band, not their girlfriends. They embraced band leadership while musing on femininity. They played hard rock while cultivating a softer image.

By the '80s, though, their career had slowed, and they turned their image over to a new label. Capitol Records had Heart recording material by hit-making composers and glammed up in corsets, shoulder-padded satin jackets, and huge hair. Nancy switched from acoustic to mainly electric guitar. They made videos for MTV, stylized period pieces with smoke machines, blowing wind, and slow-motion sequences. It was still Heart, if an exaggerated version, and to drive home that point the label also persuaded them to self-title their eighth album.

What might have been a disaster for another band worked like magic for the sisters. *Heart* earned them their first number-one single and album, and their first Grammy nomination. Despite the success, however, neither of the Wilsons cared to perpetuate the look or sound of the '80s. It was an especially difficult time for Ann, who struggled with drugs, alcohol, and weight gain, and contended with the fact that after being the voice of Heart for decades, their first number-one hit, "These Dreams," was sung by Nancy.

By the early '90s, the Wilson sisters' hometown had become an epicenter of rock music. Grunge exploded out of Seattle, upending glam metal, ushering in a new indie aesthetic and becoming a dominant cultural force. Just as Heart was closing out that overblown chapter of their own history, bands like Soundgarden began

talking about their importance. Soundgarden frontman Chris Cornell was both a friend and a staunch advocate, opining that Ann is one of music's greatest voices and slapping down those who judged her on her fluctuating weight. Cornell also inducted Heart into the Rock and Roll Hall of Fame in 2013. In 2017, Ann, one of the few singers who can do justice to Soundgarden's "Black Hole Sun," sang the song on *The Jimmy Kimmel Show* to pay a moving tribute to Cornell after his untimely death.

Ann and Nancy befriended and played with many prominent Seattle musicians, reinventing themselves once again with a Heart side project called Lovemongers in the early '90s. By this time, Nancy was married to writer/director Cameron Crowe, and she and Ann contributed to the soundtrack for his movie *Singles*, which chronicled Gen-X life in Seattle during the grunge era. Nancy would also compose music for Crowe's films

Jerry Maguire, *Vanilla Sky*, *Elizabethtown*, and *Almost Famous*—the last of which fictionalized Crowe's stint as a teenaged reporter for *Rolling Stone*—working with Crowe until their divorce in 2010.

Both sisters became mothers in their forties, and in their sixties they parted ways creatively and privately over a family incident. Ann now tours as a solo act. Nancy's project with Liv Warfield of Prince's New Power Generation called Roadcase Royale released a debut album, *First Things First*, in September 2017. It mines her love of rhythm-and-blues and funk, and its most powerful track, "The Dragon," pays tribute to Alice in Chains' late frontman Layne Staley and his struggle with drug addiction. It resonates deeply, considering all the Seattle rock giants from Jimi Hendrix to Kurt Cobain who succumbed to the rock 'n' roll lifestyle while these strong, iconic women made it through.

PAGE 54: Ann and Nancy Wilson in 1977, the year they broke their contract with their record company over what they saw as demeaning treatment. OPPOSITE: Ann playing with Heart at the Rockford Speedway, 1980. ABOVE: Nancy with Heart at a festival in Kalamazoo, Michigan, 1977.

LINDA RONSTADT

BORN: Linda Maria Ronstadt / July 15, 1946 / Tucson, Arizona

A singer's voice will change over time, deepening or thinning, becoming slightly diminished or burnished with age. So it was randomly cruel that Linda Ronstadt, who possessed one of popular music's most sublime, versatile voices, lost hers to Parkinson's disease. In 2013, she announced that she would never be able to sing again. Straightforward and purposeful in conversation, she mentioned finding other ways to be "useful" and expressed gratitude for the motor skills she still has that will likely be gone one day.

Ronstadt's body of work is so vast, varied, and honored that she hasn't left much undone. Her four-decade, shape-shifting career has encompassed country rock, rock 'n' roll, New Wave, pop, big band, American standards, ranchera, operetta, country, show tunes, Afro Cuban, jazz, and more. Her rangy, resonant singing embodies each style she slips into as if she'd been performing it all her life. Like Patsy Cline and very few others, Ronstadt has that "teardrop" in her voice. It becomes seismic as she moves from contralto toward her upper register, pausing in the sweet spot to simply ache for a few bars, then dropping back down for another dulcet verse. She says her job is to make you cry, and she does it well in any genre. But Ronstadt also has a tougher, resilient side, giving new impact to brawny, roguish tunes like the Rolling Stones' "Tumblin' Dice," Michael Nesmith's "Different Drum," Warren Zevon's "Poor Poor Pitiful Me," and many more. To hear a woman convey songs that had only been expressed by men was a revelation at the time.

Ronstadt has a keen ear for great songs and was a brilliant interpreter of them, and her radar for great players is acute. She arrived in Los Angeles from her hometown of Tucson at age eighteen, hoping to put together a country band with a rock 'n' roll rhythm section. Walking into the Troubadour on Santa Monica Boulevard one night, she stumbled upon a group called Shiloh. Her attention was drawn to the drummer—Don Henley. The backing band she'd then assemble to take on the road with her would become the Eagles. As Ronstadt heard them warm up night after night, she knew they were going to be huge.

Henley would induct her into the Rock and Roll Hall of Fame in 2014, but back then Ronstadt was on her way to becoming the biggest-selling female solo artist of the decade, landing on the cover of *Time* magazine, as well as six times on the front of *Rolling Stone*. After a couple of hit singles and several albums, her soulful mix of rock and country, and of old and new material, took off. 1974's *Heart Like a Wheel* was the beginning of a run of consecutive platinum albums that hadn't previously been achieved by a female artist, three that went to number one on the *Billboard* chart, and numerous other record-breaking feats, plus her first two Grammys (one of which she says she accidentally left in a rental car). The sultry, rocking kiss-off "You're No Good" was a number-one pop single, while its yearning B-side, Hank Williams's "I Can't Help It (If I'm Still in Love with You)," went to number two on the country chart (and earned her a Grammy); her cover of the Everly Brothers' "When Will I Be Loved" topped both

> Ronstadt's body of work is so vast, varied, and honored that she hasn't left much undone.

INFLUENCES: Janis Joplin, Dolly Parton, Joni Mitchell, Anna McGarrigle, Kate McGarrigle, Peggy Lee

INFLUENCED: Sheryl Crow, Grace Potter, Dixie Chicks, Pat Benatar

DEEP CUTS: "He Darked the Sun" / "How Do I Make You" / "Just One Look"

Ronstadt was on her way to becoming the biggest-selling female solo artist of the decade, landing on the cover of *Time* magazine, as well as six times on the front of *Rolling Stone*.

charts. 1977's *Simple Dreams* ended Fleetwood Mac's *Rumours*' twenty-nine-week run as the number-one rock album, and its singles—Ronstadt's cover of Buddy Holly's "It's So Easy" and the huapango-tinged stunning version of Roy Orbison's "Blue Bayou"—dislodged Elvis Presley from the number-one slot on the country chart. Her *Living in the USA*, led by her cover of Chuck Berry's "Back in the USA," was the first album in history to go double-platinum before it even hit store shelves. Its cover, a photo of a permed Ronstadt on roller skates in a satin jacket, gym shorts, and tube socks, is a slice of 1978.

Remarkably, it wasn't until she was on the other side of all that success that Ronstadt says she finally began to develop her voice as a serious instrument. Against the advice of her management, she made career gambles that paid off creatively and commercially. In 1980, Joseph Papp cast her as Mabel Stanley in his production of *The Pirates of Penzance* for the prestigious New York Shakespeare Festival; she played the role in the film adaptation as well, demonstrating an impressive coloratura soprano on Gilbert and Sullivan classics like "Poor Wand'ring One."

Ronstadt began revisiting the great American songbook, mining the catalogues of George Gershwin, Irving Berlin, and others in 1983 with the platinum-selling *What's New*, the first of a trilogy of collaborations with bandleader Nelson Riddle. She joined Papp again for a production of Puccini's *La Bohème*. She delved into her heritage on the album *Canciones de mi Padre* (her father was Mexican), performing boleros and ranchera in a glittering charro outfit.

As prolific a solo artist as Ronstadt was, she also collaborated extensively. A friend of Neil Young's since their Troubadour days in the late '60s, she sang backup on many of his songs; her lucent harmonies are audible on "Heart of Gold." Her duet with New Orleans music royalty Aaron Neville, "Don't Know Much," was a worldwide hit. She built a coterie of women musician friends and worked with them often, including Nicolette Larson, Jennifer Warnes, and especially Dolly Parton and Emmylou Harris, her partners on the *Trio* albums. Her final album, *Adieu False Heart*, was a project with Cajun singer Ann Savoy.

Ronstadt loved nothing more than playing music with others and hearing it played live. Her autobiography, *Simple Dreams: A Musical Memoir*, is mostly oriented around those stories, her own musical explorations, and pickin' parties from friends' homes in Laurel Canyon to motel rooms on tour. Though she admits to drug use, salacious tales don't appear. She is friends with many of her famous exes, including California governor Jerry Brown, musician J. D. Souther, and director George Lucas. She never married, not apropos of having taken the Carter Family's "I Never Will Marry" to number eight on *Billboard*'s Country chart. Adopting two children took her off the road for a while, but she went back to touring when they were old enough to come along. Now retired, she spends time working with Los Cenzontles, a band and cultural center in Richmond, California, not far from where she lives in the Bay area.

PAGE 58: Linda Ronstadt with her iconic tambourine in London, 1978. OPPOSITE: Ronstadt performing traditional Mexican songs with a mariachi band in Los Angeles, 1986. BELOW: Backstage, 1970s.

BONNIE RAITT

BORN: Bonnie Lynn Raitt / November 8, 1949 / Burbank, California

In 1982, Bonnie Raitt was eight albums into her career, and nearly as many years away from her Grammy-winning breakthrough, *Nick of Time*. Booked to appear on *Late Night with David Letterman*, which had debuted only a couple of months earlier but was already a coveted gig for hip musicians, she took the opportunity to bring along eighty-three-year-old Sippie Wallace, an idol of hers. She'd recorded two of the blues pioneer's songs before she discovered that Wallace was still alive and living in Detroit. Coaxing her out of retirement, the two spent a decade performing together and became like family to each other.

Raitt was there to promote her *Green Light* album, yet she seemed more interested in promoting Wallace. Not only did Raitt play guitar as Wallace sang her bawdy blues classic "Women Be Wise," accompanied by New Orleans stalwart Dr. John on piano, but she also had Letterman interview Wallace to discuss her life, career, and first album in decades, titled *Sippie*.

Since releasing her eponymous debut in 1971, Raitt had built a loyal following for her mix of blues, rhythm-and-blues, and singer/songwriter balladry, as well as her soulful voice, sweet and purposefully roughened with Jim Beam and cigarillos, and her extraordinary slide guitar playing—B. B. King himself would call her "the best damn slide player working today." She'd quit Radcliffe College in her junior year to pursue music, playing gigs around Boston's revered folk and blues scene and New York City's landmark Greenwich Village folk clubs. Raitt learned from the masters, opening shows for the likes of Mississippi Fred McDowell and Howlin' Wolf, honing a unique style compounded by the sheer surprise of deep blues coming from a young, freckled, redheaded white girl. But in 1982, she was far from a household name.

Devoting so much of her time on a national television show to her hero was a generous act, one that defines Raitt as an artist and a person.

Raitt was raised as a Quaker, and her parents built social conscience and mission into family life. Helping those less fortunate and fighting injustice has been at her core throughout her career, from making sure blues legends get their "proppers," to performing at the historic "No Nukes" concert and countless other benefits, to meeting with tribal leaders at Standing Rock during the Dakota Access Pipeline protest. As a child, she joined her family in fighting nuclear proliferation and collected funds for refugees around the globe. Her teen years coincided with the civil-rights, women's-rights, and anti-war movements, and Raitt was immersed in it all, including the folk music that brought it to the fore.

She got her first taste of the other thing at the heart of her artistry—country blues and slide guitar—when at age fourteen she found the album *Blues at Newport '63*. It was on Vanguard Records, the label of one of her heroes, Joan Baez, which caught her attention, as did the

> B. B. King himself would call her "the best damn slide player working today."

INFLUENCES: Sippie Wallace, Sister Rosetta Tharpe, Aretha Franklin, Big Mama Thornton, Joan Baez, Ruth Brown, Joni Mitchell, Bessie Smith, Barbara Lynn, Memphis Minnie, Victoria Spivey

INFLUENCED: Susan Tedeschi, Grace Potter, Brittany Howard, Tracy Chapman, Melissa Etheridge

DEEP CUTS: "Too Long at the Fair" / "Gamblin' Man" / "No Gettin' Over You"

syncopated, fingerpicked melodies of Mississippi John Hurt, and the Delta boogie of John Lee Hooker. But it was John Hammond's bottleneck guitar, named for the technique of sliding a glass bottle or tube against the strings, evoking a crying sound, that captured Raitt's imagination, particularly when she saw his photo on the back cover. White and middle-class, like her, and just seven years her senior, he was the son of the legendary producer John Hammond, who'd sign Bob Dylan, Aretha Franklin, and many more. Raitt loved the way slide guitar mimicked the tones of the human voice and how it was used with open guitar tunings. It reminded her of her grandfather's Hawaiian lap steel. And she found it easy to play, which it isn't for most people. Like blues in general, it's deceptively simple—some technique, a lot of "feel," and hard to get quite right. She slipped an empty bottle of Coricidin cold medicine on her ring finger and taught herself every song on that album.

Being an activist wasn't rebellious in Raitt's family, but playing the blues was, sort of. Her father, John Raitt, was a famous stage actor known for leading roles in *Carousel*, *The Pajama Game*, *Oklahoma!*, and many more. He starred on Broadway but also toured constantly (Raitt's "The Road is My Middle Name" is about him), and he taught his daughter to always give her best performance, whether on a New York City stage or a small regional theater. Raitt also loved life on the road, and between touring, recording, and playing benefits, she never took more than a couple of weeks off for the first two and a half decades of her career.

Raitt's mastery of the idiom runs so deep that her music thrived in the '80s, when synthesizers were sucking the soul out of so many recordings. Like Ruth Brown, Etta James, and many others had done

with blues and jazz, she brought blues into pop music, maintaining the integrity of the former and elevating the latter. At age forty, she became a pop star when her version of John Hiatt's "Thing Called Love" drove *Nick of Time* to the top of the *Billboard* album chart and won three Grammys (Raitt would go on to win seven more over the years). Her exquisite taste in covers led to more chart success (the puckish "Something to Talk About," the lachrymose "I Can't Make You Love Me"), but she also wrote a number of memorable songs throughout her career, from 1972's defiant "Give It Up or Let Me Go" to the lamenting "The Ones We Couldn't Be" from 2016's *Dig in Deep*.

It's her guitar playing, though, where Raitt is unparalleled, one of just two women on *Rolling Stone*'s 100 Greatest Guitarists of All Time list (Joni Mitchell is the other). For decades, she played her unpainted brown 1965 Fender Stratocaster, with a fat tone she describes as sounding "like bacon smells." Raitt was also the first woman offered a signature guitar by Fender. She initially turned it down, until 1996, when she realized she could donate the proceeds to music edu-cation for kids. Even when she's being celebrated, Raitt finds a way to use the moment to help others.

Being an activist wasn't rebellious in Raitt's family, but playing the blues was, sort of.

PAGE 62: Bonnie Raitt in San Francisco, 1977. OPPOSITE: At the Rock and Roll Hall of Fame induction ceremony, New York, in 1990—the year she won four Grammys; she wouldn't be inducted herself until 2000. ABOVE: Raitt playing in Sonoma, California, 2001.

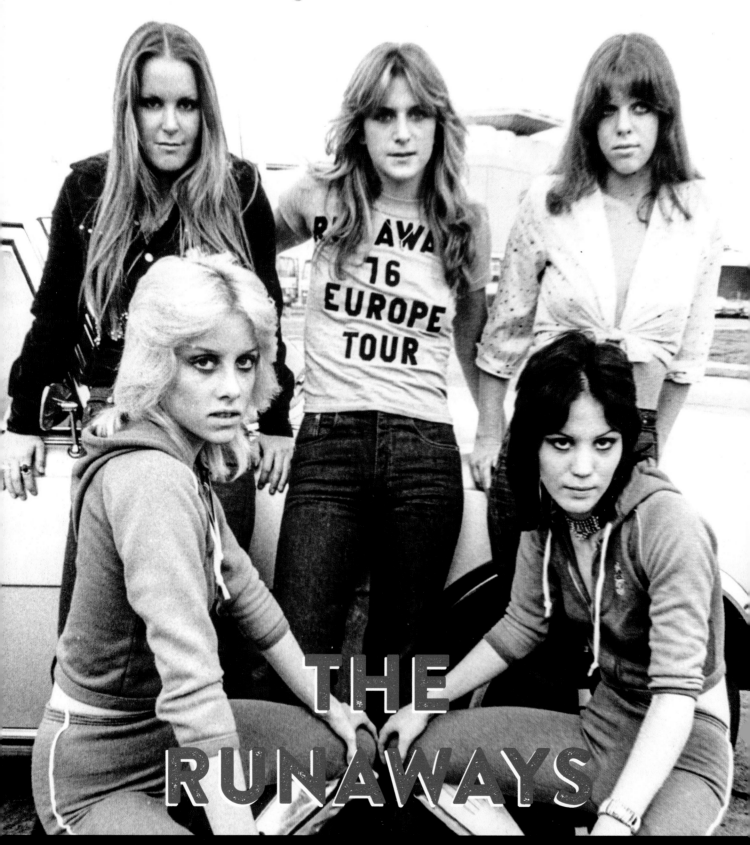

THE RUNAWAYS

FORMED IN: 1975 / Los Angeles

Cherie Currie is a wood-carving chainsaw artist. Jackie Fox attended Harvard Law School with Barack Obama. Lita Ford is a star of metal guitar. Joan Jett went to the Rock and Roll Hall of Fame. Sandy West went to prison.

The Runaways' post-band lives were as intractable as their brief teenage tether. A hard-rock act that glittered like glam, shredded like metal, and shouted like punk, they were already solid players who could write songs. They were very LA—surfers, valley girls, Sunset Strip frequenters. They formed in the wake of Rodney Bingenheimer's English Disco, a Strip gathering place for young, gender-bending rock 'n' rollers, PVC-bound fetishists, space oddities in satin and sequins, and sheer-swaddled baby groupies, finding one another at clubs like the teens-only Sugar Shack and the Starwood, or hanging around outside the Roxy where their heroes performed. Even at fifteen and sixteen, they were ambitious. They were treated like rock stars in Japan and mingled with the UK punk scene, but failed to gain much traction on their own turf.

Laced into a corset, garter belt, and thigh-high stockings, her baby-fine white-blonde hair parted in the middle, layered, and feathered, singer Currie belted out lyrics with post-adolescent disdain. She stomped, squatted, and postured in platform shoes, whipping her microphone in the air and spooling its cable around her legs. Ford's guitar attack bared her love of Deep Purple–era Ritchie Blackmore and Black Sabbath's Tony Iommi. She banged her head so hard, her long hair flew back and forth over her ensemble of T-shirt, gym short-shorts, and high silver boots. At the opposite end of the stage, Jett was covered in a snug long-sleeve jumpsuit, dressed like her idol Suzi Quatro. Hunched over with her guitar slung below her hips, she kept the rhythm down, occasionally leaning in and synching up with Fox (the third of five bassists the band would burn through, including future Bangle Micki Steele), whose coiling bass lines added surprising dimension to the songs.

Drummer West was the Runaways' co-founder and powerhouse, a hard-hitting, metal-loving rock 'n' roller with a cigarette-singed voice who rocked a '70s unisex look—feathered sun-streaked hair, pukka shell necklace, no makeup. Athletic and affable, she and Jett hit it off immediately when they were introduced in 1975 by producer, songwriter, and impresario Kim Fowley. Nearly two decades into the music business, Fowley had been looking to put together an all-female rock band, which had been done but without much commercial success. Within six months, the core Runaways lineup had a record deal with Mercury and an eponymous debut with the chugging, defiant teen anthem that would become their defining song, "Cherry Bomb."

Their second album, *Queens of Noise*, was heavier and harder, and when it was released in 1977 the Runaways were headlining shows with opening acts like Cheap Trick and Tom Petty and the Heartbreakers. The group barely made it through their summer tour of Japan,

> They were treated like rock stars in Japan and mingled with the UK punk scene.

INFLUENCES: Suzi Quatro, David Bowie, Fanny

INFLUENCED: Hole, Kathleen Hanna, Babes in Toyland, L7, Pussy Riot, the Go-Go's

DEEP CUTS: "Black Leather" / "School Days" / "American Nights"

though—Fox left, followed by Currie. The guttural, gum-chomping Jett took over lead vocals, and they extricated themselves from Fowley to release two more albums. But the fracturing was audible. Ford and West wanted to play metal, while Jett was more aligned with punk's reinvention of old-school, three-chord rock 'n' roll. The band performed its swan song on the last night of 1978 and officially broke up several months later.

The dissolution of the Runaways was marked by myriad accusations of who was at fault, along with much bitterness, controversy, and shocking allegations of sexual assault and abuse aimed at Fowley, who died in 2015. Fox went back to school and became an entertainment attorney. Currie starred opposite Jodie Foster in the film *Foxes*, playing a teenage cautionary tale who dies after hitching a ride with the wrong couple. She landed other acting roles, continued making music, and in 1989 penned her memoir *Neon Angel*. Tragedy befell West, who felt shattered after the breakup. Involvement with drugs and guns led to prison stints, and lung cancer took her in 2006.

Ford and Jett carved out post-Runaways careers in music, but they've both spoken about their struggles to be taken seriously by the industry. Ford recorded several solo albums and earned two Grammy nominations, hitting platinum with 1988's *Lita*, led by a Top 10 duet with Ozzy Osbourne and a cover of "Kiss Me Deadly." She took a fifteen-year break, moving to a private Caribbean island to raise her two sons with then-husband Nitro singer Jim Gillette. Ford returned to music with new recordings in 2009 and a 2016 memoir *Living Like a Runaway*, in which she details her volatile engagement to Tony Iommi, who she still calls one of her guitar idols, and other details of rock 'n' roll life. She remains one of metal's few female lead guitarists.

But it's Jett who remains iconic. As a young teen, she already knew she was going to play rock 'n' roll, and her single-minded vision has led her through a lengthy and varied career. After the demise of her band, she was rejected by numerous major labels. Nevertheless, she persisted. She founded Blackheart Records and showed them all what a girl can do. In 1982, Jett and her band the Blackhearts' cover of "I Love Rock 'n' Roll" was a number-one hit in several countries, including the United States. They ran Tommy James's "Crimson and Clover" back into the Top 10 and several other songs into the Top 40, and were nominated for a Grammy for "I Hate Myself for Loving You." As a producer, Jett made records with the Germs and Bikini Kill, among many other projects. She worked in film and television, and in 2010 produced *The Runaways*, a semi-biographical film with Kristen Stewart and Dakota Fanning delivering uncannily faithful performances as Jett and Currie when they were just starting out as the "queens of noise."

It's Jett who remains iconic.

PAGE 66: [top, L–R] Lita Ford, Sandy West, Jackie Fox, [bottom, L–R] Cherrie Currie, and Joan Jett on their first overseas tour in London, 1976. OPPOSITE, TOP: The Runaways give attitude on the beach in Los Angeles, 1976. OPPOSITE, BOTTOM: The Runaways' greatest-hits compilation didn't come out until 1987, eight years after the band had broken up. ABOVE: Jett's debut solo album, *Bad Reputation*. RIGHT: Jett performing while wearing a T-shirt for the Ramones, with whom the Runaways shared tours and a stripped-down rock sensibility, undated.

SIOUXSIE SIOUX

BORN: Susan Janet Ballion / May 27, 1957 / London

Siouxsie Sioux's music is phantasmagoric, dark, and danceable. There's a chilling hollow in her voice, which at times dips flat but retains its force. The early albums with her band Siouxsie and the Banshees were exquisite and disturbing. They could be soundtracks to slowly going insane, or comfort to isolated, musically inclined teens, which describes Sioux growing up in suburban Chislehurst, southeast of London. Inventive guitarist John McGeoch created an unsettling but utterly compelling soundscape with his MXR 117 flanger, the source of the band's distinct "warped" resonance, the effects pedal stretching and reverberating his note patterns like a fun-house mirror. Peter "Budgie" Clarke (who'd played on the Slits' landmark *Cut*) was punk's most fascinating drummer, whose relentless tom-tom attack gave the band a tribal consciousness.

The musical slippery slope matched the band's lyrical content, often co-written with bleached blonde bassist Steven Severin. Sioux's lyrics, and their unnerving delivery, hinted at her discordant, disturbing home life, marred by alcoholism and violence. "Spellbound" (which was used to creepy effect in *American Horror Story: Hotel*) describes a nightmarish childhood where walls provide no security and even treasured toys turn on you, where your earliest memories feel like psychosis. "Candyman" is the true story of Sioux's sexual assault at age nine.

Her family failed to acknowledge it; the song "Happy House" is a sarcastic suburban mask, a place where feelings are swallowed.

Onstage, Sioux was pure power and presence. She danced like a punk rock Salome, or a New Wave Marlene Dietrich, a goth-dolly in ghostly makeup with a dandelion-like circle of wild black hair teased in every direction and the painted, pointed lip line of a silent movie star. Her unique look predated the band, and though it evolved over the years, she was never seen on- or offstage without it. Her geometric "panda eye" eyeliner was an exaggerated version of the look she'd loved on '60s pop stars like Dusty Springfield, as well as the face paint of Native Americans whom she favored over cowboys as a child, as her stage name indicates.

By the early '70s, Sioux was hanging out at the King's Road clothing shop run by Malcolm McLaren and Vivienne Westwood, which went through several iterations but is best known for its mid-'70s form, SEX, where fetish-wear became street fashion. Sioux and several other stylish kids (including Severin and Billy Idol) from the Bromley area where she grew up were dubbed the Bromley Contingent by journalist and photographer Caroline Coon, who documented much of the British punk explosion. They loved the glam rock of David Bowie and Bryan Ferry, but seeing the Sex Pistols gave them the impetus to

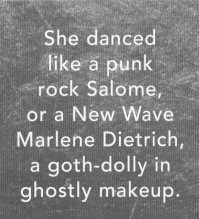

She danced like a punk rock Salome, or a New Wave Marlene Dietrich, a goth-dolly in ghostly makeup.

INFLUENCES: Dusty Springfield, David Bowie, Patti Smith

INFLUENCED: Shirley Manson, PJ Harvey, Marilyn Manson, Beth Ditto, Savages

DEEP CUTS: "Love in a Void" (with the Banshees) **/** "Slowdive" (with the Banshees) **/** "Godzilla" (with the Creatures)

play. Their insurgent look was a part of what put punk on the radar of the British press and made it a phenomenon. Before they'd even written a song, Siouxsie and the Banshees—with the Pistols' Sid Vicious on drums and future Adam Ant guitarist Marco Pirroni—made their debut at the watershed moment in 1976 known as the 100 Club Punk Festival, alongside the Clash, the Sex Pistols, the Damned, the Buzzcocks, and others. They couldn't really play anything; it was mostly improv and Sioux's recitations.

But what started as performance art became a thirty-year career. Siouxsie and the Banshees would expand their sound with elements of cabaret and carny (*Peepshow*), Indian tablas (*Superstition*), and string arrangements (*The Rapture*). Forever flying slightly below the radar, they remained culturally relevant, co-headlining the inaugural Lollapalooza festival, and writing songs for Tim Burton's *Batman Returns* and Paul Verhoeven's trashy cult classic *Showgirls*. Sioux and Budgie's side project, the Creatures, was a drum-and-vocal exotica-pop excursion that reflected the music of the balmy locales where the seemingly sun-averse band recorded, such as Andalusia and Hawaii. Their horn-blown version of Mel Tormé's "Right Now" was an unlikely hit in 1983. The couple also married in 1991 and announced their divorce in 2007, shortly before Sioux released her solo debut, the glammy-pop *Mantaray*. More than four decades after she became a punk-and-goth idol, her album sounds influenced by some of the contemporary artists she inspired, such as Shirley Manson and Beth Ditto.

PAGE 70: Siouxsie Sioux and the Banshees at London's Vortex Club, 1977. OPPOSITE: Sioux in front of Parliament in London, 1980. LEFT: Sioux mixes together a typically unique lacy bondage look in New York, 1984. ABOVE: The Banshees' 1981 *Once Upon a Time* singles collection.

THE SLITS

FORMED IN: 1976 / London

The Slits started as musical neophytes incited by punk and in love with reggae, and they embodied the rebellious nature of both. They played a raucous combination of genres; and as they progressed as a unit, they incorporated deeper grooves, tribal beats, and spacey dub into their unconventional sound. In their best-known lineup, natty-dreaded wild-child singer Ari Up, striking dark-eyed drummer Palmolive, stylish blond guitarist Viv Albertine, and Tessa Pollitt, the bassist with a hedge of brown hair and a man's tie around her neck, the Slits were innovative and incendiary. BBC1 Radio legend John Peel called them mesmerizing.

Their very name was provocative, a crude reference to female genitalia, but it was also defensive, obliterating anyone's power to use like words to disparage them. The name was also a clear indication that they weren't especially interested in rock stardom, at least not in the beginning. Even now, it's hard to imagine a band called the Slits headlining Wembley Arena.

They didn't want to follow any rock 'n' roll template. Punk freed them, it allowed them to be anarchic while they figured out their instruments, their innate rhythms, and what messages they wanted to convey. They were aggressive and bold, completely subverting mid-century Western female archetypes, drawing on everything from childhood nursery rhymes to the Sex Pistols to tribal cultures. Their performances were improvisational in the way that they were so new to playing music that anything could happen, but their chemistry made the mayhem sound purposeful. Albertine's guitar went off like an intermittent power tool as Palmolive and Pollitt's rhythm section repeatedly built and tore down each song.

They were fronted by one of rock's most impetuous performers, the uninhibited fourteen-year-old Ari Up. A force of pure teenage id, she possessed unrivaled bravado. Her voice was powerful, and she could push it to belt, giggle, or yelp at will. She once urinated onstage, wore white undies over black pants, and changed outfits in a bank during business hours as a gathering crowd looked on. Her physicality was extreme but completely natural, a relentless expression of her emotions and thoughts through every inch of her body. On- and sometimes even offstage, she'd wrench and spin in rhythm, or "riddim," as she'd say in a confluence of English, German, and Jamaican patois.

Up was raised in a musical household through which celebrities would often pass. Her mother Nora Forster was a German music promoter who brought home famous friends and lovers, including Jimi Hendrix, Yes' John Anderson, and Barry Gibb, when Up was a child. By the mid-'70s, Forster was dating Chris Spedding, who was working with the Sex Pistols at the time and introduced the family to punk rock. In an economically depressed London full of squats, Nora Forster's warm, open home attracted many musicians, including the Clash's Joe Strummer. The latter was like a big brother

> They didn't want to follow any rock 'n' roll template.

INFLUENCES: Sex Pistols, the Clash, Lee "Scratch" Perry, Sister Nancy, Jimmy Cliff, Patti Smith, Chrissie Hynde, Augustus Pablo, Don Cherry

INFLUENCED: the Raincoats, Nirvana, Björk, Bikini Kill, Neneh Cherry, Courtney Love, Huggy Bear, Kim Gordon

DEEP CUTS: "Animal Space" / "Love und Romance" / "Instant Hit"

to the then-tween Arianna Forster, giving her both guitar lessons and her nickname, Ari Up (as in "hurry up").

As extroverted as Up was, the Slits were truly a collective. Albertine was the group's fashionista, a chic art-school dropout dressed in clothes from SEX. Her longtime friend Chrissie Hynde encouraged her to join the band and helped her see herself as the sort of guitar player she wanted to be. Tessa Pollitt's heavy bass thrum was unusual for the times and integral to the sound the Slits were after. Palmolive, who'd grown up in Spain under dictator Francisco Franco's repressive reign, wrote songs that added an enigmatic depth to the cheeky social commentary of the others.

The Slits were deeply enmeshed in the music scene by friendship, mentorship, family, romantic relationships, and even management; but far beyond the social connections, they were an essential part of UK punk. They demarcated the movement with their approach to playing, up-yours attitude, look, and the subject matter of their lyrics—the tedious nature of conventional life, conspicuous consumerism, drugs, and acerbically funny love songs with a bitter aftertaste. Their three Peel Sessions are legendary and blow away any notion that they couldn't play their instruments. Their debut *Cut* is a post-punk milestone. Its radical cover, featuring Up, Albertine, and Pollitt bare-breasted and slathered in mud, once again challenged notions of female sensuality, as there's no mistaking their warrior countenance. Their second album, *Return of the Giant Slits*, included more sonic explorations, African rhythms, dub, and earth-conscious lyrics. Sadly, it marked the unraveling of the band.

Up and Pollitt resurrected the Slits with new members in 2005, recording and touring for audiences that now span three generations of fans. It ended with Up's tragic death at forty-eight in 2010, predating her mother Nora and stepfather John Lydon (aka Rotten), both of who helped raise her three sons.

Albertine declined to join her former bandmates but started playing and recording music again on her own. She wrote *Music Music Music Clothes Clothes Clothes Boys Boys Boys* (2014), a revealing memoir of not only her punk years but also detailing the aftermath, her struggles with marriage, fertility, cancer, and reconciling her past and present; and a follow-up, *To Throw Away Unopened* (2018), about her family's dysfunction.

Palmolive, who left the Slits before *Cut* and briefly joined the Raincoats, is now Paloma McLardy. She embraced Jesus and, along with husband Dave, is active in their Cape Cod, Massachusetts church and community. But in November 2017, she drummed with the Raincoats at The Kitchen performance space in New York City. They were celebrating the release of *Pitchfork* editor Jenn Pelly's book on the Raincoats' debut album for the 33 1/3 series. Bikini Kill performed as well—their first time in two decades. With Ari Up gone, the Slits' original lineup can never reunite, but their fear of being written out of music history is forever quelled.

Cut

the slits

PAGE 74: Albertine and Pollitt onstage, undated. OPPOSITE: The Slits, undated.
BELOW: Ari Up with the Slits in New York, 1978. LEFT: The Slits' 1979 debut album, *Cut*.

They were an essential part of UK punk.

POISON IVY

BORN: Kristy Marlana Wallace / February 20, 1953 / San Bernardino, California

It started with hitchhiking, which could have ended horribly and sometimes did in 1972. Heading back to her apartment from Sacramento State, where she studied art, Kristy Wallace took a ride with two men. She recognized the one in the passenger's seat; he wore unusual clothes and had intrigued her when she saw him on campus. His name was Erick Purkhiser, and they shared a class in "art and shamanism." Although they've both confirmed the story of how they met, as has the driver of the car, it may be apocryphal. In the first known photo of them as a couple, they're lean, long-haired, blue-jeaned hippies, if that's actually them. In the thirty-seven years they ended up being together, they were often referred to as man and wife, and indeed they only did part when Purkhiser died in 2009; but sometimes they said they weren't actually married. Relocating in the mid-'70s, first near Purkhiser's home turf in Ohio, and then to New York City, they rechristened themselves Poison Ivy Rorschach and Lux Interior and established the Cramps, creating not just a band but also inventing their own lifestyle and building their own mythology.

The two bonded over a love of collecting records and other kinds of American kitsch, and they'd spend their entire life together amassing rare vinyl, psychotronic movies, and all sorts of ephemera. There was no Internet, and little or no journalism devoted to this stuff. The only way to discover it was to go find it, and, if you were lucky, talk with people who knew about it.

> The Cramps' sound was dubbed "psychobilly."

Rorschach and Interior did both. They'd visit the K Street Mall in Sacramento and buy cutout albums because they liked the covers. They'd spend whole days in Ohio thrift stores, poring over 45 rpms, purchasing stacks of them for five or ten cents apiece. They fell in love with the transcendent magic of black doo-wop groups, the way the vocal harmonies conveyed an other-worldly feeling, the way the recordings had an echo to them. The slightly warped sound, as if the hole in the 45 was a bit off-center, had a hallucinatory quality that the Cramps wanted in their music. They tapped into early rockabilly and its roots in blues and country so sinister that it made devil-worshipping metal seem puerile.

The Cramps' sound was dubbed "psychobilly," the word lifted from Johnny Cash's song "One Piece at a Time" in which he builds a Cadillac out of odd parts. It was a perfect analogy, as the band was its own sort of Frankenstein, a conglomeration of hillbilly music and pentatonic blues soaked in slapback, trashy B-movie aesthetics, and horror comic imagery. Onstage it looked like burlesque performance art on acid, but it rocked. Rorschach's primitive, violent guitar sound and Interior's ghoulish intoning were the band's linchpins. Crunching chords, ringing riffs, and plucking simple note patterns on her 1958 Gretsch 6120 semi-hollowbody and a feedback-loving Fender Pro Reverb tube amp, Rorschach stood coolly as she created the Cramps' sonic miasma, while Interior jumped, whooped,

INFLUENCES: Cordell Jackson, Wanda Jackson, the Collins Kids, Hasil Adkins

INFLUENCED: Southern Culture on the Skids, the White Stripes, the Raveonettes

DEEP CUTS: "Rockin' Bones" / "Thee Most Exalted Potentate of Love" / "The Band That Time Forgot"

howled, and writhed on the floor as he sang. But she was much more than a foil for his onstage mania. Rorschach wrote or co-wrote nearly all of their original songs and produced or co-produced most of their records. She also managed the band when no one else could get it done. Her guitar playing, a noisier reinvention of early rock 'n' roll, was influential, heard in future generations of garage rockers and twisted outlaw country bands. So was her style—close-fitting animal prints, metallic boots, bejeweled bikini tops, glittering miniskirts, tiaras topping her cascade of orange curls, and always Cleopatra eyeliner with dark red lipstick.

The Cramps were also punk rock in their simplicity, black leather, and no bassist.

The Cramps were also punk rock in their simplicity, black leather, and no bassist (at first, anyway), part of CBGB's "Class of '76." They made their debut at the club that year with guitarist Bryan Gregory, and drummer Miriam Linna, who'd go on to co-found Norton Records, one of the preeminent reissue labels of the early rockabilly and garage rock that weaned the Cramps and countless other bands, and chronicle decades of rock 'n' roll in her magazine *Kicks*. Through eight studio albums, along with singles, extended plays, and live albums, twenty-two or so band members would join and leave Rorschach and Interior. From their earliest recordings made at the legendary Sun Studios in Memphis, with Big Star's Alex Chilton producing, to their final studio album, *Fiends of Dope Island*, the Cramps would strike a balance between tetchy old obscure covers and originals that paid tribute to their progenitors, who had made rock records when rock was truly rebellious and frightening.

PAGE 78: The dark majesty of Poison Ivy, 1978. OPPOSITE: The Cramps play London's the Forum in 1991, the year they had their only Top 40 hit in the UK with "Bikini Girls with Machine Guns." ABOVE: Lux Interior and Ivy, undated.

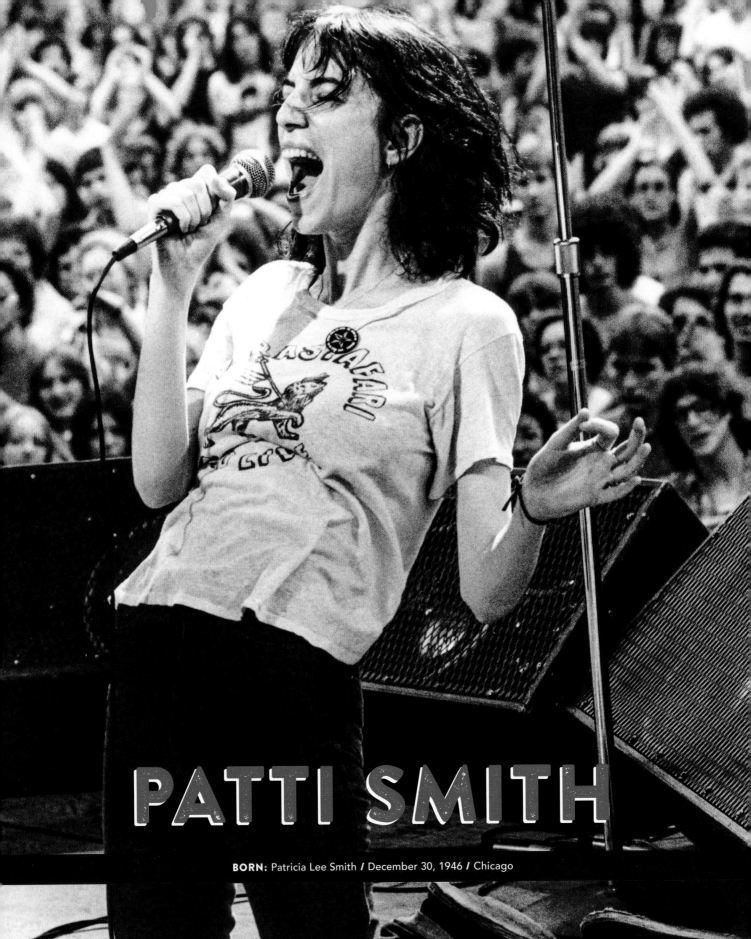

PATTI SMITH

BORN: Patricia Lee Smith / December 30, 1946 / Chicago

The voice—impertinent, suggestive, totally free—sounded as if it didn't give a damn. But Patti Smith says she got into rock for the opposite reason: She wanted to save it from what she saw as its bloated, stagnant self; she wanted to use it to connect with other misfit souls. She'd already found her voice as a poet. Drawn to New York City's mushrooming downtown music scene in the mid-'70s, she found she had a voice as a rock singer, one that defied constructs of gender and art itself. Androgynous as her appearance, Smith's voice had absolute conviction, whether delivering roiling imagery or calling for any sort of revolution. With sneers and warbles, she could recite, improvise, or embellish, and you'd never doubt her. Her words made pictures pace over the pulse of her band's three-chord jams. Poetry is one thing, but Smith had that cadence when she spoke/sang, the one that explains without words why rock 'n' roll was originally a euphemism.

She is called the godmother of punk, but that's inadequate, considering the extent of her influence. What she forged at CBGB with the Patti Smith Group wasn't performance art but rather the artful performance of a rock 'n' roll conjurer, and in 1975 it earned her a deal with Arista Records. She says she never imagined a career in music, but no one walks into Electric Lady Studios, built by and for Jimi Hendrix, records a monumental debut album like Horses, and then slinks back to

> Smith's voice had absolute conviction, whether delivering roiling imagery or calling for any sort of revolution.

her job at a bookstore. On some level, Smith had been planning this for her entire life.

She spent most of her childhood in Woodbury, New Jersey, south of Philadelphia and just across the Delaware River. She was the oldest of four, her mother a waitress and her father a machinist (though it was her own brief blue-collar work experience that inspired the song "Piss Factory"). Gangly, awkward, and not academically gifted, Smith was nonetheless exceptionally bright, a voracious reader who immersed herself in art, poetry, and music and had a well-defined aesthetic from a young age. She dropped out of college to give birth to a daughter, who she gave up for adoption and never saw again, then headed for New York City in 1967.

Smith chopped off her hair so she wouldn't look like a folkie and dyed it purply-black with henna. She found work at Manhattan's legacy bookstores, including Scribner's, Argosy, and the Strand. She started reading her poetry at open-mic nights and landed occasional off-off-Broadway theater and cabaret gigs. She went to Paris twice, tracing the steps of her beloved romantic poets and busking on the street. She wrote for music magazines, including Creem, which published three of her poems and later made her a pin-up "Creem Dream," posed topless with a copy of Iggy and the Stooges' Raw Power clutched to her chest. She dabbled in rock, co-writing songs with Rick Derringer and Blue Öyster Cult, whose keyboardist and guitarist Allen Lanier was her longtime partner.

INFLUENCES: Grace Slick, Arthur Rimbaud, Janis Joplin

INFLUENCED: PJ Harvey, Siouxsie Sioux, Shirley Manson, Karen O, Exene Cervenka, Kathleen Hanna, Courtney Love

DEEP CUTS: "Distant Fingers" / "Beneath the Southern Cross" / "Nine"

On February 10, 1971, Smith gave her first reading at the St. Mark's Poetry Project, with Lenny Kaye accompanying her on guitar. Peppering her speech with "like" and speaking in a South-Jersey-via-Lower-East-Side accent, she rips into "Mac the Knife" on account of it being Bertolt Brecht's birthday and then follows with her poem "Oath" and its "Christ died for somebody's sins but not mine" line that would (mostly) make its way to the opening bars of her cover of Van Morrison's "Gloria," the first track on *Horses*. She had sought out Kaye after reading an article he'd written that she liked, and the two became friends. Eventually, they'd hone their act at clubs like Max's Kansas City and CBGB, and the Patti Smith Group would grow to include bassist Ivan Král, keyboardist Richard Sohl, and drummer Jay Dee Daugherty.

Following her biggest commercial success, Smith decided to quit the business and have a family.

Outside of her band, Smith became romantically involved with many of her male collaborators: Sam Shepard, who co-wrote and co-starred in the play *Cowboy Mouth* with Smith; Todd Rundgren, who produced her fourth album, *Wave*; Television guitarist Tom Verlaine, whose singing influenced her, or vice versa; poet Jim Carroll, who encouraged her to keep writing; and other handsome, lanky dudes. None, though, was as profound to Smith as her relationship with artist Robert Mapplethorpe, as she details in her 2010 book

Just Kids. They lived together in the Chelsea Hotel. She supported him financially and nurtured him. He photographed her for the cover of *Horses*, seeming genderless in a men's white shirt and black trousers with a black ribbon draped around her neck, bathed in natural light. It became one of rock's most iconic images.

Smith's second album, *Radio Ethiopia*, wasn't as accessible as her debut, but her third, *Easter*, took off on the strength of "Because the Night," given to her by Bruce Springsteen. The two shared a recording engineer, Jimmy Iovine, but they also would have crossed paths at Max's Kansas City, where Springsteen would sometimes kill a few hours after his own gigs, waiting until sunrise, when buses and trains resumed service back to New Jersey. Smith completed the song with a verse about her new boyfriend, Fred "Sonic" Smith of the MC5, and her recording made it to number 13 on the *Billboard* Hot 100.

Following her biggest commercial success, Smith decided to quit the business and have a family. After *Wave* was released in 1979, she married Fred Smith (who died in 1994 at age forty-six) and moved to Detroit, where she remained for a decade and a half and raised two children: daughter Jesse and son Jackson. In 1988, she released *Dream of Life*, which yielded a song that would become a staple when she returned to public performance in the mid-'90s: "People Have the Power." The song was often invoked at political events for candidates and causes that Smith cares about.

Since reviving her career, Smith has released half a dozen albums and numerous books of poetry, art, fiction, and memoir. And when the stage at CBGB went dark permanently on October 15, 2006, it was Smith who signed off. "Although we mourn the closing of CBGB, we should remember CBGB not merely as a place," she said. "It is a state of mind."

PAGE 82: Patti Smith plays Central Park in 1976 just before going into the studio to record *Radio Ethiopia*. OPPOSITE, LEFT: A typically edgy portrait from 1976. OPPOSITE, RIGHT: Her third album, 1978's heavily religious *Easter*.

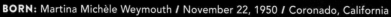

TINA WEYMOUTH

BORN: Martina Michèle Weymouth / November 22, 1950 / Coronado, California

The diffident personality, military family, Catholic education, folk-guitar playing, art school—these are common denominators among nascent rock 'n' rollers, and they were all part of Tina Weymouth's formative years. But she may be the only rock star whose career began with a hand bell. At thirteen, she toured with the Potomac English Hand Bell Ringers, responsible for six bells that she'd play when the conductor pointed at her. She's also one of the few rock musicians who admits to not fully understanding rock 'n' roll, not that that's an apt description of the music she makes, although she has been inducted into its Hall of Fame. Rarest of all is her forty-one-year marriage to drummer Chris Frantz, her rhythm-section partner in Talking Heads and the Tom Tom Club, with whom she has two grown sons.

> She may be the only rock star whose career began with a hand bell.

It's also uncommon to be in even one band that created a totally unique sound. Weymouth has been at the center of two. Much of the Talking Heads catalog, eight studio albums and two live albums, rides on her spacious groove and melody, her bass adding rhythmic heft to the band's imaginative, cerebral quirk. Original, intellectual, philosophical, and arty, the band rocked nonetheless, largely due to the contributions of Weymouth and Frantz. As Talking Heads expanded into African music and polyrhythms, Weymouth's playing became even funkier and more fun. When she and Frantz branched off with the Tom Tom Club, they created the genius "Genius of Love," a song so exceptional that it has been sampled as many as 146 times, according to recent estimates, but nothing has come close to its original form.

It was Frantz who talked Weymouth into teaching herself bass, bringing her albums by Suzi Quatro, another self-taught woman wielding a Fender Precision. Weymouth got the same bass and painted over the original sunburst finish with battleship gray, a color she'd used a lot as an art student at the Rhode Island School of Design. It was camouflaged, sort of like Weymouth herself, her hair chopped so short that if you glanced quickly in the early days of Talking Heads, you might not have realized there was a woman in the band. The "boyish" look also averted attention from pimps and other derelicts as she walked around her New York neighborhood in 1974, when she, Frantz, and David Byrne moved from RISD to a commercial space on Chrystie Street, just three blocks from punk-rock epicenter CBGB.

All the members of Talking Heads cut their hair short. It was a conscious decision, because at CBGB the weirdest thing anyone could do was to appear normal. Even their band name was a reference to the pallid pundits of television past. Their first CBs gig was opening for the Ramones, uniform in their leather jackets, ripped jeans, and shaggy hair. Talking Heads walked out in polo shirts and casual slacks. But when they plugged in and played,

> The "boyish" look also averted attention from pimps and other derelicts.

INFLUENCES: Suzi Quatro, Carol Kaye, Duck Dunn

INFLUENCED: Este Haim, Kim Gordon, Kim Deal, Justin Meldal-Johnsen

DEEP CUTS: "The Man with the 4-Way Hips" (with Tom Tom Club) / "Punk Lolita" (with the Heads feat. Debbie Harry and Johnette Napolitano) / "Right Start" (with Talking Heads)

they were punk, avant-garde, and spartanly funky. Led by Weymouth's staccato riff, the first song they wrote together and became known for was "Psycho Killer," a reminder that Ted Bundy looked normal, too.

Talking Heads carved out a unique niche in New Wave, growing more creative and complex on each of their first four albums through their 1980 magnum opus *Remain in Light* (which the Library of Congress added to its National Recording Registry in 2017). Produced by Brian Eno and inspired by African musician Fela Kuti, it contained the song "Once in a Lifetime," a modernist anthem with a compelling rhythmic imbalance hung on a distinct Weymouth bass riff. The expansive tour to promote it, however, took five extra musicians and lots of extra gear. It left them insolvent, and, with growing tensions between them, the group took a lengthy hiatus.

Weymouth and Frantz started a project that became the Tom Tom Club, returning to Compass Point Studio in Nassau, Bahamas, where *Remain in Light* was recorded. Said to be haunted, its owner, Island Records honcho Chris Blackwell, had consecrated it with chicken blood and feathers to ward off malevolent spirits and other calamities. In Studio B, on a hill perched above the sea, they recorded rhythm beds for three songs, including "Genius of Love" and what would become its B-side, "Lorelei," and "Wordy Rappinghood." Blackwell, who was in the adjacent studio producing Grace Jones's

Weymouth and Frantz built songs like a house.

Nightclubbing, liked the nascent tracks so much that he green-lit a full album for his label.

Weymouth and Frantz built songs like a house, from the foundation to the roof, doing it all by hand and on tape. When they added handclaps to "Genius," they stood in a circle, with reggae legends Sly Dunbar and Robbie Shakespeare on loan from the Jones sessions. Weymouth and two of her sisters, Laura and Lani, added the vocals, a tragedy about lost love, drugs, and death masked by the whimsical melody, playful beats, and name-checked funk heroes like Hamilton Bohannon. Not only did they create one of the most inventive, influential dance tracks of all time, the Tom Tom Club did what Talking Heads hadn't—they went to number one on *Billboard's* Club Songs chart, and even played *Soul Train* in 1984.

Talking Heads reunited and had their greatest commercial success in the mid-late '80s. The Tom Tom Club continued to record sporadically, most recently 2012's "Downtown Rockers," a shout-out to many of their musician friends from their CBGB days. Through it all, Weymouth has been a stealthy influence, on anyone who regards the album artwork she contributed to, or who listens for the bass lines she created that percolate through Talking Heads and Tom Tom Club songs, or who saw her onstage anchoring a maelstrom of sounds with her bass and was inspired to attempt it themselves.

PAGE 86: Tina Weymouth with the Talking Heads, 1980. ABOVE: The Talking Heads' *More Songs About Buildings and Food* (1978) and *Remain in Light* (1980). OPPOSITE: In concert with the Talking Heads in New York in 1978, the year of their first Top 30 hit, a cover of Al Green's "Take Me to the River."

DEBBIE HARRY

BORN: Angela Tremble or Trimble (adopted as Deborah Ann Harry) / July 1, 1945 / Miami

BLONDIE IS A GROUP.

In 1979, buttons were printed with that message to inform casual music fans that Blondie was in fact a band, and not its peroxided singer Debbie Harry. Not that anyone could take their eyes off Harry. It's impossible not to acknowledge her exceptional beauty; eye-of-the-beholder notwithstanding, the geometry of her face is simply a fact. Just as remarkable is that Harry wasn't afraid to cultivate a glamorous image in the mid-'70s at CBGB, the infamous Bowery club where New York punk broke and where New Wave germinated, and where beauty was out of favor. It worked for her and the band because of everything else she is, smart and tuned-in, funny and sarcastic, imaginative and cool, all of which she conveyed in her nonchalant voice.

Blondie is still a group, except on Twitter, where Blondie and Harry have been one and the same since 2009. Of course she tweets. Harry is as relevant and important as ever, and not only for the timelessness of her music and style. Musicians, visual artists, and performance artists seek her out, and she's just as aware of and interested in them. Blondie's 2017 album *Pollinator* shows how far the band's influence has traveled, only to return to the "queen bee"—contemporary songwriters and musicians Sia, the Strokes' Nick Valensi, Charlie XCX, Dev Hynes, and TV on the Radio's Dave Sitek are all among contributors to the band's eleventh release.

Their prior album was the danceable and diverse *Ghosts of Download*, so named because so much of it was done on computers, both programming and sending music back and forth between collaborators, including Colombian electronica collective Systema Solar ("Sugar on the Side"), EDM deejay Hector Fonseca ("Mile High"), as well as singer/DJ Guy "Miss Guy" Furrow, and Gossip's Beth Ditto. It was packaged as a double album with *Blondie 4(0) Ever*, celebrating the band's fortieth anniversary with an album of re-recorded hits. Together, the two discs draw an arc from Blondie's early days to generations of young artists whom they inspired.

Harry and Chris Stein, her Blondie co-creator, lifelong collaborator, and ex-partner (it's complicated), have always had their eyes and ears wide open to New York City's prodigious, sundry art and music

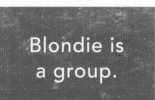

scenes. More than any other band, they spun disparate influences into songs, embodying New York's unique clash of cultures and the greater things that occur where they intersect. The hit that definitively broke them out of CBGB's burgeoning scene was "Heart of Glass." Riding on the pulse of disco, with Harry's aloof vocals airborne over the ebb and flow of shimmering synthesizers, it was sonically and technologically ahead of its time. Dance music was still anathema to rock 'n' rollers, but Blondie's genre mashups would change everything. They took reggae to number one with a cover of "The Tide is High," a '60s rocksteady song done up with steel drums and a horn section. Meeting Brooklyn graffiti artist and hip-hop pioneer Fab Five Freddy inspired Blondie's "Rapture," the first time a song with any kind of rap hit number one on

INFLUENCES: Janis Joplin, Grace Slick, Lou Reed, the Ronettes, the Shangri-Las, Marc Bolan

INFLUENCED: Cyndi Lauper, Gwen Stefani, Shirley Manson, Madonna, Kathleen Hanna, Hayley Williams, Joan Jett, Beth Ditto

DEEP CUTS: "Rip Her to Shreds" (with Blondie) / "Shayla" / "Well Did You Evah!" (with Iggy Pop)

the *Billboard* chart. Freddy would go on to host *Yo! MTV Raps*, but in 1980 he was spray-painting Campbell's soup cans onto New York subway cars, a homage to another friend of Harry's — artist Andy Warhol.

Though born of punk rock, Blondie was a pop band, not just musically but in the sense of the pop art promulgated by Warhol, who even painted a digital image of Harry on his Commodore Amiga. Harry's

"Blondie" was the sort of character that she and Chris Stein envisioned: the '30s-cartoon-meets-'60s-girl-group-performer-meets-punk-singer. Harry's version of the blond bombshell was exaggerated and art-damaged, in torn T-shirts, short-shorts, and only the top and sides of her hair bleached, her natural dark brown color sticking out beneath it and at the roots. She had some styling help — friend and then-up-and-coming designer Stephen Sprouse dressed her in sharp suits and asymmetrical tops, including the diaphanous handkerchief-cut dress that she wore in the "Heart of Glass" video, and artist/nightlife notable Anya Phillips put her in hot pink on the cover of Blondie's second album, *Plastic Letters*. But Harry's own punk/New Wave aesthetic is still imitated, even though she's not done with it.

As a solo artist and actor, Harry continued to do prescient work. She appeared in David Cronenberg's 1983 futuristic horror film *Videodrome* as the somewhere-between-human-and-cyber-creation Nicki Brand, presaging humanity's soon-to-be-interactive

lives. That same year, Harry starred on Broadway, along-side Andy Kaufman, as the titular wrestler in *Teaneck Tanzi*, which closed after one night, just as wrestling began its ascent to the cultural juggernaut it is today. In 1988, John Waters cast her as villainous "hair hopper" Velma Von Tussle in his original film *Hairspray*, which became a cult classic in the '90s, and a phenomenon as a Broadway show and film remake in the aughts. Even the cover art of Harry's 1981 debut solo album, *KooKoo*, was prophetic. It featured her face pierced by four giant acupuncture pins, so shocking that some record stores refused to display it—and a decade before facial piercings could be done at any mall in America.

PAGE 90: Performing with Blondie in Amsterdam, 1977. OPPOSITE, LEFT: Blondie at the Paradiso, Amsterdam, September 21, 1977. OPPOSITE, RIGHT: Blondie's self-titled debut, 1976. BELOW: Harry at New York's MPCS Studio, 1977.

Like her friend and sometimes-tour mate Cyndi Lauper, Harry is also involved in the LGBTQ community. Over the years, she has shared a reciprocal love with the performers at renowned Manhattan drag events like Wigstock and Click + Drag, and clubs such as Jackie 60 and Squeezebox, often joining them onstage. Harry remains the quintessential New York artist, completely engaged in the art and culture of the present, just as she has always been.

> Though born of punk rock, Blondie was a pop band.

CHRISSIE HYNDE

BORN: Christine Ellen Hynde / September 7, 1951 / Akron, Ohio

At the height of '70s UK punk, Chrissie Hynde watched as all her musician friends began their ascent to infamy while success eluded her.

She had the look—wiry, leather-clad, and a touch androgynous in buttoned-up shirts and fitted jackets, her eyes obscured by a thick fringe of dark bangs and concentric circles of kohl eyeliner. She had the songs, inspired in part by the raw power of Iggy Pop, the inventive guitar approach of Joni Mitchell, and a deep appreciation of American soul music and its British Invasion elucidation. She had the attitude—adventurous and unsentimental, she turned her experiences into rawboned lyrics and deployed them with a knife-thrower's precision. She'd played with a nascent version of the Damned, jammed with the Clash's Mick Jones, gave Johnny Rotten a little instruction on guitar, and convinced her friend Viv Albertine to join the Slits, but nearly half a decade went by and none of her attempts to form a band had panned out.

> She had the look—wiry, leather-clad, and a touch androgynous.

Hynde grew up a budding Anglophile in suburban Akron, Ohio, wanting out and dreaming of England. Obsessed with music, she learned guitar and would hang around outside venues after shows to meet her heroes. She was enrolled at Kent State during the 1970 protest that ended with the shooting of four students, including her acquaintance Jeffrey Miller, whose body lies prone in the most famous photo captured on that day. At college, she studied art, waited tables, took copious amounts of drugs, and had savage entanglements with bikers. In 1973, Hynde took off for London, landing a gig as a writer for the *New Musical Express*, reviewing albums and interviewing stars such as Brian Eno, and fellow ex-pat Suzi Quatro. For a short time, she worked at SEX, the London clothing shop and punk hangout.

No one would have bet on the brash American who was a few years older than her punk cohort, but Hynde would outlast, outlive, and outsell most of them, even beating them into the Rock and Roll Hall of Fame in 2005. She finally found her band in 1978, not in London but three hours west in Hereford, near the border of Wales. Guitarist James Honeyman-Scott, bassist Pete Farndon, and drummer Martin Chambers were all accomplished local musicians who knew one another. Joining forces with Hynde, they became the Pretenders. Their eponymous 1980 album, produced by Chris Thomas (*The Beatles*, *Dark Side of the Moon*), is one of rock's most astonishing and original debuts.

The cover of *Pretenders*—just the band dressed in black and red against a stark white backdrop, their name in spare deco lettering above them—reveals much of Hynde before a note is even played. Standing with her three British blokes, it's clear that England was her destiny. There's an austerity to her, physically, musically, and in the way she communicates, that makes American excess feel moribund. Her songs are taut and as hard as her stare. Tenacious, fearless, and carnal, she's capable of observing even her own most intimate moments with the analytical eye of a journalist.

INFLUENCES: Suzi Quatro, Ray Davies, David Bowie

INFLUENCED: Shirley Manson, Deap Vally, Courtney Love, Savages, Alanis Morissette, Kathleen Hanna, Melissa Etheridge, Babes in Toyland, L7

DEEP CUTS: "Cuban Slide" / "Porcelain" / "Night in My Veins"

Hynde's fondness for odd time signatures, lack of regard for traditional song structure, and modulating octaves kept listeners—and even her bandmates—on a nerve's edge. Her sinewy alto is expressive, trembling for a revelatory instant, then snapping back with resolve. Her phrasing, bluntly Midwestern with European curves, is so distinct that it takes repeated spins to decode many of her lyric passages.

Side one of *Pretenders* is a gripping post-punk arc of sex and violence, with glimpses of Hynde's Ohio past on songs like "Precious," "Up the Neck," and "Tattooed Love Boys." Her opaque power chords are brightened

Tenacious, fearless, and carnal, she's capable of observing even her own most intimate moments with the analytical eye of a journalist.

PAGE 94: Chrissie Hynde playing in Detroit, 1984. PAGE 95: The Pretenders eponymous debut (1979). ABOVE: Hynde knocking out power chords with the Pretenders in Central Park, 1980. LEFT: Hynde with the Pretenders in New York, 1994.

by Honeyman-Scott's guitar jangle and seared by his scorching solos. Snippets of sound effects—wailing sirens, video-game bleeps, and landline bleating—might have sounded gimmicky in another context, but here they heighten the band's concise, chorus-less interplay. The album's second side lays back a bit with the twinkling but tragic "Kid," the smoldering reggae-vibed "Private Life" (later covered by Grace Jones), the propulsive bass-driven "Mystery Achievement," and their first big hit, "Brass in Pocket." A self-possessed soulful strut, it showed Hynde could seduce anyone, from fans to the fickle British music press, with her tough persona and without revealing an inch of flesh, just as easily as she could issue the inevitable kiss-off.

The band released an EP containing their next two hits, "Talk of the Town" and "Message of Love." They rushed to make a second full-length album, *Pretenders II* (1981), which suffered creative and critical short shrift as a result. Bound to be a product of their sudden success, it nonetheless contained some gems, including "Day After Day," one of the more poetic ruminations on the banality and beauty of relentless touring. The album pulls

other real-time pages from Hynde's life, including "The Adulteress," alluding to her tumultuous romance with the Kinks' Ray Davies. The relationship didn't last, but Hynde gave birth to their daughter Natalie in 1983.

Hustling into the studio was fortuitous, because both Honeyman-Scott and Farndon (who'd been fired from the group for his drug use) would be dead within two years. Both were swift and senseless tragedies, but Hynde carried on with the album *Learning to Crawl* (1984), addressing her new professional situation and her new baby. The Pretenders transitioned from a cogent quartet to a larger cast of players who revolved around Hynde's vision, releasing seven more albums with a lot of hits and just a few misses. She also took time off to raise Natalie and a younger daughter, Yasmin, from her six-year marriage to Simple Minds' Jim Kerr. Her life apart from the band encompassed duets with Gloria Estefan and Frank Sinatra, singing Chip Taylor's "Angel of the Morning" with an acoustic guitar at the mythical Central Perk café on the television show *Friends*, opening (and closing) a vegan restaurant in her hometown of Akron, taking part in a number of campaigns and actions for the animal-rights group PETA, and in 2014 releasing a solo album.

Rarely one to indulge in deconstructing her lyrics or her life, it took decades for Hynde to finally unpack some of the shocking stories behind her songs. In her 2015 memoir *Reckless*, she set off a cultural firestorm with comments about the sexual assaults she'd experienced—but it was already out there, in the songs. That's how you get closest to Hynde—a true rock 'n' roller, a loner who is also a leader, a determined artist whose image involves a degree of obfuscation so that fans will focus on what's important: the music.

PAT BENATAR

BORN: Patricia Mae Andrzejewski / January 10, 1953 / New York City

The video that launched MTV in 1981—the Buggles' *Video Killed the Radio Star*—is well known and often referenced. The video that played next—Pat Benatar's *You Better Run*, which made her the first woman to be presented on the brand-new format—is not. She'd already released two albums, had a Top 10 hit, and won her first Grammy. But suddenly she was on nationwide television multiple times a day, all of five feet tall, strutting in front of her band in shiny black spandex and a pixie haircut, double-tapping at the camera lens when she roared the chorus as if it was an actual threat. New artists had never before experienced that kind of exposure, and it was game-changing. Before the decade was done, Benatar scored fifteen Top 40 hits, three Top 10 albums, and four Grammys for Best Female Rock Vocal Performance. Only Tina Turner and Sheryl Crow have won as many in that category.

Her voice was already known, a theatrical mezzo-soprano with muscle-flexing, punch-throwing power. Having planned to study opera at Juilliard, and having spent years singing glossy pop covers and show tunes, Benatar had to cultivate her vocal rough edges to have a career in rock. The image, though, came naturally. She grew up in Lindenhurst, on Long Island's blue-collar south shore, a little scrapper who says she knocked out a neighborhood kid's teeth when he yelled at her to stop singing. Being so small, she had to be resolute, and as an adult it served her well in navigating the music business. She has often spoken of the harassment and humiliation she dealt with—chased around a piano, hit on by sleazy radio program directors, and the time her record label airbrushed off her top and airbrushed on larger breasts in a print ad.

Benatar's take-no-crap persona was exemplified on guitar-fired hits like "Heartbreaker," "Hit Me with Your Best Shot," "You Better Run," and "Treat Me Right" (which she co-wrote), but she also covered Kate Bush's aching "Wuthering Heights," and wrote love songs like "Promises in the Dark" that showed vulnerability. Synthesizer and piano crept into the music as she moved through the '80s, with grand ballads like "Shadows of the Night," and the bombastic, impelling pop of "Invincible." As the MTV monster grew and devoured more videos, Benatar's became increasingly cinematic, and she used them to mine feminist themes. She transforms from Rosie the Riveter to Nazi-fighting pilot in "Shadows," and threatens a pimp in "Love is a Battlefield," leading a group of captive women out of a dance hall with Michael Jackson/*Thriller*-like choreography. No matter how dramatic the presentation became, though, her music remained accessible. You didn't have to be a record geek, arty New Wave fan, or punk rocker to "get" Benatar—she was everyperson's rock star. Drug- and drama-free, and married for almost all of her career, she characterized herself as fairly normal as well.

Having dominated the '80s, Benatar went on to explore a range of styles, from jump blues, Chicago blues, and torch songs, to soulful acoustic productions, and back to hard rock. Through it all, her guitarist,

> Being so small, she had to be resolute.

INFLUENCES: Heart, Robert Plant, Ruth Brown, Big Maybelle, Diana Ross, LaVern Baker, Etta James, Suzi Quatro

INFLUENCED: Hayley Williams, Karen O, Avril Lavigne, Martina McBride, Alanis Morissette

DEEP CUTS: "I'm Gonna Follow You" / "True Love" / "Rated X"

Benatar
fought her
way into
rock 'n' roll.

musical director, and husband of thirty-six years—Neil Giraldo—has been by her side. In the early days, he helped her craft a rock 'n' roll sound out of her too-well-trained-for-rock voice. The couple never stopped writing, recording, and touring. When their daughters were born, Haley in 1985, and Hana in 1994, they all went on the road together in the family bus; Benatar maintains that rock 'n' roll is easy compared with motherhood.

It may seem easy in retrospect, but Benatar fought her way into rock 'n' roll and then fought to stay, proving every naysayer wrong. Told that female artists couldn't draw a male audience to concerts and certainly wouldn't fill arenas, she was vindicated when in 1982 she arrived back home in New York at the end of a tour to find that she'd sold out Madison Square Garden. Like her friend and colleague Melissa Etheridge, Benatar often heard the tired line from radio programmers that "We already have one woman on the playlist." She persisted, of course, and is finally getting credit for paving the way. In 2018, Benatar and Etheridge were honored at the Women's International Music Network's She Rocks Awards, along with Exene Cervenka, Kate Pierson and Cindy Wilson of the B-52s, and Fanny. She was also an interviewee on Brooke Baldwin's *American Woman* CNN series, examining the careers of pioneering women in public life.

Benatar continues to tour, and she's also paying her success forward. In January 2017, she released "Shine," her first new song in more than a decade, in honor of the Women's March on Washington. A collaboration with songwriter/producer Linda Perry, the song benefits the B. A. Rudolph Foundation, which supports women studying public service and STEM and headed for a career in government. Benatar, Perry, and Giraldo also recorded the ballad "Dancing Through the Wreckage" for the soundtrack of the 2017 documentary *Served Like a Girl*, which follows female veterans as they raise awareness of 55,000 among them who are homeless. Benatar already had a profound impact on rock; now she's making one on the rest of the world.

PAGE 98: Pat Benatar in Philadelphia, 1980. OPPOSITE: Benatar playing Los Angeles in November 1979, just three months after the release of her debut album. ABOVE: In New York, 1981.

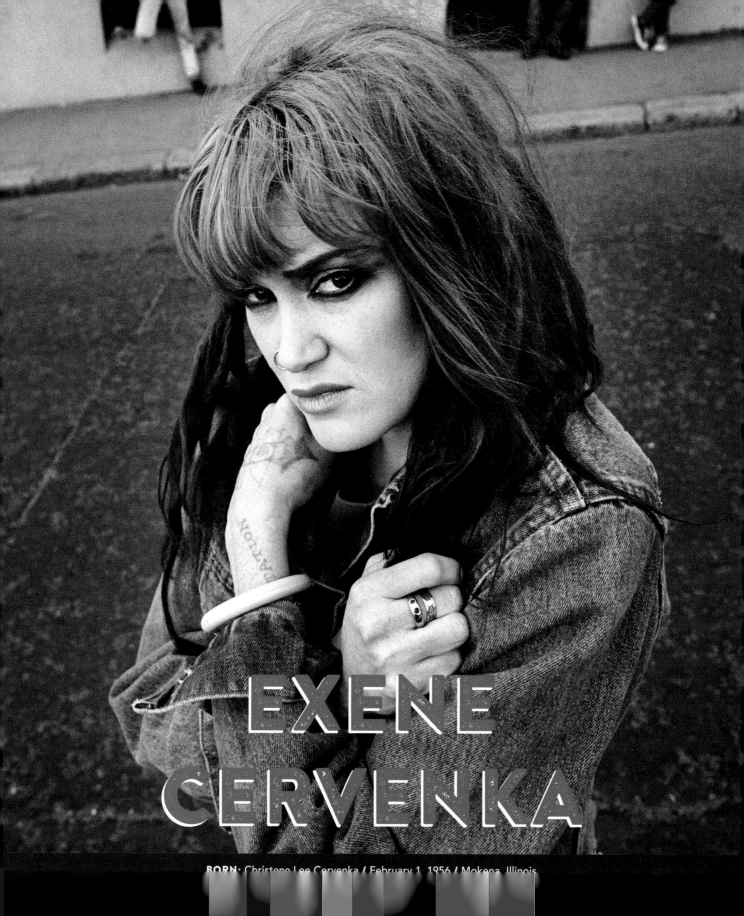

EXENE CERVENKA

BORN: Christene Lee Cervenka / February 1, 1956 / Mokena, Illinois

Along with her band X, singer, poet, and artist Exene Cervenka articulated America's slide from the late '70s into the early '80s. A palpable shift was rippling through the culture as a volatile, creative decade transitioned into the Reagan years. Punk reacted, becoming angrier and increasingly political, but X took a more intimate view.

The band coalesced in Los Angeles, where Cervenka had landed a job in 1976 as the first-ever librarian at Beyond Baroque Literary Arts Center in Venice. She and bassist/singer John Doe met there at a poetry workshop, and he brought her into his nascent group. Her lack of musical training informed X's unique sound as much as her poetry. Cervenka and Doe's forlorn harmonies made them sound as if they were a couple on the verge of collapse, their voices looming over each other like shifting shadows in a film noir. With platinum-blond, silver-clad rockabilly guitarist Billy Zoom and classically trained drummer DJ Bonebrake, they melded early the starkness of rock 'n' roll, classic country's chilling imagery and ironic humor, and the DIY urgency of punk.

Cervenka's look also commanded attention. She was the anti-LA girl, her wraithlike face punctuated by black eyeliner, scarlet lipstick, and a deconstructed, bleach-streaked Bettie Page hairdo, wearing dresses and jewelry from a mix of decades past. She'd spent her teen years in Florida developing a love of all things vintage, a pursuit facilitated by the state's large population of seniors. When they'd die, their adult children would often chuck their belongings. She and sister Mirielle built a rich collection of their cast-offs, everything from clothes to home goods, sometimes Dumpster-diving for the best stuff.

Cervenka was the heart of X's aesthetic, a mix of poetry and penury, of art and iconography. It was kitsch steeped in Holy Roller brimstone and cheap whiskey. It was glamorous old Hollywood cut up with kitchen shears and stapled back together in punk's image. Even her name, Exene, was as punk as it gets. Altered from her given name, Christene, she'd literally put an X over herself, taking herself out of the mainstream, branding herself a weirdo, or a blank like Richard Hell when he sang that he belonged to a blank generation. It was also a possible dig at those who took umbrage at replacing the Christ in Christmas with an X.

X the band named their 1980 debut *Los Angeles* after their adopted home city, building its stories in shards of gritty urban low-living, drinking, drugs, and sexual violence. Its 1981 follow-up, *Wild Gift*, followed Doe and Cervenka's marriage, tracing the downhill slide of low-rent domesticity, beer-soaked rows, and failing tests of fidelity. It was a wry contrast to the prognosticators who began to talk about "cocooning," proselytizing for people to couple up and build a nest, that same year. Their third album, *Under the Big Black Sun*, is like a pulp novel haunted by Cervenka's sister Mirielle,

> Cervenka was the heart of X's aesthetic, a mix of poetry and penury, of art and iconography.

INFLUENCES: the Doors, Patsy Cline, Sister Rosetta Tharpe

INFLUENCED: Shirley Manson, Courtney Love, Bikini Kill, Bratmobile, L7, Deap Vally

DEEP CUTS: "Motel Room in my Bed" (with X) / "Breathless" (with X) / "Poor Little Critter on the Road" (with the Knitters)

and critical eye. In 1985 she released *Twin Sisters*, a spoken-word recording of an event she did with Watts-born poet Wanda Coleman. She'd gotten to know Coleman, a former Emmy-winning television writer who some called the "unofficial poet laureate of LA," at Beyond Baroque. Coleman had recently won a National Endowment for the Arts grant and a Guggenheim Fellowship, but Cervenka was drawn to the cadence with which she performed and began to do public readings with her.

Poetry, spoken word, and art were always central to Cervenka's creative life, as well as a means of support while X was inactive — their last studio album was 1993's *Hey Zeus*, though they'd reunite to play periodically over the years, including a fortieth-anniversary tour in 2017. Poetry had brought her into a rock 'n' roll career that she'd never considered. It was also a point of bonding between her and her second husband, actor Viggo Mortensen; their son Henry has performed at Beyond Baroque.

Cervenka remains outspoken, unafraid to engage on difficult topics, from the way female musicians comport themselves to how the music industry betrays performers, from the failure of American politics to pejoratives and their misappropriation. She espouses Libertarian views and speaks nostalgically of the '60s and '70s. But she's also relentlessly positive and grateful, continuing to celebrate the virtue of art, the strength of women, and the dark splendor of Americana.

> Cervenka exorcised her intense grief in many of the album's songs.

who was killed in a car crash on her way to an X gig at the Whisky A Go Go in 1981. Cervenka exorcised her intense grief in many of the album's songs, her writing becoming more pointed and poignant.

Cervenka also looked outside the band for artistic expression. Her first collaboration with No Wave artist Lydia Lunch, *Adulterers Anonymous* (1982), was a book of poetry that mined love and lies and skewered Reagan's America. It was a surreal, visceral collage with flashes of sarcasm that characterized Cervenka's dry wit

PAGE 102: Exene Cervenka, 1984. OPPOSITE, TOP: With her then-husband John Doe in New York, c. 1983. OPPOSITE, BOTTOM: X's debut album, *Los Angeles*. ABOVE: Cervenka performing in London, 1979.

KIM GORDON

BORN: Kim Althea Gordon **/** April 28, 1953 **/** Rochester, New York

How did someone who grew up mostly uninterested in music become an iconic, bass-playing *Girl in a Band*? For Kim Gordon, who named her memoir after an annoying question repeatedly asked of her—"What's it like to be a girl in a band?"—it was a series of unlikely, though not unprecedented, turns. A middle-class kid from Los Angeles, she moved to New York City in 1980, drawn by the downtown art scene and the legacy of Andy Warhol's Factory. A visual artist, she paired up romantically and professionally with guitarist Thurston Moore, who mostly disdained the art world. Yet Gordon brought that sensibility to their band, Sonic Youth, which was as much a literate, experimental art project as it was a vital link between punk rock and grunge.

No matter how huge the band became during their three-decade run, she always thought rock stardom was "goofy" and stood off to the side of the stage, migrating toward the center only when her band signed with a major label and it was expected of her. At the height of Gordon's status as the "godmother of grunge," which was about as anti-fashion as music got, she styled up the movement with an influential clothing line; and long after flannel and unwashed hair fell out of vogue, she was still sitting by runways at New York's Fashion Week and elegantly attired at the glamorous Met Gala. Outside of playing in her band with only "boys," she worked on projects with numerous women and helped bolster their careers; but she's not afraid to openly criticize others who she thinks are getting it wrong, from referring to the Spice Girls' act as "repulsive" to critiquing singer Lana Del Rey over what constitutes feminism.

Gordon had rhythm and a good sense of both visual and aural space, but she barely played or sang when she, Moore, and guitarist Lee Ranaldo started Sonic Youth in 1981. She held down root notes with her bass and often spoke lyrics in a deep, tuneless voice, sometimes extemporaneous words that were secondary to the band's guitar maelstrom, at least in the beginning. She was inspired by late-'70s No Wave bands that decimated rock clichés with dissonance and disregard for even the three-chord song structure that safety-pinned punk together. No Wave pushed punk's DIY aesthetic into free jazz, funk, or feedback with abandon. It resonated with Gordon, who found it liberating enough to feel she could participate. She carved out a groove in Sonic Youth's improvisational jams, eventually finding euphoria in performance.

The band eventually wound their detuned strings and electric squall into songs, though they never gave up the noise. They spent the '80s bouncing between indie labels, releasing five studio albums and several EPs and singles (including a "side project" as Ciccone Youth, reconstructing Madonna hits), culminating in their 1988 indie apotheosis *Daydream Nation*, a critically

> She always thought rock stardom was "goofy."

> She carved out a groove in Sonic Youth's improvisational jams.

INFLUENCES: Mars, Nico, the Slits, Lydia Lunch, Au Pairs, Patti Smith, Siouxsie Sioux, the Raincoats, Catherine Ribeiro, the Shangri-Las

INFLUENCED: Sleater-Kinney, Bikini Kill, Bratmobile, Kurt Cobain, PJ Harvey, Kim Deal

DEEP CUTS: "Shaking Hell" (with Sonic Youth) / "Sacred Trickster" (with Sonic Youth) / "Addicted to Love" (with Ciccone Youth)

She found
catharsis in
writing her
2015 memoir.

PAGE 106: Kim Gordon shows her patriotism, undated.
ABOVE: Gordon playing with Sonic Youth at the Johnny
Ramone Cancer Research benefit in New York, 2004.
OPPOSITE: Sonic Youth's major label debut, *Goo*.

acclaimed noise-rock landmark that funnels the band's atonal tempest into songs loosely packed with pop-culture references from Warhol to Joni Mitchell to prescient cyberpunk author William Gibson.

The album launched them from underground to major label as they signed with Geffen imprint DGC, and things began to change for Gordon. She has talked about the unwanted weight of suddenly being expected to carry the sensuality of the band and experiencing sexism for the first time while on tour as an opening act for Neil Young—not from Young, who loved Sonic Youth, but from his crew. But on the group's DGC debut, *Goo*, she also stepped up to her new center space onstage, writing and singing the band's first hit, "Kool Thing," which sarcastically riffed on race and gender, and exploring the external pressure on women to be perfect via singer Karen Carpenter's body dysmorphia on "Tunic (Song for Karen)."

During the '90s, Gordon's new rock-star status led her to creative collaborations outside Sonic Youth. She started producing albums in 1991, with Hole's *Pretty on the Inside* as the first of several credits.. She formed the noise-indie band Free Kitten with Pussy Galore guitarist Julie Cafritz (Boredoms drummer Yoshimi P-We, Pavement bassist Mark Ibold, and DJ Spooky would later participate as well). Along with friend Daisy von Furth, she co-created X-Girl—a fashion line of the slim-cut ringer T-shirts, miniskirts, and '60s-inspired A-line dresses that she wore on- and offstage—and launched the acting career of Chloë Sevigny, who became the face of the brand. Gordon would later model for several companies, from Calvin Klein to Uggs. She became a video producer when Kim Deal approached her

to make videos for "Cannonball" and "Divine Hammer," hits for her post-Pixies band, the Breeders. Suspicious of MTV, Deal put her trust in Gordon, seeing that she and Sonic Youth had handled it well and maintained their artistic integrity. Gordon also tried to get riot grrrl to cross over into the mainstream during their "media blackout" when she cast Bikini Kill's Kathleen Hanna in the Sonic Youth video for "Bull in the Heather." She took acting roles, playing a cold-blooded (but fashionable) Hong Kong crime boss in *Boarding Gate* by Olivier Assayas, whose 2002 film *Demonlover* featured a Sonic Youth soundtrack, as well as cameos in Todd Haynes' interpretive Bob Dylan biopic *I'm Not There* and in television shows such as *Girls* and *Portlandia*. And at age forty-one, she had a daughter, Coco, with Moore.

Sonic Youth continued to record and tour until 2011, when both the band and Gordon's twenty-seven-year marriage ended over Moore's long-term affair with book editor Eva Prinz. Gen X fans were more vocally upset about Gordon and Moore's breakup than the band's; as the first generation of latchkey kids and widespread divorce, they'd idolized the two as a rock 'n' roll power couple who gave them relationship goals. But Gordon moved on. She found catharsis in writing her 2015 memoir as well as in an outpouring of support from musicians she inspired, such as Sleater-Kinney's Corin Tucker, who changed the lyrics of the song "I Wanna Be Your Joey Ramone" from "I wanna be your Thurston Moore" to "I wanna be your Kim Gordon" in concert. Gordon also plays in freeform electric guitar duo Body/Head with friend Bill Nace, occasionally designs clothes for other fashion lines, and continues to work as a visual artist.

THE GO-GO'S

FORMED IN: 1978 / Los Angeles

How is it possible that in the history of rock, only one all-girl band had a number-one album that they wrote and played entirely themselves? The Go-Go's held the top spot on the *Billboard* 200 for six weeks in 1982 with their debut, *Beauty and the Beat*. They were the first, and no one has done it since.

If the band was an anomaly, so was their music. Spurred by punk and shaped by '60s girl groups, with a wave of their native Southern California's surf rock, the Go-Go's blithe, guitar-driven pop sounded like nothing else on the radio at the time. For the sake of reference, *Beauty and the Beat* was finally bumped from number one by Vangelis' *Chariots of Fire* soundtrack, and though nominated for a Best New Artist Grammy that year, the Go-Go's lost to Sheena "My Baby Takes the Morning Train" Easton. They were New Wave without synthesizers, but they also drew from retro style and imagery.

On the surface, their songs were spangled and simplistic, as bouncy as a pogoing dancer, but *Beauty and the Beat* showed emotional range and writing chops, particularly of guitarists Jane Wiedlin and Charlotte Caffey. Singer Belinda Carlisle's slightly keening, often trilling soprano was distinct. She sounded like a cheerleader who'd fallen in love with punk rock, which is exactly what had happened. The band had spent two years coming up in the Los Angeles punk scene and playing to gobbing skinheads in England, but their pop sensibility was undeniable.

Caffey wrote the early-'80s classic "We Got the Beat." It was their biggest hit, reaching number two on the Top 100, just behind Joan Jett's "I Love Rock 'n' Roll," and it also opens Cameron Crowe and Amy Heckerling's era-defining film *Fast Times at Ridgemont High*. The song spins around drummer Gina Schock's double-barrel snare attack, upon which bassist Kathy Valentine plays its identifying riff. Caffey deploys a hang-ten solo, and a drum-and-vocal clap-along mid-section make it interactive. An earlier version of "We Got the Beat" was the group's first single (featuring founding member and original bassist Margot Olavarria), released in 1980 on British indie Stiff Records when other labels were wary of signing an all-female band, ostensibly because none had been all that successful. Ironically, the song's crowd-rousing power ultimately helped them secure a deal with IRS Records, when the label's Miles Copeland witnessed an audience going berserk upon hearing it played live.

Wiedlin wrote *Beauty and the Beat*'s other hit, "Our Lips Are Sealed," in 1980 about her brief on-tour romance with the Specials' Terry Hall, based on lyrics and letters he'd sent her afterward (Hall has a co-write credit on the song). Though some of the words and phrases sound like they sprang from the mind of a

> On the surface, their songs were spangled and simplistic, as bouncy as a pogoing dancer.

INFLUENCES: Suzi Quatro, X, Buzzcocks, Blondie, the Runaways, the Ronettes, the Angels, the Shangri-Las, Lesley Gore

INFLUENCED: the Donnas, Green Day, Hayley Williams, the Bangles, Haim, Best Coast

DEEP CUTS: "Surfing and Spying" / "Johnny Are You Queer" / "Get Up and Go"

talk show *

dude, the Go-Go's made a girl-power anthem of it, the theme of an assured sisterhood that didn't require anyone's approval. That seemed to characterize the way the band operated offstage as well. There were always women working with them—their manager, their lawyer, and some of their roadies.

Even the cover of *Beauty and the Beat* took an equalizing approach, a photo of the band wrapped in white towels and turbans, so low-budget that their tan lines are visible. Slathered in white facial masks, they're unified in appearance, not to be measured against one another. The band repeated this on the cover of their second album, *Vacation*, the women waterskiing in a line like a resort postcard from the '50s, dressed in matching outfits, hands on one another's shoulders for support.

Despite the look of concordance, the band was already fracturing. Wiedlin left in 1984, unhappy about not being allowed to sing the songs she had written, and having tested the waters outside the group by recording with the band Sparks. Carlisle wanted to go solo; from the outset, the press had singled her out as the breakaway star. Valentine wasn't getting many of her songs on the albums, even though she co-wrote the band's next two hits—"Vacation" and "Head Over Heels." With diminishing returns on their second and third releases, along with assorted health and drug-related issues, the Go-Go's broke up in 1985, although they'd periodically reunite to record and tour in the decades that followed.

Carlisle went on to a prolific solo career, again drawing from great women songwriters, including pop superpower Diane Warren ("I Get Weak"), Ellen Shipley ("Heaven on Earth"), and her former bandmates Caffey and Wiedlin, and working with actor/director Diane

Keaton, who directed music videos for her. Wiedlin continued to record on her own as well, hitting the Top 10 with the song "Rush Hour," and acted in numerous films and television shows. Valentine played with a number of different musicians and bands, and co-wrote the Go-Go's "reunion" song "Has the Whole World Lost Its Head" with Wiedlin in 1994. Schock worked with numerous artists, wrote songs for films, and co-wrote songs for Miley Cyrus and Selena Gomez. Caffey played in the Graces with Meredith Brooks and

> **Carlisle wanted to go solo; from the outset, the press had singled her out as the breakaway star.**

future Springsteen backup singer Gia Ciambotti, and co-wrote a number-one hit with Keith Urban. She also collaborated with Anna Waronker on projects including *Lovelace: A Rock Musical*, based on the life of adult-film star Linda Lovelace. And in 2018, the band themselves landed on Broadway in a most unlikely setting—the Gwyneth Paltrow–coproduced *Head Over Heels*, which sets their songs of the 1980s to an Elizabethan love story of the 1580s, proving that the Go-Go's timelessness runs in both directions.

PAGE 110 / OPPOSITE, TOP: The Go-Go's in concert at New York's groundbreaking New Wave- and punk-incubating "rock disco," Hurrah, 1980. ABOVE, TOP: Classic Go-Go's swag, best attached to the front of a denim vest. ABOVE, BOTTOM: A photo shoot for *Creem* magazine, 1981.

CYNDI LAUPER

BORN: Cynthia Ann Stephanie Lauper / June 22, 1953 / New York City

After a 2013 appearance at Sirius XM, Cyndi Lauper graciously signed autographs for anyone who asked. When handed a copy of her 1993 album *Hat Full of Stars*, a critically acclaimed commercial flop, she paused for a moment and looked at it reflectively. "That's a really good one," she said in her unmistakable Queens, New York accent. She had her little black pug Gordie in tow, who all but disappeared when she cuddled him against her dark outfit. Her hair was the color of pale cotton candy; this was relatively tame for Lauper, whose look was long demarcated by electric hues.

Lauper was promoting the debut of her reality show on WE tv, *Still So Unusual*, a mischievous look into her private life with husband David Thornton and their teenage son Declyn. She also talked about her *Kinky Boots* project and its imminent arrival on Broadway. Adapted for the stage from the 2005 film of the same name, Lauper wrote the music and lyrics. Six months later, she'd become the first solo woman to take home a Tony award for Best Original Score. With her Emmy and four Grammys, the win put her an Oscar away from being an EGOT.

The way that Lauper regarded one of her lowest-selling albums with a bit of melancholy, but also with recognition of its artistic merit, was poignant. She has said there isn't a song in her catalog she won't sing. Perhaps that's because her choices were never expedient, not in her music, nor her style, nor her activism. She didn't look or sound like anyone else. She steered her music in the direction she wanted, recording albums of standards, blues, and country/rockabilly, in addition to dominating the Broadway musical. She tackled heavy subject matter such as AIDS, abortion and reproductive rights, child sexual abuse, and racism. She started out and has remained a staunch LGBTQ ally and advocate, founding the True Colors Fund to help homeless LGBTQ kids.

Beginning with her 1983 solo debut, *She's So Unusual*, Lauper forged a buoyant, quirky sound, but there was substance beneath the candy-colored surface, even in her biggest hits. "Girls Just Wanna Have Fun," written by the late songwriter Robert Hazard, could have been vacuous, but in Lauper's voice it was empowering. "Time After Time" is a pining ballad, but in its video Lauper gives her character an element of defiance, pushing back when her boyfriend criticizes her half-shaved head, and taking off when she wants to go. Her masturbatory masterpiece "She-Bop" was declared obscene by Tipper Gore's PMRC (Parents Music Resource Council) but declared awesome by pop fans. The fourth single, Jules Shear's "All Through the Night," made her the first woman to have four hits in *Billboard*'s Top Five from the same album. And just a month after winning two Grammys for her debut, Lauper stepped into the WWF ring and became part of wrestling's storyline, performing alongside her friends Captain Lou Albano, the Fabulous Moolah, and Wendi Richter, to the fascination of some and the shock of others.

Habitués of late-'70s Manhattan clubs like Trude Heller's in Greenwich Village,

She didn't look or sound like anyone else.

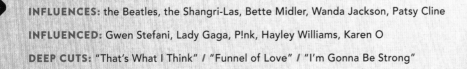

INFLUENCES: the Beatles, the Shangri-Las, Bette Midler, Wanda Jackson, Patsy Cline

INFLUENCED: Gwen Stefani, Lady Gaga, P!nk, Hayley Williams, Karen O

DEEP CUTS: "That's What I Think" / "Funnel of Love" / "I'm Gonna Be Strong"

Great Gildersleeves on the Bowery, and the Upper West Side's Trax would have noticed the flame-haired singer before her ascent to fame when she fronted Blue Angel, a slick, sax-y rockabilly band with whom Lauper got her first record deal. Her vocals practically burst out of their lone self-titled album. No band could contain her four-octave voice, a singular expression that was befitting of a unique, outlandish exterior. As a solo artist, Lauper cultivated an eye-catching look that became her trademark. New Wave fashion of the '80s abounded with vivid colors and sharp angles on everything from hair to shoulder pads, but Lauper mixed neon with retro pieces and with "junking," wearing piles of jewelry and other accessories. Her hair was an ever-shifting rainbow, sometimes shaved and spiked, or molded into various shapes, making it not so unusual for twenty-first-century middle-schoolers and middle-aged office workers to dye their hair purple or green or blue.

Lauper was and still is a pop star for outcasts because she'd been an outcast herself, drawn to people on the margins who she kept in her heart and commemorated in her music. Her songs offer the promise of self-realization: Today you are a teenage dork, tomorrow you'll be an iconoclast.

> Her hair was an ever-shifting rainbow, sometimes shaved and spiked, or molded into various shapes.

PAGE 114: Cyndi Lauper in concert, 1984.
PAGE 115: Lauper's "All Through the Night" single (1984). LEFT: In her trademark thrift-store chic, 1984. OPPOSITE: Performing, 1984.

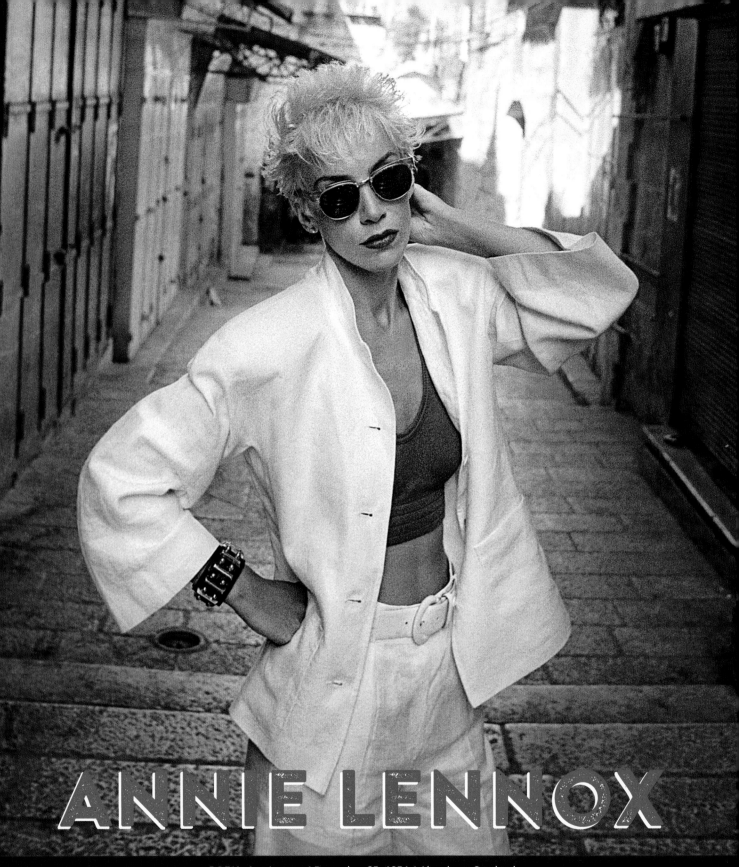

ANNIE LENNOX

BORN: Ann Lennox / December 25, 1954 / Aberdeen, Scotland

Annie Lennox was lying on the floor, despondent, curled into a ball. She and ex-boyfriend Dave Stewart had taken a bank loan of several thousand dollars to buy music equipment for their fledgling electronic duo; but, like their romantic relationship, none of it seemed to be functioning. It was 1980, and the band they'd been in for nearly four years, the Tourists, had broken up, too. The New Wave–pop quintet had recorded a sort of one-dimensional version of blue-eyed soul singer Dusty Springfield's "I Only Want to Be With You" on a lark, and it became a minor hit in the UK, landing them radio and TV appearances along with an opening spot on tour with Roxy Music. They barely had enough success to be drubbed by the music industry, including some biting critiques in the British press. Lennox felt scarred by the experience. When Stewart finally got the synthesizers working and began pounding out a riff, she bolted up and poured her jaded, depressed feelings into "Sweet Dreams (Are Made of This)." Lennox and Stewart became Eurythmics, and the song was their 1983 breakthrough, a number-one hit in the US.

It was the video, however, that really introduced Lennox to the world. MTV was just two years old, and music videos, mostly shot by record labels with no intended outlet, were rudimentary—usually just some variation on a band playing live. Eurythmics' conceptual, surrealistic approach set them apart. They appeared in the boardroom of a record label with a live cow wandering around the conference table, then out in a pasture with the herd, visual metaphors for what they'd experienced in their first band. Lennox, her hair cropped short and dyed tiger-lily orange, sang in a beefy contralto that lifted off into soaring R&B melisma between verses over the jagged, repeating synth riffs. Her pale eyes were rimmed in black, and she stared down the camera like a boss as she sang and banged her black-gloved fist on the ebony table, dressed in a men's double-breasted business suit and tie, wielding a riding crop. It was the first of many personas she'd adopt throughout her career, each one serving as a creative portal and a shield for the inherently shy singer.

Lennox's self-taught vocal technique was her way of rebelling against three years of classical study at the Royal Academy of Music in London, where she had arrived at age seventeen. Raised in northeast Scotland, she grew up hearing BBC1 spin American soul music on her transistor radio. As a teenager, she'd go to Aberdeen clubs to watch bands cover Motown and Stax/Volt songs. Her father, a shipyard worker, played a form of Highland bagpipe music called *piobaireachd*—an expressive, lamenting solo style that Lennox likened to American blues. Born too late to be a hippie and too early to be a punk, she was inspired by both movements' radical reinventions of cultural norms.

Eurythmics infused New Age into their New Wave. Their name was adapted from a performance art/movement therapy called *eurythmy* that Lennox had learned about as a child, and it also reflected their melding of sounds. Using synthesizers and

> It was the video, however, that really introduced Lennox to the world.

INFLUENCES: Dusty Springfield, Aretha Franklin, Debbie Harry, Tina Turner, Joni Mitchell, David Bowie

INFLUENCED: Amy Winehouse, Joss Stone, Adele, P!nk, Beth Ditto

DEEP CUTS: "Womankind" / "Train in Vain" / "Belinda" (with Eurythmics)

drum machines, they channeled a post-punk, European iciness, which they tempered with a love of red-hot American rhythm and blues. Lennox's voice conveyed both. Over their decade as a band, the chill of windswept arrangements and electronic instruments on songs such as "Love is a Stranger" and "Here Comes the Rain Again" gave way to more rhythm and less blues, replaced by boisterous horn sections and prominent guitar parts on "Would I Lie to You," and even bringing in the Queen of Soul herself, Aretha Franklin, on "Sisters Are Doin' it for Themselves" (Franklin would also include the song on her 1985 album *Who's Zoomin' Who?*).

The duo used the nascent art of video-making to their advantage, employing images that juxtaposed modernism with nature, as well as heavily costumed narratives that allowed Lennox to become a variety of characters, from CEO to torch singer to escort. Her male personae garnered the most attention. Nominated for the Best New Artist Grammy in 1984 (the duo lost to Boy George), she hit the red carpet as "Earl the Rocker" in a greasy black Elvis pompadour with muttonchop sideburns and stubble and remained in character, performing "Sweet Dreams" to a slightly confused audience. Eurythmics also played with gender in videos like "Who's That Girl," casting singer Peter "Marilyn" Robinson as one of Stewart's "girls," and pairing Lennox with a woman presenting as a man.

Even when she wasn't in character, Lennox often wore tailored men's suits and kept her hair in a pixie cut. She consciously embodied equality in her partnership with Stewart, refusing to be objectified as a female pop star and suggesting gender as a spectrum. It was a powerful public image.

When she and Stewart parted ways in 1990, Lennox began a solo career with 1992's *Diva* and its sentimental ballad, "Why," writing almost all the songs herself for the first time. Her sound softened to a sumptuous adult pop, crossing over to the rising VH1, the video channel that would later name her "Greatest Living White Soul Singer" for an audience who'd outgrown MTV. A collection of covers, *Medusa*, followed in 1995 and then came *Bare* in 2003. As her career progressed, Lennox embraced aging in her lyrics and her look. She did photo shoots with scant makeup or clothes that were stark and stunning and was always artistic and empowering. Lennox's solo output

> Born too late to be a hippie and too early to be a punk, she was inspired by both movements' radical reinventions of cultural norms.

healthcare, a living wage, and protection from violence.

Still, the honors kept piling up, including an Oscar, a Golden Globe, and a Grammy for "Into the West," which Lennox co-wrote and recorded for the soundtrack to *The Lord of the Rings: The Return of the King*. In 2014, she turned her love of blues toward jazz and the Great American songbook on *Nostalgia*, interpreting George Gershwin's "Summertime," Duke Ellington's "Mood Indigo," and the devastating "Strange Fruit," landing her first number one on *Billboard*'s Jazz Albums and Traditional Jazz Albums charts and scoring a nomination for a Traditional Pop Vocal Album Grammy. Her script-flipping performance of Screamin' Jay Hawkins's "I Put a Spell on You" at the awards the following year was a reminder that all her accolades were well-deserved.

was somewhat sporadic—she also raised a family and got involved in humanitarian work. She is a longtime advocate for the fight against HIV and AIDS, working with the late Nelson Mandela, the United Nations, and other organizations, and giving a TED Talk on the problems and the progress. Deeply affected by the poverty and powerlessness afflicting women and girls that she witnessed in her travels around the world, she founded The Circle, an NGO dedicated to fostering global feminism, raising money, and implementing programs to give women access to education,

PAGE 118: Annie Lennox in Jerusalem, 1987. OPPOSITE: Lennox, undated. ABOVE: Performing with Eurythmics, 1983. LEFT: Eurythmics' fifth album, *Be Yourself Tonight* (1985).

THE BANGLES

FORMED IN: 1981 / Los Angeles

They started out as the Bangs, more precisely the Supersonic Bangs. Before that, they were the Colours, spelled with a *u* like the British do, evidence of their Anglophilia. Susanna Hoffs, Vicki Peterson, and Debbi Peterson were three Southern California girls who loved the Beatles, the Byrds, and all things '60s, who dressed in mini-skirts and go-go boots and played garage pop that jangled with Hoffs's Rickenbacker guitar. It was 1981, a time when thrift stores were rife with hip castoffs from decades past, and most of it could be acquired on the cheap.

Hoffs was a recent graduate of UC Berkeley, where it's eternally the '60s. She'd prowled its record stores for vintage vinyl, rediscovering the Top 40 of her childhood and digging deeper into more obscure bands. She went to punk rock shows and fed off the artists' energy and do-it-yourself ethos. She moved back to her parents' Los Angeles home after graduating with an extensive extracurricular music education and a fervent desire to start a band.

Hoffs met the Peterson sisters via the classifieds in *The Recycler*, a local newspaper which also birthed Metallica and Mötley Crüe that year. Vicki Peterson had been playing guitar since grade school. She was even more motivated after seeing a girl her age singing on *The Ed Sullivan Show*; it was eight-year-old Susan Cowsill, Peterson's future bandmate and sister-in-law. By high school, she had convinced younger sister Debbi to play drums with her. The new trio bonded over their shared love of '60s pop and garage bands like the Seeds and the 13th Floor Elevators. They hired bassist Annette Zilinskas and saved money from their day jobs to fund

the Bangs, becoming the Bangles after a band of the same name threatened to sue.

Los Angeles was wide open to burgeoning bands at the time. Punk had demystified the process of making a record and playing gigs, and there were plenty of venues to play. The scene itself was transforming as punk waned and new groups pushed its aesthetic in different directions—metal, glam, New Wave, power pop, roots, and the one the Bangles fell into: the Paisley Underground. A number of like-minded musicians had gravitated toward the city, the last wave of baby boomers. They loved the Beatles just as older boomers had, but they'd come of age when John, Paul, George, and Ringo were bending sounds and minds on *Rubber Soul*, *Revolver*, and *Sgt. Pepper*. They were inspired by the jangle and harmonies of the Byrds, Grass Roots, and Buffalo Springfield, the baroque pop of the Zombies, the fuzz-tone guitars of the Yardbirds, and deeper cuts from Lenny Kaye's influential 1972 garage-rock compilation *Nuggets*.

The Dream Syndicate, the Rain Parade (founded by Hoffs's ex David Roback), Long Ryders, Green on Red, and the Three O'Clock (whose Michael Quercio coined the Paisley Underground moniker) pedaled in varying degrees of pop, twang, and psychedelia. They all knew one another and played gigs together; it was a convivial scene. The Three O'Clock eventually signed

> Los Angeles was wide open to burgeoning bands at the time.

INFLUENCES: the Mamas and the Papas, Joni Mitchell, the Hollies, the Shangri-Las, the Cowsills, Dusty Springfield, Carole King

INFLUENCED: Haim, Wilson Phillips, Sheryl Crow, Best Coast, Aimee Mann

DEEP CUTS: "The Real World" / "Getting Out of Hand" / "Dover Beach"

with Prince's Paisley Park Records. Prince was a Bangles fan as well and was drawn to the melodic, psychedelic-kissed pop these bands were creating.

But the Bangles were the only ones to achieve mainstream chart success. Their vocal arrangements were superb, with the distinct sweet timbre of Hoffs's voice and the multilayered sound of the Peterson sisters' familial harmonies. Although they all wrote and sang, they had a star in the Audrey Hepburn–like Hoffs, whose dark hair, dark eyes, and small stature stood in contrast to the big-blonde ideal of the '80s. They were college smart and street smart. When Miles Copeland, New Wave star-maker and the brother of Police drummer Stewart Copeland, came calling in 1982, they were so wary of signing a management deal that they allegedly brought a tape recorder to their first meeting.

Shortly after their debut EP was released, Zilinskas left for the cowpunk quartet Blood on the Saddle and was replaced by Michael Steele, who'd been the

> **The Bangles also had extraordinary taste in cover songs.**

Runaways' first bassist. Steele wasn't looking for another all-girl band after her less-than-stellar Runaways experience; but with similar taste in music to Hoffs and the Petersons, she wanted in. Steele also wrote and sang, and her introspective contralto added another dimension to the band's harmonies. They were signed to Columbia, the label of Dylan and Springsteen, and in 1984 released *All Over the Place*. The 1986 follow-up, *Different Light*, put them in the Top 10, led by the Prince-penned single "Manic Monday." The third single, the novelty-ish "Walk Like an Egyptian," gave each band member their own verse (except Debbi Peterson). It was a massive worldwide hit. Absurdly, it made the list of banned songs by Clear Channel radio stations after 9/11.

Though they amassed a catalog of literate, well-structured pop originals, the Bangles also had extraordinary taste in cover songs, and they recorded and performed them live with aplomb. It was the covers where they revealed both the breadth of their musical knowledge and the skill to reinvent songs and inhabit them as a female foursome. Debbi Peterson's lead vocals on the Merry Go-Round's "Live" and "Going Down to Liverpool" are high points on *All Over the Place*, as is Michael Steele's version of Big Star's "September Gurls" on *Different Light*. In concert, they'd wail on "7 and 7 Is" as ferociously as Arthur Lee and Love had on the Sunset Strip twenty years earlier. With four-part vocals and Vicki Peterson's blazing guitar riffs, their 1987 version of Simon & Garfunkel's "Hazy Shade of Winter" for the *Less Than Zero* soundtrack was a return to their rocking roots, capturing the energy of the group on record in a way they hadn't since their first EP.

Presciently, it was produced by Rick Rubin, a master of bookending the careers of great artists like Johnny Cash and Glen Campbell with recordings that took their music full circle. The Bangles, Mach I, were near the end. Their biggest hit followed; in 1989, "Eternal Flame" went to number one in nine countries including the United

States, but the treacly ballad sounded less like the Bangles than any of their previous commercial endeavors. They disbanded and stayed that way for a decade.

Hoffs made two solo albums and a series of oldies covers compilations with power-pop songwriter Matthew Sweet, who also joined her in the fictional band Ming Tea when she was enlisted to contribute music for her film-director husband Jay Roach's *Austin Powers* series. She reunited the Bangles to work on *Austin Powers: The Spy Who Shagged Me*, and they've recorded and toured on and off since then (except for Michael Steele, who left the band in 2004). Debbi Peterson played in the short-lived Smashbox, with Gina Schock (Go-Go's), Sara Lee (Gang of Four, B-52's), and Wendy & Lisa (Prince), and then a duo called Kindred Spirit. More recently, she sang and played guitar in Broken Sky with John Wicks of British pop group the Records, and has recorded with Matthew Sweet and others. Vicki Peterson married musician John Cowsill and formed Continental Drifters and the Psycho Sisters; she also toured with the Go-Go's in 1994–1995 when guitarist Charlotte Caffey was on maternity leave. Her latest project is the twangy garage band Action Skulls, with her husband and Billy Mumy (Will Robinson on *Lost in Space* and half of the novelty song duo Barnes & Barnes). Sometimes Peterson is seen playing the 2008 Daisy Rock Bangles signature guitar, a semi-hollow body with vintage mini-pickups, an ode to the sound she, Debbi, Susanna, and Michael coopted and made their own at a time when everything felt possible.

PAGE 122: The Bangles ignore the boys at LA's Will Rogers Beach, undated. OPPOSITE: The Bangles in Chicago, 1984. LEFT: Their second album, *Different Light* (1986). BELOW: Performing on a TV show, undated.

MELISSA ETHERIDGE

BORN: Melissa Lou Etheridge / May 29, 1961 / Leavenworth, Kansas

t's impossible to overstate the impact Melissa Etheridge had when she walked onstage at the 2005 Grammys, in jeans and a Beau Brummel-ish velvet jacket, playing her Fender Thinline Telecaster as she strolled to the microphone, looking every bit the rock star—and completely bald.

Etheridge was a nominee, but she was also part of a tribute to Janis Joplin. Kris Kristofferson, the author of "Me and Bobby McGee," which Joplin posthumously took to number one, introduced the segment. A barefoot Joss Stone opened with a dramatic "Cry Baby," reeling across the stage in a flowing sleeveless satin gown, with long, wavy golden hair and an armful of gold bangles. It only made Etheridge's entrance more pronounced. Singing "Piece of My Heart" in her recognizable rasp, she brought the crowd, including Joplin's sister Laura and brother Michael, to its feet.

The two-time Grammy winner's look itself was a big deal. Diagnosed with breast cancer in October 2004, Etheridge had undergone a lumpectomy and several painful rounds of chemotherapy and radiation. Naming her album *Lucky*, released earlier in the year, was fortuitous. Not only did she beat cancer, she was nominated for Best Solo Rock Vocal Performance for the album's single "Breathe." The illness had forced her to cancel part of a North American tour, but it was not going to force her to wear a wig. As she sang, the camera stayed on her, riveted, just like the audience in Los Angeles and those watching the broadcast around the world. Etheridge changed the word "man" in the song's first line to "one" with an eye roll and a smirk, as if to mock the absurdity of an out lesbian singing to "the only man."

She was arresting. In that brief performance, Etheridge crystallized what little is left of rock's rebellious nature. It's emboldening, and it can change the world.

At least it can change perceptions, and Etheridge made that part of her career. Growing up in Leavenworth, Kansas, she knew she was going to be a rock star long before she understood her sexuality. At twenty-one, she made a permanent move to Los Angeles. In 1986, Island Records founder Chris Blackwell, who'd also signed the Slits and produced Grace Jones (among many others), discovered Etheridge singing at a gay bar in Long Beach, California. He liked her hard rocking persona and craggy, expressive voice. People saw her akin to Bruce Springsteen, a hero of Etheridge's who later became a friend. A dozen years prior, then-rock critic Jon Landau had written of Springsteen as "rock and roll future." Blackwell saw women as rock and roll future.

Etheridge's singing style is rooted in the blues shouters who had to get loud when their acoustic music was brought from the Mississippi Delta to noisy Chicago bars. She writes heart-wringing songs that mine love, circumstance, hopelessness, fury, and redemption, and blows them up to arena-rock size. Many of her characters, like the one in "All American Girl" with a dead-end office job, an HIV-positive boyfriend (a likely death sentence at the time), and an unwanted pregnancy, live in the margins

> Etheridge crystallized what little is left of rock's rebellious nature.

INFLUENCES: Janis Joplin, Big Mama Thornton, Bruce Springsteen, Bonnie Raitt

INFLUENCED: Serena Ryder, Joss Stone, Brittany Howard, Joan Osborne, Susan Tedeschi

DEEP CUTS: "Resist" / "Miss California" / "Respect Yourself"

Her candor
was ahead of
its time.

where escape is a daydream. Early on, fans found her lyrics and her delivery so intimate that they formed a particular bond with her; for years, she received copious amounts of confessional letters and personal gifts.

Etheridge earned Grammy nods for her first and third albums, but it was her fourth release, *Yes I Am* (1993), that was the real breakthrough, with its Top 10 hits "Come to My Window" and "I'm the Only One." Unsatisfied with tacit acceptance of her sexuality, Etheridge put it front and center, helping to shift public perception of LGBTQ issues. The album's title reaffirmed her official coming-out months earlier at the Triangle Ball during President Bill Clinton's inauguration. Standing with her friend k. d. Lang and having just had a kiss planted on her lips by Cassandra "Elvira" Peterson, she said, "I'm very proud to have been a lesbian all my life."

Part of the trust Etheridge built with her fan base was her openness about her private life. In long-term, committed relationships, she and her partners were very public, attending events as couples, speaking frankly about having children via artificial insemination and choosing their friend David Crosby as the biological father. Her candor was ahead of its time. More than two decades before the United States Supreme Court declared marriage equality the law of the land, she helped redefine what it means to be a family. In 2014, she married Linda Waller, two days after their shared fifty-third birthday.

Etheridge continues to fight for causes in which she believes, including marriage equality around the globe, indigenous communities, and environmental activism. In 2006, she won the Best Original Song Oscar for "I Need to Wake Up," which she wrote for Al Gore's film documentary *An Inconvenient Truth*. More recently, she helped raise money for the legal defense fund of the protestors at Standing Rock in North Dakota.

Since defeating cancer, she has also become a proselytizer for marijuana, which she credits with improving her physical and mental health. The singer who had never done drugs and rarely drank joined with other "ganjapreneurs" in 2015 to sell her own "Private Reserve Cannabis Infused Wine Tincture." She received some backlash after admitting that she smoked with her two oldest kids, but still takes every opportunity to extoll the life-enhancing virtues of weed. Though she has a California medical use card, Etheridge was arrested for possession in August 2017 as she crossed the US-Canada border into North Dakota. She's practically beaming in her mug shot, looking healthy, her skin aglow. She also looks exultant, like someone on the cusp of yet another social revolution, someone who knows they're on the correct side of history because they've been there before.

PAGE 126 / OPPOSITE: Melissa Etheridge, 1990. ABOVE: Etheridge performing, undated.

KIM DEAL

BORN: Kimberley Ann Deal / June 10, 1961 / Dayton, Ohio

"Mrs. John Murphy" was supposed to be a joke. Married when she joined the Pixies in 1986, Kim Deal comically billed herself under her husband's name, deriding the tradition that once accompanied the institution. She mocked both punk rock's uniformity and the stuffiness of button-down office work by showing up for gigs at Boston's scuzziest clubs in the clothes she'd worn at her day job, playing bass in sensible heels, pantyhose, and a skirt suit, topped with a lacquered poof of '80s-style secretary hair. If any doubt lingered that Deal enjoyed skewering middle-class values, the name of her side project—the Breeders—poked fun at her child-bearing contemporaries.

Yet Deal didn't suffer a misfit upbringing in Huber Heights, Ohio, the Dayton suburb where she has lived, on and off, for most of her life. She and twin sister Kelley were smart, popular, social. Their parents are still married, and the siblings live near them, pitching in to help care for their mother, who has Alzheimer's. Family is paramount. During the Pixies' nascent period, Kim unsuccessfully tried to persuade Kelley to play drums for the band. Later on, when the Breeders became Kim's full-time gig, she brought Kelley in to play guitar. As teens, the Deal twins had performed at local bars, truck stops, and restaurants, sometimes with their folks sitting at a table in the back, singing a range of covers, from Hank Williams to Elvis Costello. "Mrs. John Murphy" left Dayton when her new husband, an Air Force contractor from Boston, wanted to move back home.

The marriage didn't last, but Deal ended up part of a band that had a monumental influence on '90s rock and beyond. The Pixies' restrained verses and cacophonous choruses (loosely inspired by another Boston band, the Cars) became a standard dynamic. So did the anti-style of walking onstage wearing whatever you happened to have on, which Deal's bandmates did, too, as well as her ubiquitous "unwashed hair, don't care" appearance. Kurt Cobain loved the sound of their first full-length release, *Surfer Rosa*, so much that he nabbed its engineer, Steve Albini, to work on Nirvana's *In Utero*; PJ Harvey did the same with *Rid of Me*. The Pixies' oblique rock was punctuated by the rants and shrieks of Charles Thompson, aka Black Francis, aka Frank Black, who wrote absurdist lyrics about death, molestation, incest, Christianity, environmental ruin, and other fun fare, and was lauded as one of the most important singer/songwriters of the era.

Even in a supporting role, Deal's presence is pervasive in her ghostly "Oooohs" on "Where is My Mind" (used in the film *Fight Club* and many other movies and commercials) and her lilt on the chorus of "Here Comes Your Man" (also film and commercial fodder). She adds a glinting undertone to "Monkey Gone to Heaven" as Black Francis sings about a man undone by tons of sludge. The rare times she takes the lead are fan favorites, like "Gigantic," which has since been re-recorded for an iPhone commercial by singer Phoebe

> As teens, the Deal twins had performed at local bars, truck stops, and restaurants.

INFLUENCES: Chrissie Hynde, Tina Weymouth, Sara Lee, Suzi Quatro, X, Kendra Smith, Mo Tucker, Marianne Faithfull, Kim Gordon, T-Rex

INFLUENCED: PJ Harvey, Josephine Wiggs, Sleater-Kinney, Karen O, Bikini Kill, Luscious Jackson, Veruca Salt, Bratmobile

DEEP CUTS: "Break My Body" (with the Pixies) / "Drivin' on 9" (with the Breeders) / "So Sad About Us" (with the Breeders)

Bridgers, who wasn't even born when the Pixies broke up. Deal's voice is girlish with a Midwestern flatness to it, and a peculiar patina of innocence. When she performs, the corners of her mouth curl upward toward her high cheekbones into an unsettling smile, reminiscent of the suburbs that produced her in the way their uniform brick homes, manicured lawns, and peculiar quiet seem to be masking something uncanny.

Deal's fan club included Cobain, who publicly wished she'd written more Pixies songs. At odds with Thompson about her contributions to the band, she started the Breeders with friend Tanya Donelly from Throwing Muses as a side gig and an outlet for the songs she'd been writing. When Donelly left to form Belly, Deal brought in her twin, who had to quit a job as a technical analyst for an Air Force defense contractor in Dayton to record the band's second album, *Last Splash*, and go on tour.

> Deal's voice is girlish with a Midwestern flatness to it, and a peculiar patina of innocence.

The Breeders shared the Pixies' dynamics and surrealist predilection, with a more profound pop sensibility, atmospherics, and the vocal twinning of the Deal sisters. In 1993, the year Thompson told the rest of the Pixies they were officially kaput, Deal's band released the million-selling song "Cannonball." Buzzing with feedback, shot through with Josephine Wiggs's sliding, leaping bass notes, and Kelley Deal's off-kilter supporting guitar hook, it was an inescapable hit. It was also on the tip of every music critic's pen, named the number-one single of the year by the *Village Voice*, *NME*, and *Melody Maker*, and many "Best of the '90s" thereafter. "Divine Hammer" followed, Deal's irresistibly poppy double entendre, whether she's a betrayed Sunday school believer smashing the patriarchy or dying for a heavenly hookup. Though the band was plagued by addiction, broke up, and all moved on to numerous other projects, they reunited in 2013 to celebrate the twentieth anniversary of *Last Splash*. It was the same year Deal quit the Pixies, who'd reunited in 2004, for good.

PAGE 130: Kim Deal leading the Breeders with a cigarette and beer in San Francisco (where they had recorded *Last Splash* and its breakout hit, "Cannonball"), 1994. LEFT: In 1995, when she was playing with her post-Breeders band, the Amps. OPPOSITE: Performing, c. 1993.

L7

FORMED IN: 1985 / Los Angeles

As the '90s dissolved into the new millennium, L7 was broke, fractured, and fed up. For a decade and a half, they'd occupied a unique niche—an all-girl, head-banging, hard-rock band that plied abrasive guitars, raging vocals, and blunt social and political commentary. They called themselves "slob girls," their hair and clothes ratty, their bassist Jennifer Finch barefoot onstage. Offstage, they made scatological and STD jokes. They were more metal than punk and more grunge than grunge. Butch Vig produced their 1992 breakthrough, *Bricks Are Heavy*, just after he'd done their friends' album—Nirvana's *Nevermind*. They scored a hit with "Pretend We're Dead," a slacker send-up with a chorus of encouragement and a big, bounce-along guitar hook.

But after five albums, numerous tours, countless journalists asking them ridiculous gender-specific questions, and MTV spots highlighting their female bravado, they had no record label, no management, no money, and no bassist (Finch had quit); and few seemed to pay much attention when they fizzled out in 2001. Dropped by their major label, Slash/Reprise, they'd formed their own, Wax Tadpole Records, and made the 1999 album *Slap-Happy* by the good graces of a friend who let them use his studio. They introduced a few new sonic elements to their boxy song structure—sampled voices, polka beats, slow tunes, even a first attempt at three-part harmonies, a departure

> They called themselves "slob girls," their hair and clothes ratty, their bassist Jennifer Finch barefoot onstage.

from their usual screaming and gang vocals, but reviews were mixed. Once a main-stage act at Lollapalooza, L7 had lost favor to funk-based, seven-string "Samurais," punkier upstarts, and more radio-friendly female acts. The group promoted their new indie record by flying a plane over the Lilith Fair crowd at the Rose Bowl in Pasadena, California, with a banner that read BORED? TIRED? TRY L7. They did the same the next day over the Warped Tour outside the Stone Pony in Asbury Park, New Jersey. The East Coast banner read WARPED NEEDS MORE BEAVER . . . LOVE, L7.

Those stunts were tame by comparison to what the band had become known for. They once raffled off a one-night stand with drummer Dee Plakas. Guitarist Suzi Gardner was the first woman to have her breasts molded by the infamous Cynthia Plaster Caster, who'd spent decades collecting the impressions of rock's most famous phalluses. Director John Waters cast them as the fictional band Camel Lips in his film *Serial Mom*, dressing them in prosthetic vulvas. They wrote a song for the film, based solely on the title Waters gave them: "Gas Chamber." Their song "Shitlist," from *Bricks Are Heavy*, was both a song and an actual list that they updated when they were pissed off, which was often. Singer/guitarist Donita Sparks dropped her pants on live television in England. Even more notoriously, Sparks, frustrated by problems with the sound onstage

INFLUENCES: Frightwig, Girlschool, the Runaways, Kat Bjelland, X

INFLUENCED: Evanescence, the Donnas, the Distillers, 7 Year Bitch

DEEP CUTS: "Fast and Frightening" / "Metal Stampede" / "This Ain't Pleasure"

at the Reading Festival in 1992, yelled "Eat my used tampon, fuckers!" after she'd pulled hers out and hurled it into the crowd (earlier that summer, Bratmobile's Allison Wolfe had done the same thing at Fugazi fans while attending a Washington, D.C. rally). In the years that followed, L7 fans would pelt the band with clean ones, sometimes with fond messages written on them in red-ink Sharpie.

It had taken the band seven years and three albums to get to that Reading stage, which they shared with Nirvana, Nick Cave, and others. Sparks moved to Los Angeles from Chicago at nineteen, landing a job at the *LA Weekly*. That's where she met Finch, who had briefly played in a trio with Courtney Love and future Babes-in-Toyland guitarist/singer Kat Bjelland. They added Gardner, whose punk-rock bona fides included singing on Black Flag's college radio hit "Slip It In," and found Plakas after firing a male drummer for calling them misogynistic names, according to Sparks. The LA metal scene was not a friendly place for them; they found greater acceptance and support from male musicians in Seattle, where grunge was bubbling up.

Early on, L7 built activism into the band. Their song "Wargasm," written after the first Gulf War, called out purveyors of ersatz patriotism. They also played benefits for

They once raffled off a one-night stand with drummer Dee Plakas.

non-profits such as Act Up LA, AIDS-awareness advocates, and the environmental group Greenpeace. In 1991, they founded Rock for Choice to help protect women's reproductive rights and counter growing efforts to undermine *Roe v. Wade*, organizing its first major benefit concert, which featured Nirvana, Hole, and other allies. In 2015, they reunited to tour, and in 2017 they released a crowdfunded documentary, *L7: Pretend We're Dead*. But when they started making records again, they delved right back into rock punditry with "Dispatch from Mar-a-Lago" and "I Came Back to Bitch," their first new songs in eighteen years.

PAGE 134: The slob girls of L7, undated. OPPOSITE: L7, c. 1994. ABOVE, TOP: Their third album, *Bricks Are Heavy* (1992), was produced by Butch Vig, who started Garbage the following year. ABOVE, BOTTOM: The band at the Lollapalooza music festival in Mountain View, California, 1994.

KATHLEEN HANNA

BORN: November 12, 1968 / Portland, Oregon

Riot grrrl is a punk-rock subgenre, a collective, a consciousness, a clarion call. It was a fanzine, or zine, that both directed and chronicled its crusade. It was meant to encourage, inspire, and support women, but it also had a profound influence on the most iconic rock star of the '90s, Nirvana's Kurt Cobain. Bikini Kill's Kathleen Hanna notably wrote "Kurt Smells Like Teen Spirit" on his bedroom wall, inspiring the title of his generation-defining anthem, but that was the least of it.

Hanna is one of riot grrrl's most enduring figures, and at times its lightning rod. Though she reinvented herself musically after Bikini Kill ended, with the electro-punk Le Tigre and her alter-ego-turned-dance-punk band the Julie Ruin, she has continued to write, talk, and make art in an ardent feminist voice that helps keep the spirit of the movement active. Bikini Kill's "Rebel Girl," on the 1993 album *Pussy Whipped*, became a defining song for Hanna. It depicts not only the cool self-assurance of the "rebel girl," but also the expansive way women can relate to one another and the power within that paradigm. That Joan Jett had produced and appeared on the original single only gave the band extra cred.

Starting out as a spoken-word artist, Hanna both inspired and was inspired by the indie music scene in Olympia, Washington, where she attended Evergreen College. A meeting with her literary hero Kathy Acker convinced her that music was a more expedient way to reach people than poetry slams. It turned out to be good advice, eventually; at the time, the punk scene was so male-dominated that early crowds who heard Bikini Kill perform songs about female empowerment and abuse were predominantly male. But Hanna and her friends would get their message out in other ways as well.

Hanna had read and submitted material to an ideological feminist-oriented zine called *Jigsaw*, edited by Tobi Vail, an Olympia drummer, singer, and guitarist with an exhaustive knowledge of music. Vail was friends with Cobain; they collaborated on music and dated for a time. She wouldn't join Nirvana but had a huge impact on Cobain, who often advocated for women's and LGBTQ rights in interviews, in songs, and in his life. Instead, Vail, Hanna, and bassist Kathi Wilcox formed Bikini Kill, the band and the zine. They'd later add Billy Karren on guitar. Along with the band Bratmobile—Allison Wolfe, Molly Neuman, and Erin Smith—and their cohort, they set about a grassroots movement to enfranchise women and create their own place in rock and beyond, complete with manifestos and reclamation of pejoratives that had been used to diminish them.

Raised during the '70s, riot grrrl musicians had come of age realizing that not only were the promises of the women's movement unfulfilled, but even the counterculture music they loved made no space for them. Despite

> Hanna, who sometimes performed in a bra with provocative words scrawled across her stomach, was criticized for her looks and demeanor.

INFLUENCES: Poly Styrene, the Raincoats, the Slits, Siouxsie Sioux, Ronnie Spector, Mecca Normal, Beat Happening, Yoko Ono

INFLUENCED: Sleater-Kinney, Bratmobile, Pussy Riot, Tegan and Sara, Beth Ditto, Deap Vally

DEEP CUTS: "False Start" (with Bikini Kill) / "What's Yr Take on Cassavetes" (with Le Tigre) / "Ha Ha Ha" (with the Julie Ruin)

Hanna's approach was radical.

American Women) and Naomi Wolf (*The Beauty Myth*), and exemplified during Anita Hill's 1991 testimony before Congress that she'd been sexually harassed by Supreme Court nominee Clarence Thomas.

Hanna's approach was radical. From the stage, she instructed "girls to the front" and "boys to the back" of the room, a manifestation of the safety and sovereignty riot grrrl demanded for women everywhere as a matter of natural law. Bikini Kill's lyrics dealt with childhood trauma, unleashing suppressed anger, and sexual politics, but the message was just as much about Hanna's delivery. Her voice was convincing; it boomed when she sang, lurching into powerful trills. She pogoed and thrashed through the band's performances. In between songs, she used her pulpit to roar about issues: violence, sexual assault, and inequality, often with autobiographical anecdotes.

As the movement grew, riot grrrl suffered a backlash, and not just from haters who showed up to the gigs to taunt, threaten, or even harm the band members. In

their celebrated forbears in the punk explosion of the '70s, or maybe because of them, violence and misogyny had crept into punk, metal, and the emerging grunge scene. Mosh pits made slam dancing look gentle by comparison. At the time, a feminist backlash pervaded throughout the country and the culture, articulated by writers like Susan Faludi (*Backlash: The Undeclared War Against*

THE C.D. VERSION OF THE FIRST TWO RECORDS.

covering them, media often belittled them, using words like "angry" and "warpath" to describe the music and the mission, or revealing private details about their lives. Hanna, who sometimes performed in a bra with provocative words scrawled across her stomach, was criticized for her looks and demeanor, for showing her body as part of the act, even for wearing her hair in a ponytail, as if doing anything feminine was averse to the mission. As the '90s progressed, contemporaries like Sleater-Kinney, PJ Harvey, Hole's Courtney Love, and Garbage's Shirley Manson found success, but the movement itself remained relatively underground. By the end of the decade, pop culture's prevailing idea of female empowerment was the Spice Girls.

A generation later, however, riot grrrl is being rediscovered and re-evaluated. In 2009, New York University's Fales Library opened the riot grrrl Collection (started by then-Senior Archivist and Evergreen alumnus Lisa Darms), an archive of letters, journals, photographs, recordings, and of course zines that recognize the movement as historically important. It continues to expand. Hanna was the subject of a 2013 documentary film, *The Punk Singer*, chronicling her career, her struggle with Lyme disease, and her marriage to Beastie Boy Adam "Ad-Rock" Horovitz. Hanna has also been involved with the Willie Mae Rock Camp for Girls, named for Willie Mae "Big Mama" Thornton, as an instructor and fundraising chair. Younger musicians are drawing inspiration from riot grrrls, who helped shift the language, sound, and perception of feminism. Hanna and her "sisters" launched a cultural ferment, the last generation to do so without the Internet—only with flyers, fanzines, and fortitude.

PAGE 138: Kathleen Hanna playing with Bikini Kill at Washington, D.C.'s St. Stephen's Church, 1992. OPPOSITE, TOP: *The C.D. Version of the First Two Records* (1994). OPPOSITE, BOTTOM: Bikini Kill at New York's Wetlands club, 1994. ABOVE, TOP; Hanna performing with Le Tigre in London, 2005. ABOVE, BOTTOM: Le Tigre's second album, *Feminist Sweepstakes* (2001).

COURTNEY LOVE

BORN: Courtney Michelle Harrison / July 9, 1964 / San Francisco

One of rock's most polemic figures is also one of its most audacious, astute, and unpredictable. By her own account, Courtney Love set out to become a rock star with famous friends, and that's exactly what happened when she formed the band Hole in 1989 with Eric Erlandson. The three albums they released in the 1990s reflect the decade and Love's trajectory through it, from squalid rock clubs to mega-music festivals, from a turbulent marriage and parenthood with Nirvana's Kurt Cobain to his suicide and the aftermath, from selling millions of records to landing critically acclaimed, award-winning film roles.

At times, it all felt driven by Love's sheer will. Like many artists, an intractable self-loathing feeds her bottomless ambition, but hers has a more destructive side than most. For every lurch forward in her career, she spiraled into self-sabotage fueled by drugs, rage, feuds, and meltdowns. She would be on the red carpet in couture, and then in court as a defendant in a smart black suit. She could be tranquilly serving herself tea from a china pot while having a conversation with Barbara Walters, or hurling her makeup compact at Madonna's head and crashing the stage live on MTV. There was no way to know what she'd do next.

Love's unhinged charisma was magnetic, but she and her band had the goods. Her tortured vocals caterwauled over the blare of her and Erlandson's guitars, blending No Wave nihilism into punk rock power chords and the timbre of metal with Pixies dynamics. Love's songs, like herself, were visceral and confrontational, jabbing at the ways second wave feminist moms had failed their Gen-X daughters and all the shitty things that followed as a result. She tore apart female archetypes in her lyrics and her look, perversely called "kinderwhore"—baby-doll dresses with stockings, everything messy, ill-fitting, or torn, topped with a bleached mop of hair, glaring red lips, and tear-smudged eyeliner. It was inexpensive to cultivate via thrift shops and provided a bit of shock value until it became part of the fashion rubric of the '90s. Love says she lifted the look from the Divinyls' Chrissy Amphlett, but both she and friend/frenemy/former bandmate Kat Bjelland, singer/songwriter of Babes in Toyland, became its mainspring. Love, though, took it mainstream. For her, kinderwhore was part Bette Davis in *Whatever Happened to Baby Jane?* and part fetishizing the girlie things that her hippie, intellectual childhood lacked.

There is also the matter of her tumultuous relationship with Cobain, whose rocket ride to fame with the band Nirvana ended with a self-inflicted gunshot to the head. Courtney and Kurt were the First Couple of grunge, joined by love, heroin, and their baby daughter Frances Bean. They would be forever linked in rock 'n' roll infamy and tragedy. During their roughly three-year relationship,

INFLUENCES: Fleetwood Mac, Chrissie Hynde, PJ Harvey, the Pixies, the Runaways, Lydia Lunch, Exene Cervenka, Patti Smith, Chrissy Amphlett, Pussy Galore, Linda Perry

INFLUENCED: Brode Dalle, Avril Lavigne, Hayley Williams, Beth Ditto, Deap Vally

DEEP CUTS: "Burn Black" / "Rock Star" / "Gold Dust Woman"

She was barely thirty and a widow with a young child, wrestling with grief and addiction, struggling to keep her own band together.

foreshadowing future work; even in the midst of menacing guitar, she lifts a couplet from Stevie Nicks's "Rhiannon" and mutilates Joni Mitchell's "Both Sides Now."

Between the album's ferocious veritas, Love's outsized persona and adroit manipulation of the music business, and her coupling with Cobain, a major-label bidding war erupted over Hole, the first for a female-fronted band, ending with Geffen and a reported million-dollar advance. Their follow-up, *Live Through This*, was melodically and lyrically a huge creative leap. Love not only roars, she sings—it's not pretty, but it delivers. Fury-filled, erudite, and evocative, Love honed a lifetime of chaos into adeptly structured songs with huge hooks and a damaged sheen to match her own. The album's release exactly one week after Cobain's 1994 death caused a deluge of conspiracy theories, dissection, and discussion, but it remains one of the grunge era's most gripping documents.

Love's star continued to rise as an actor in films such as *The People vs. Larry Flynt*. Her portrayal of Althea Flynt, junkie, stripper, and wife (all of which Love had been in her own life) of the controversial publishing magnate earned her a Golden Globe nomination and several critic's choice awards. Other roles followed, including *Man on the Moon*, in which she starred opposite Jim Carrey in his role as eccentric comic-turned-wrestler Andy Kaufman. In 1998, Hole released a third album, *Celebrity Skin*, a far more poppy effort that sparkled

drama and conjecture hounded the introverted Cobain and the extroverted Love, who was vilified throughout their tether and denounced after his death. How was she supposed to behave? She was barely thirty and a widow with a young child, wrestling with grief and addiction, struggling to keep her own band together (Hole bassist Kristen Pfaff died of a drug overdose two months after Cobain). "People go back to work," she said. "This is what I do."

Love spoke/screamed her way through Hole's 1991 debut album, *Pretty on the Inside*. Co-produced by Kim Gordon, it shares Sonic Youth's noise-rock sound and anarchic arrangements. Still, Love reveals her soft core,

with the bling of Love's glamorous new Hollywood life (and new beau actor Edward Norton, who she dated for three years), and bassist Melissa Auf der Maur's sweet girl harmonies. It earned them four Grammy nominations. As the '90s came to an end, riot grrrl had waned, pop music was on the rise, and Love seemed happy and healthy.

By the early 2000s, however, Hole had broken up. Love continued acting in films, and she published a cogent critique in Salon.com of how artists are mistreated and ripped off by the recording industry, which was on the cusp of imploding. Love was, too. She made two solo albums with songwriter/producer Linda Perry, 2003's panned *America's Sweetheart* and a 2010 comeback, *Nobody's Daughter*. In between, though, she'd fallen back into a cycle of drugs, courtrooms, and rehab. She says she never properly grieved Cobain's death until 2010. Since then, she's been involved in numerous creative collaborations on music (including a new Hole lineup), fashion, books, and film, as well as television cameos on *Empire*, *Sons of Anarchy*, and more. She also mended her relationship with Frances Bean after years of on-and-off estrangement. Despite the pandemonium of Love's life, she managed to keep her daughter out of the public eye.

PAGE 142: Courtney Love gets ready to rage, undated. OPPOSITE: Performing with Hole in California, 1995. LEFT: With Hole, 1995.

PJ HARVEY

BORN: Polly Jean Harvey **/** October 9, 1969 **/** Bridport, England

Visceral, spiritual, experimental, and dark, PJ Harvey's music challenges both listeners and herself. Uncomfortable if she felt comfortable, Harvey used each of her albums as a locus for where she should go next. The intensity of her songs reflects the internal roiling she felt making them; though highly guarded about her personal life, stories of breakdowns and thoughts of retirement from the music business have trickled out over the years. Yet each time she came close to retreating, Harvey instead emerged with a stunning, shape-shifting piece of work.

The singer, songwriter, and multi-instrumentalist (saxophone, guitar, cello, piano, vibraphone, and more) grew up on a farm in England's rural West Country, the first known settlers of which date back to the Mesolithic era. Harvey was surrounded by history, folklore, and her parents' record collection, heavy on blues and Beefheart (she'd later work with Captain Beefheart alum Eric Drew Feldman). Her folks quarried hamstone, a honey-colored limestone unique to the region, used to build churches and other structures for centuries. Her stonemason mother and her own pursuit of sculpture early on gave her some basic tools for writing and building albums, fusing her imagination and introspection with the right surroundings and the right personnel.

"PJ Harvey" was technically a trio when their astounding debut *Dry* was released in 1992. Harvey's lamenting vocals and guitar dirge borrow the Pixies' muted verses and surging choruses. Erotic and self-immolating, the album opens with her pleading and bargaining as she's being left for another ("Oh My Lover"), and goes on as she relives and grapples with the devastation. Her use of feminist ("Happy and Bleeding") and biblical ("Hair," "Water") imagery and pagan iconography ("Sheela-na-gig") provoked cultural debate, particularly after she distanced herself from the word "feminist" in an interview. But *Dry*'s follow-up, *Rid of Me*, was a furious reprisal. Harvey flexed female power ("50 Foot Queenie") and challenged gender concepts, slipping into the skin of a man to feel what it would be like to "calculate my birthright" ("Man-Sized"), matching her caterwaul with waves of guitar distortion.

By 1993, Harvey was struggling with fame, shutting herself off from prying press and overzealous fans. She evolved her music and her façade in tandem with a variety of characters in performance and on videos for her songs, from face-obscuring retro sunglasses and feather boas worn with leopard print, to heavy makeup and period clothing. She'd moved back to be near her parents while she was finishing *Rid of Me*, and her first official album as a solo artist, *To Bring You My Love* (1994), drew heavily from the blues and '60s and '70s rock records she'd heard them play when she was a child. She lifted Captain Beefheart's first line from his first album, *Safe as Milk*, and opened with it: "I was born in the desert." A "spaghetti Western" thread runs through

> Harvey flexed female power and challenged gender concepts.

INFLUENCES: Kate Bush, Chrissie Hynde, Kim Deal, Patti Smith, Marianne Faithfull, Björk, Bessie Smith

INFLUENCED: Karen O, Alanis Morissette, Courtney Love, Portishead, Savages

DEEP CUTS: "Water" / "Reeling" / "Guilty"

it, from the opening track to "The Dancer" at the end. In between, songs like "Send His Love to Me" ring with Spanish-influenced acoustic guitar, and on "C'mon Billy" she finds futile her attempt to tame an outlaw.

Harvey continued reinventing herself on her albums (as well as projects with longtime collaborator John Parish). The uneasy *Is This Desire* (1998) is moody and melancholic, the rage washed away by synthesizer, electronic beats, and piano. The haunted, desolate *White Chalk* (2007) is a modern reading of the British folk tradition and Victorian chamber music. It took her two years to make the edgy, lo-fi *Uh Huh Her* (2004), on which she played all the instruments but drums.

But it was *Stories from the City, Stories from the Sea* (2000) that began an eerie circle of concurrence. Inspired in part by a several-month stay in New York City, she namechecks the city's sights and sounds in the celebratory way unique to inter-lopers. She weaves that narrative through another of a love affair, heightened by a duet with Thom Yorke of Radiohead, who'd opened shows for her when PJ Harvey was still a trio. Melodic and drum-driven, with vocals as sweeping as a skyline view, it's easily her most accessible work. She was awarded Britain's prestigious Mercury Prize for the album on September 11, 2001, phoning in her acceptance from a hotel room in Washington, D.C. that was on lockdown due to the attacks. A decade later, Harvey became the prize's first two-time winner for her song cycle of war, imperialism, and decline, *Let England Shake*. She'd researched it for years, immersing herself in books, art, and documentaries on war. Her rhythmic idiosyncrasy embellished with equally oddball instrumentation like autoharp and bugle, she developed a completely different voice, high-pitched and aged.

Harvey further swapped the personal for the sociopolitical on *The Hope Six Demolition Project*, based largely on her travels to Afghanistan, Kosovo, and Washington, D.C. with photojournalist Seamus Murphy, whose work had helped inspire her previous album. Murphy's footage, a juxtaposition of the life of citizens, soldiers, and the places where the two intersect, comprised the video for "The Orange Monkey." It may not be her best, but its artistic and sociological achievement is that it sees people who are too often unseen. Ironically, she

recorded the album in front of an audience unseen by her. Harvey turned the recording sessions into an art installation called *Recording in Progress*. Billed as a "mutating, multidimensional sound sculpture," she and the musicians and producers recorded in a "glass box." Ticketholders could see in, but Harvey and her cohort couldn't see out. Whatever she'll do next will no doubt surprise, possibly shock, and hopefully stun.

Harvey continued reinventing herself.

PAGE 146: PJ Harvey performing in New York, 1995. OPPOSITE, TOP: Performing in Belgium, 1995. OPPOSITE, BOTTOM: Harvey's second album, 1993's *Rid of Me*. RIGHT: In New York, 1993.

SHERYL CROW

BORN: Sheryl Suzanne Crow / February 11, 1962 / Kennett, Missouri

At twenty-nine, Sheryl Crow had finally gotten her big break. Signed to a major label, paired with a hot producer, and handed a big budget to record her debut album, everything just felt . . . wrong.

Her route there had been circuitous. Crow graduated from the University of Missouri with a degree in music composition and became a grade-school teacher, playing in bar bands on nights and weekends. Her side hustle as a jingle singer took off when one McDonald's spot paid her more than two year's teaching salary, and she left Missouri for Los Angeles to seek opportunity. On a lark, she auditioned as a backup singer for Michael Jackson, and he chose her. Crow toured the world with him for a year and a half before returning to Los Angeles.

She landed odd gigs, such as a small singing role on the ill-fated police musical TV show *Cop Rock*. She waited tables at a restaurant known to attract music industry types, hoping to pass her demo tape into the right hands even though she could be fired for doing so, and she was.

> Her side hustle as a jingle singer took off when one McDonald's spot paid her more than two year's teaching salary.

But this was her moment. She'd found a home at A&M Records, the last "boutique" label that believed artist development was part of the deal. Her producer, Hugh Padgham, had won Grammys for his work with Phil Collins and Sting. As the sessions progressed, though, Crow had the sinking feeling that the music was too slick, it wasn't representative of her. Several months and nearly half a million dollars in, she acted on her instincts, asking her label to kill the project.

Miraculously, A&M obliged the then-unknown singer/songwriter, allowing Crow to make another album on her terms. Her actual debut, *Tuesday Night Music Club*, grew out of her weekly jam sessions with a group of musicians. It was rock with pop melodies and an undercurrent of Americana, the kind of music someone who grew up listening to classic rock and Top 40 radio in the '70s might spin into a new confection for the '90s. It was light-hearted with a heavy bottom. Its sound was contemporaneous, yet it conveyed a hint of nostalgia. It won three Grammys and it made Sheryl Crow a star.

Thirty-two Grammy nominations later, with nine wins and more than 50 million records sold, Crow has made a career of following her inner compass. After her highly collaborative debut, she disengaged for a while, producing and writing most of her eponymous second album by herself. Her instincts were right again: The soul-searching mix of love, social ails, hope, and yearning was a hit and earned her another pair of Grammys.

Throughout her career, Crow's social conscience lilted its way into the radio-ready hits she crafted. She wrote about war, guns, abortion, and other polemic subjects from which many stars would shy away. In 1996, Wal-Mart banned the sale of *Sheryl Crow*, which could have been catastrophic as it was a major music retailer at that time. Crow spoke out against the 2003 invasion of Iraq while her friends the Dixie Chicks inadvertently committed

INFLUENCES: Fleetwood Mac, Bonnie Raitt, Rolling Stones, Delaney & Bonnie, Carole King

INFLUENCED: Grace Potter, KT Tunstall, Cam, Haim

DEEP CUTS: "The First Cut is the Deepest" / "Home" / "C'mon, C'mon"

career suicide for doing the same. Even her beach-y summer song "Soak Up the Sun," from 2002's *C'Mon, C'Mon*, is a strike at materialism. Yet she managed to stay above the fray, equally at home in a duet ("Picture") and on tour with the far more conservative Kid Rock.

When Crow felt like singing opaque references to her busted relationships with famous men, she did that, too. In interviews, she was frank about her attraction to complicated, creative partners such as actor/writer Owen Wilson, guitarist Eric Clapton, and cyclist Lance Armstrong, to whom she was engaged for five months. She spoke openly about her struggles with depression

long before first-person essays flooded the Internet, as well as her diagnosis with breast cancer at forty-four.

As Crow's music encompassed more country and rhythm-and-blues, she left Los Angeles and settled in a different entertainment mecca, Nashville, only three hours from where she grew up. Crow longed to be a mother, something her friend Stevie Nicks has publicly said she sometimes regrets not experiencing, and is now raising two adopted sons as a single mom. She makes records in her home studio, including one aptly titled *Be Myself* (2017), scheduling sessions around caring for her kids. Her songs still balance pop ebullience with a critical eye, tackling topics such as overexposure on social media; a president with ties to Russia; and keeping partisan discourse cordial, or at least constructive.

No matter what the mood or the matter, Crow seems to project her genuine self. With a lean, athletic build, bright blue eyes, and mile-high cheekbones, her appearance hasn't changed much in her two-and-a-half-decade career. The vintage rock duds that characterize her style have become classic, perennially turning up in department stores as timeless-looking reproductions. Since retail caught up with the well-worn denim-and-leather look she rarely deviated from, Crow developed her own women's clothing line with a rock 'n' roll flourish.

Crow's sartorial choices reflect not only her music but also her journey: the laid-back Midwestern rock 'n' roller who moved to California and absorbed its breezy West Coast mojo, only to return home. From Laurel Canyon hippie chic, to Malibu surf culture, to Hollywood glam, to Los Angeles consciousness-raising, and ultimately to family life on a Tennessee ranch, it's all part of Crow's captivating persona.

PAGE 150: Sheryl Crow, 1997. LEFT: Performing at Farm Aid in Columbus, Ohio, 2003. OPPOSITE: In concert at Woodstock, 1999.

She wrote
about war, guns,
abortion, and
other polemic
subjects from
which many
stars would
shy away.

ALANIS MORISSETTE

BORN: Alanis Nadine Morissette, / June 1, 1974 / Ottawa, Canada

She portrayed a Zen-like God in the 1999 film *Dogma*, cast by fellow lapsed Catholic Kevin Smith. She planted a kiss on Sarah Jessica Parker's lips during a round of "Spin the Bottle" in 2000 on *Sex and the City*. But the most clever stunt casting of Alanis Morissette was when she starred as herself on HBO's *Curb Your Enthusiasm* in 2002, performing for an eco-benefit at Larry David's house. Mildly injured in a minor fender-bender in David's driveway, she played the gig wearing a large, restrictive neck brace, sitting up stiffly, looking almost as uncomfortable as the grimacing audience. Her voice warbled comically as she sang the line "I know I won't keep on playing the victim" from "Precious Illusions" off her album *Under Rug Swept*, which was new at the time.

Known for her whirling, emotive performances, it would have seemed like watching a bird with clipped wings had Morissette not been so natural and so funny playing herself. Seven years earlier, she'd released *Jagged Little Pill*, a gale force of girl rage and late–Gen X perfectionism that earned five Grammys. The album transformed Morissette, who'd been a teen star in Canada, into a global rock star and new feminist voice at age twenty-one.

Her singing was righteously indignant and gapingly vulnerable. Onstage, she reeled, long wavy hair flying around her face as her body caught up with her mood. As a lyricist, Morissette articulated generational, gender, and spiritual anxieties. Songs like "Hand in My Pocket" and "All I Really Want" identified the breaking point of a peer group unfairly labeled "slackers" as they struggled against economic and cultural forces stacked against them, and sometimes gave up. "Perfect" conveyed the heartbreak of overachievers in the language of their pushy parents. "Forgiven" was a skeptic's struggle with faith. "You Oughta Know" was a clarion call to women harmed by bad relationships, vastly amplified by Morissette's vocal muscle. Direct and explicit, it was a warning that secrets were not safe in the throes of heartache, and that their expression could turn any indignities back onto the heartbreaker. Ironically (much more so than her song "Ironic," which was anything but), the one secret Morissette kept was the identity of "Mr. Duplicity." Only Carly Simon's "You're So Vain" has caused as much conjecture. The mystery was used as a subplot on the *Curb* episode as well; Morissette "unburdens" herself by whispering who the song is about into David's ear.

Another "Perfect Illusion" lyric Morissette sang on the show gets at the core of her: "I know who I'm not, I still don't know who I am." It took her a long time to figure that out. *Jagged Little Pill* was a tidal wave, and as poised an artist as she was at such a young age, it knocked her out of alignment. She traveled to India, one of many spiritual quests and a source of material for her next album, *Supposed Former Infatuation Junkie*. She struggled with depression, anxiety, and eating disorders. She bottomed out after the breakup of her four-and-a-half-year relationship with actor Ryan Reynolds, then composed and released the cathartic *Flavors of Entanglement*.

> Her singing was righteously indignant and gapingly vulnerable.

INFLUENCES: Heart, Tori Amos, Sinéad O'Connor, Björk

INFLUENCED: Hayley Williams, Avril Lavigne, P!nk, Joss Stone

DEEP CUTS: "Right Through You" / "Not All Me" / "Narcissus"

Even in the depths of despair, Morissette revealed a sense of humor; while making the breakup album, she re-arranged the Black Eyed Peas' "My Humps" as a solo piano ballad and recorded a YouTube video of it, which has been viewed millions of times.

In 2010, she found happiness, marriage, and motherhood with deejay Mario "MC Souleye" Treadway, until postpartum depression seized her. Again, Morissette explored her way into recovery, this time with nutrition and meditation, tying the spiritual threads that run throughout her work and life into something tangible. She blogs about her relationship with food and what works for her, as well as mindfulness practices and how to use consumerism as a more beneficial tool. The same person who showed us more than two decades ago that venting trauma beats internalizing it now manifests how to deal with the aftermath.

Jagged Little Pill is still very much a part of Morissette, though, who is giving her landmark album new life by turning it into actual theater. Expanding the original concepts with *Juno* writer/director Diablo Cody and Grammy- and Tony-winning Broadway star Idina Menzel, *Jagged Little Pill* the musical could turn a new generation on to the healing power of female self-expression.

> Even in the depths of despair, Morissette revealed a sense of humor.

PAGE 154: Alanis Morissette, c. 1995. OPPOSITE: Performing in 1996, riding high on the multi-platinum *Jagged Little Pill* (1995). ABOVE: Performing in Rome, undated.

GWEN STEFANI

BORN: Gwen Renée Stefani / October 3, 1969 / Fullerton, California

I n the mid-'90s, Gwen Stefani bounded to fame in sneakers and hip-hugging track pants as the singer of No Doubt. Upbeat and playful, the Orange County, California band took cues in equal measure from '80s second-wave ska groups like Madness and the life-size cartoons at Disneyland in their hometown of Anaheim. No Doubt bubbled up like a school of Day-Glo fish swimming against a tide of disconsolate grunge, and Stefani established herself as a rock star and style icon.

But the platinum blonde with the sunny disposition was just getting started. In the new millennium, Stefani launched herself into pop infamy as a solo artist and created a trendy fashion line. She made her acting debut in a Martin Scorsese film. She appeared as a judge on *The Voice*, NBC's popular reality talent show, and she created an animated series for television based on her obsession with Tokyo's Harajuku culture and street style. On top of it all, she became a mother of three boys. Underneath it all, she continued to draw on her life, love, and heartbreak for inspiration.

> No Doubt bubbled up like a school of Day-Glo fish swimming against a tide of disconsolate grunge, and Stefani established herself as a rock star and style icon.

It was Stefani's heartache that helped catapult No Doubt, founded by her brother Eric in 1986, from ska-punk ignominy to international hit-makers. Their breakthrough album, *Tragic Kingdom* (a pun on Disney's Magic Kingdom), marks the moment she took the lead on songwriting. Much of it chronicles her feelings after her then-boyfriend, No Doubt bassist Tony Kanal, ended their seven-year relationship. The two remained in the band together, performing songs such as "Don't Speak," "Sunday Morning," and "Hey You!" as fans listened to their breakup play out in their songs.

But it was the first single from *Tragic Kingdom*, "Just a Girl," that really unleashed Stefani and No Doubt. The song is full of her frustration with the double standard to which women are held, sparked by her parents keeping tabs on her well into her twenties and extended to her experiences in the world. Stefani had gone from her close-knit, supportive family right into a band "family" that she'd joined as a teenager, and on "Just a Girl" she asserts her independence. The lyrics, pointing to anachronistic ideas about women, are sopped in sarcasm and delivered in fast and furious meter with an upstroked, ska-inspired guitar riff. Stefani affects an artless voice at first, only to deliver a gut-punch chorus proclaiming that enough is enough.

As No Doubt released seven singles over a three-year period, Stefani carved out her own identity—a glamor-girl-next-door who'd grown up a foot-stomping punk rocker and skanking "rude girl." Stefani paired her fondness for athleisure wear with bejeweled bindis and other glittering accessories she discovered during the

INFLUENCES: Debbie Harry, Pauline Black (the Selecter), Cyndi Lauper, Madonna

INFLUENCED: P!nk, Hayley Williams, Katy Perry, Avril Lavigne, Lily Allen, Best Coast

DEEP CUTS: "Different People" (with No Doubt) / "Don't Let Me Down" (with No Doubt) / "Where Would I Be"

> **Stefani carved out her own identity—a glamor-girl-next-door who'd grown up a foot-stomping punk rocker and skanking "rude girl."**

years she'd spent around Kanal's Indian family. Raised in the shadow of Los Angeles, she'd admired old Hollywood glamor and adopted the blond locks, ivory makeup, and cherry-red lipstick of stars like Marilyn Monroe, who she grew up idolizing, and Jean Harlow, who she'd later portray in Scorsese's *The Aviator*. It was Blondie's Debbie Harry, however, who she saw as a role model, both as a female singer fronting a male group, and as a style ideal. Stefani, whose grandmother and great-grandmother were seamstresses, sewed her own clothes and did (and often still does) her own makeup. So-called "Gwennabes" began copying her, much like the Madonna-wannabes of the '80s.

Stylist Andrea Lieberman turned Stefani on to haute couture, refining the singer's already-keen fashion sense. By 2004, she had debuted her own fashion line, L.A.M.B., an acronym for her first solo release, *Love. Angel. Music. Baby.*, which came out a few months later. The album cuts a wide swath through the '80s dance music of Stefani's teen years, from electronic pop to New Wave to funk to synthpop and beyond. "The Real Thing" punched up its borrowed beat and melody from New Order's "Bizarre Love Triangle," with guest appearances by that band's Bernard Sumner and Peter Hook. "Hollaback Girl," with its high school marching band drum corps and cheerleader handclaps, became Stefani's first number-one song. Its

title was also appropriated by the founders of Hollaback!, a worldwide organization dedicated to ending street harassment, especially of women and the LGBTQ community.

In 2014, Stefani joined the cast of celebrity judges on *The Voice*. Her husband of a dozen years (and dad of their three sons), former Bush front-man Gavin Rossdale, appeared that season as an "advisor" to her team. The two divorced the following year, however, and Stefani began a relationship with *Voice* co-star and country singer Blake Shelton. She documented her ups and downs with Rossdale in song: longing for marriage but opting to stay unattached ("Simple Kind of Life" from No Doubt's 2001 album *Return of Saturn*); forecasting the end of a relationship ("Ex-Girlfriend," from the same album); a breakup metaphor ("Early Winter" from 2006's *The Sweet Escape*); and moving between stages of grief ("Used to Love You" from 2016's *This Is What the Truth Feels Like*); as well as her nascent romance with Shelton ("Make Me Like You" from *This is What the Truth Feels Like*). She even wrote a song about staying friends with her first flame Kanal ("Cool" from *Love. Angel. Music. Baby.*). But while relationships have given Stefani hit-making fodder, it's what she has done on her own that makes her a pop-culture idol.

PAGE 158: Gwen Stefani performing with No Doubt in Las Vegas, 2015. OPPOSITE: At the New Orleans Jazz and Heritage Festival, 2015. ABOVE: With No Doubt in Toronto, 2009.

SHIRLEY MANSON

BORN: Shirley Ann Manson / August 26, 1966 / Edinburgh, Scotland

t was only the third day of February, and one of the most rad happenings of 2018 had already taken place. Shirley Manson, singer of Garbage and one of rock's most outspoken and fervent feminists, headlined Girlschool LA, a three-day festival of performance and panel discussions aimed at creating opportunities for women and non-binary musicians. Manson was backed by an all-female string quartet and choir, and then joined by special guest Fiona Apple for a duet of "You Don't Own Me," Lesley Gore's 1963 declaration of independence. Barely a week after #GrammysSoMale had been the takeaway from the 2018 awards, followed by Recording Academy President Neil Portnow's response that "women need to step up," Apple wore a handmade T-shirt that read KNEEL, PORTNOW. (Manson also called for him to step down). Both the song and the setting had tremendous resonance.

The idea to sing "You Don't Own Me," which Gore recorded at just seventeen, came from Manson's Garbage family—bandmate Duke Erikson's daughter, Roxy. The suggestion itself would have been unthinkable when Manson assumed the role of band frontperson in 1994. Landing in the American Midwest from her native Edinburgh—where she was a club kid and musician and had worked at Miss Selfridge department store—she couldn't have stepped into a more divergent, dude-centric world. Erikson, and Garbage co-founders Steve Marker and Butch Vig,

all came from the recording and engineering side of the music business, which is almost uniformly male; as of 2018, the number of women who've won a Grammy for Producer of the Year (non-classical) is zero. Vig was already renowned for being at the center of the grunge vortex, having produced Nirvana, L7, Smashing Pumpkins, and others at Smart Studios—the Madison, Wisconsin, recording hub he and Marker had built. They wanted their new project to be the antithesis of grunge: heavy pop with lots of electronic studio wizardry. And they needed a singer.

Marker famously saw Manson's band Angelfish during the solitary spin they received on MTV's *120 Minutes*. Manson famously bombed her first audition, but the three experienced studio denizens quickly realized that her voice and aesthetic was exactly what they were missing. Manson's singing went against the grain of '90s popular music, which was a lot of over-emoting. She invoked a lower register, and there was a soft quality with an ocean-like depth to her voice, a quiet power hinting that a fury beneath it could be unleashed if you pissed her off. She wrote lyrics. And she was glamorous, her outfits a mix of post-punk and goth-y club kid chic with pale skin, lots of dark eyeliner and lipstick, and a shock of red hair. She got the band styled as well. They wanted out of grunge but hadn't thought about their look, and she had them paint their nails,

Manson's singing went against the grain of '90s popular music.

INFLUENCES: Debbie Harry, Chrissie Hynde, Patti Smith, the Sugarcubes, Elastica, Marianne Faithfull, Kim Gordon, Siouxsie Sioux

INFLUENCED: Karen O, Amy Lee, Hayley Williams, Screaming Females

DEEP CUTS: "Subhuman" (with Garbage) / "Deadwood" (with Garbage) / "Suffocate Me" (with Angelfish)

shed their flannels, and slip into modish suits.

Their self-titled debut was packed with the guys' experimental genius and Manson's gloomy cool. It was a '90s-style wall-of-sound, layers of beats and hooks, fuzzed-out bass, samples, and found sounds. Originally conceived as just a studio project, the songs were so densely constructed that when the band decided to tour, they had to figure out ways of detonating the samples. *Garbage* yielded several hits, including "Stupid Girl," "Queer," and "Only Happy When It Rains," and scored the band three Grammy nominations. After four studio albums and numerous world tours, however, the foursome felt burned out. They took a seven-year hiatus in 2005, during which they all worked on separate

> Manson
> relentlessly kicks
> at the parameters
> around women.

projects, returning with three more albums and a coffee-table book, *This Is the Noise That Keeps Me Awake*, filled with vivid color photographs and an oral history of the band.

Manson needed the break. She traveled, and she married Billy Bush, Garbage's sound engineer (her first marriage, to Scottish artist Eddie Farrell, ended in 2003). She made her acting debut, playing a shape-shifting cyborg on *Terminator: The Sarah Connor Chronicles*, and participated in a documentary on cutting, a subject of which she has firsthand knowledge. Bullied in childhood, she self-harmed as a teen and suffered low self-esteem for years, well into her tenure with Garbage. Nearing fifty when the band released its sixth album, *Strange Little Birds*, Manson continued to express her generation's syndrome, a relentless feeling of failing, on songs like "Empty."

The quick-witted, self-deprecating Manson, though, is anything but failing. Garbage made her a rock icon, as did the NME when they gave her their 2018 Icon Award. In 2017, *Forbes* named her Activist of the Year for her advocacies of animals; AIDS and cancer research; and the LGBTQ and other communities. But her greatest impact is in her ability to articulate a response to the sexism and ageism she has experienced, sharing the tools she used to control her own agency and define herself, rather than allow herself to be defined. Insightful, intelligent, and vociferous, Manson relentlessly kicks at the parameters around women in all fields, not just the arts.

PAGE 162: Shirley Manson performing with Garbage at New York's Madison Square Garden, 2001. LEFT: Manson trying out a country-western look. OPPOSITE: With Garbage in Holland, 1998.

SLEATER-KINNEY

FORMED IN: 1994 / Olympia, Washington

The angular guitar parts seem to be having their own conversation, sometimes call and response, sometimes a call to arms. The vocals are disparate, one strident and sweeping; the second, lower-register, burbling beneath it; and an occasional third harmony floating over them both. Sleater-Kinney's musical interaction sounds like no other. Once in a while their influences peek out from behind their spiky riffs, but they play as if they've invented their own language. Corin Tucker and Carrie Brownstein's back-and-forth is clairvoyant, and drummer Janet Weiss possesses the uncanny ability to read them both from the back of the stage and give them a big rock foundation on which to play.

As students at Evergreen State College, Brownstein and Tucker were both part of riot grrrl. Tucker's duo with drummer Tracy Sawyer, Heavens to Betsy, made one of the movement's earliest 45s, a 1992 split single with Bratmobile. Brownstein's Excuse 17 formed in 1993, releasing their debut on CD via Chainsaw Records, founded by musician and queercore pioneer Donna Dresch. Chainsaw also released Sleater-Kinney's first two albums with Australian indie rock drummer Laura MacFarlane. In both bands, you can hear the nascent elements that would make a more enduring project.

Sleater-Kinney began as a casual jam (the name came from the street where their practice space was located), then a brief romantic relationship between the two

> Publications began bestowing titles on Sleater-Kinney such as "best rock band in America."

singers, then a musical partnership that spawned seven albums in ten years. There were shared themes with riot grrrl—sexual politics, self-image, gender equality—as well as a DIY feel, fueled by defensible rage at being hurt, or patronized, or underestimated. Their self-titled 1995 debut was spare and sinewy and clocked in at a very punk-rock 22 minutes, 45 seconds short. But on each subsequent release, their interplay became increasingly sophisticated and the songs more distinguished. By their third album, *Dig Me Out*, they'd found Weiss, who played at the speed of punk with the expansive style of classic rock. Like many bands, the addition of the right drummer took them from good to great.

Time, *Rolling Stone*, *Esquire*, and other publications began bestowing titles on Sleater-Kinney such as "best rock band in America." Pearl Jam took them on an arena tour as their opening act in 2003. They signed with Sub Pop and in 2005 released *The Woods*, with its sprawling, heavy guitar freakouts and scant rambles like "Modern Girl." By then, Brownstein was suffering from debilitating anxiety, Tucker wanted to spend more time with her four-year-old son Marshall and have a second child (which she did in 2008, daughter Glory), and Weiss had other offers. The band went on "indefinite hiatus." Weiss and Brownstein played together in Wild Flag with Helium's Mary Timony and the Minders' Rebecca Cole. Tucker made solo albums and played with REM's Peter Buck, among others.

INFLUENCES: Bikini Kill, Poly Styrene, the Slits, PJ Harvey, Chrissie Hynde, Sara Lee, the Avengers, Mecca Normal

INFLUENCED: the Yeah Yeah Yeahs, Beth Ditto, Erase Errata, Screaming Females, Le Butcherettes

DEEP CUTS: "A Quarter to Three" / "Light Rail Coyote" / "Little Babies"

SLEATER-KINNEY DIG ME OUT

Brownstein attempted a more structured life, briefly working for Wieden+Kennedy in 2007, the Portland advertising agency responsible for Nike's "Just Do It" campaign, and upending both the ad and rock worlds by using the Beatles' "Revolution" to sell sneakers. She'd later draw on the experience in sketches for *Portlandia*, the IFC TV comedy series she co-created and starred in with *SNL* alum/drummer Fred Armisen, lampooning her adopted home city. Her deadpan foil to Armisen's unhinged characters was the show's heart, and led to supporting roles in *Transparent* and the Todd Haynes film *Carol*, among others. She also wrote the *Monitor Mix* blog for NPR Music and contributed to *All Songs Considered*, and in 2015 published a memoir, *Hunger Makes Me a Modern Girl*.

Through most of their break, the trio remained friends. Brownstein got her bandmates work on *Portlandia*; Tucker appeared in a couple of episodes, and Weiss was the show's location scout for five years. When Sleater-Kinney reunited in 2015 with their acclaimed eighth album *No Cities to Love*, they supported female artists like Minneapolis rapper Lizzo, who they brought on tour as an opening act. Two decades after riot grrrl, it's encouraging to see women turn its philosophy into real opportunities for one another.

PAGE 166: Sleater-Kinney backstage at San Francisco's The Fillmore, 2002. OPPOSITE, LEFT: Sleater-Kinney's third album, *Dig Me Out* (1997). OPPOSITE, RIGHT: Performing in San Francisco, 2000. ABOVE: At the ArthurFest in Los Feliz, California, 2005.

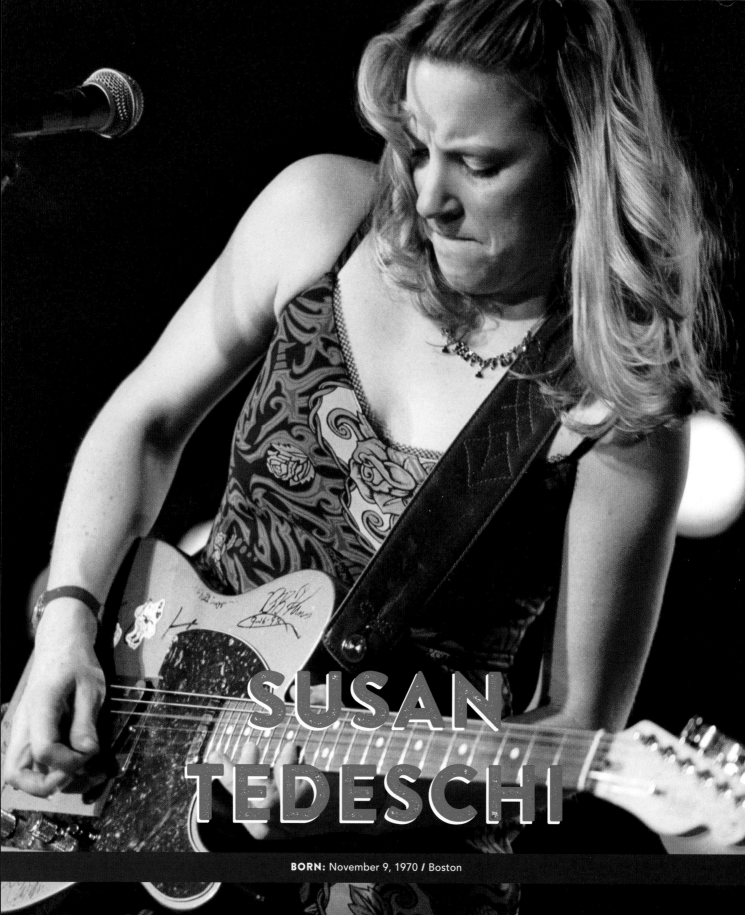

SUSAN TEDESCHI

BORN: November 9, 1970 / Boston

On her first gig at a New York City blues bar, Susan Tedeschi dressed more like one of the Upper East Side office workers who'd arrived for happy hour than an ax-wielding blues singer with a gospel-drenched voice. Image-making wasn't really on the agenda for the Berklee College of Music alumnus. She was a serious musician with a bachelor's degree from the school that stars are more famous for dropping out of than graduating. When the blond, blue-eyed Tedeschi stunned the crowd with a throaty wail and pulled on the strings of her Telecaster, no one paid any attention to what she wore, either.

She'd begun to master the music from playing in the Boston blues scene, the '90s version of the place that nurtured Bonnie Raitt, the J. Geils Band, Treat Her Right, Morphine, and others with a connection to the genre. Even Boston's garage bands, like the Remains and the Lost, were steeped in the primordial ooze of the blues. Tedeschi's blues was electric, soulful, and gritty. She was signed to Rounder Records' Tone-Cool imprint, also based in Massachusetts. Her 1998 label debut, *Just Won't Burn*, contained a couple of chestnuts—Junior Wells's "Little by Little" and Ruth Brown's "Mama, He Treats Your Daughter Mean," and it offered surprising originals written by Tedeschi and her band, including the album's blazing first track, "Rock Me Right." The singer and guitarist also made a bold move in covering John Prine's "Angel from Montgomery," a

> Tedeschi stunned the crowd with a throaty wail.

staple for Raitt (years later, Tedeschi would sing with Prine on his duets album).

Just Won't Burn turned out to be an apt title. It was a slow burn, but over the course of two years it went gold, selling half a million copies. Tedeschi won two prestigious W. C. Handy Blues Awards and snagged a Grammy nomination for Best New Artist only to lose to Christina Aguilera. In the process, though, Tedeschi became the "it-girl" with whom to play. She toured with Buddy Guy and B. B. King, played Willie Nelson's Fourth of July Picnic, Farm Aid, and recorded a version of "Crazy" with the bandanna-sporting, weed-proselytizing American icon. She performed on *Austin City Limits* with Jimmie Vaughan and Double Trouble, and joined the Lilith Fair, singer Sarah McLachlan's feel-good sisterhood of the traveling bands.

On tour with the Allman Brothers in 1999, she met guitarist Derek Trucks, and the two bonded over their shared love of obscure blues, jazz, and guitar gear. The nephew of Butch Trucks had just officially joined the Allmans that year, but he'd been unofficially jamming with them since childhood and was well on his way to being named one of the best players of all time. Their wedding in 2001 was surprising, less because Tedeschi is eight years his senior than because she favors Fender guitars and Trucks is a Gibson guy (that's a joke among guitarists, as both brands inspire loyalty). But in reality the two different instruments, the former pointed and trebly, the latter round and sustained, are, as Trucks has said, "a great marriage of sound."

For a decade, they raised a family together but kept their music endeavors separate. In 2011, however,

INFLUENCES: Bonnie Raitt, Aretha Franklin, Janis Joplin, Sister Rosetta Tharpe, Big Mama Thornton, Toni Lynn Washington

INFLUENCED: Grace Potter, Larkin Poe, Samantha Fish, Joanne Shaw Taylor

DEEP CUTS: "Hurt So Bad" / "Gonna Move" / "Revolutionize Your Soul"

She was a serious musician with a bachelor's degree from the school that stars are more famous for dropping out of than graduating.

they formed the Tedeschi Trucks Band, a soulful eleven-piece roots outfit that grooves and swings with New Orleans jazz, Indian raga jams, Delta slide, hippie funk, and Tedeschi's ardent blues belting, powerful enough to stand strong in the center of the shivaree of instrumentation and improvisation. She was the missing piece in Trucks's previous all-dude incarnations, a woman's voice, spiritual and commanding, and a conversational guitar style that complements his inventive six-string excursions. And playing in their family band, Tedeschi finally won a Grammy after many nominations—Best Blues Album for their first collaboration, 2012's *Revelator*.

AMY WINEHOUSE

BORN: Amy Jade Winehouse / September 14, 1983 / London **DIED:** July 23, 2011 / London

The vision of Amy Winehouse enshrined in our minds is kind of a caricature, with her jet-black beehive weave and winged eyeliner. Tattooed and emaciated, she embodied the rock 'n' roll look of danger and its specter of death.

But when her debut album *Frank* was released in 2003, she appeared much different—radiant, fearless, ambitious, and so excited about making music. Barely out of her teens, which she'd spent much of singing at a London jazz club, she was a nascent superstar, a self-assured burnished brunette who could scat while picking guitar, whose lyrical insights on love and relationships belied her youth.

The voice was already there. A soulful, sophisticated intersection of jazz and blues, Winehouse divined something primal through her sultry phrasing. *Frank* was named in part for Frank Sinatra, the vocal phrasing master who'd been a staple in the Winehouses' North London home. Her parents' music heavily influenced the young artist, as did their divorce when she was just nine. The subsequent teenage mayhem that ensued—drinking, smoking weed, tattoos, piercings, bulimia, antidepressants, older boyfriends—charted the course of her career and of the rest of her life.

Shaped as she was by the music of past generations, and what she'd later come to call "elitist" jazz, Winehouse's sound was never anachronistic. Working with songwriter and producer Salaam Remi, she mixed old and new into a seamless, beguiling pearl of an album. They sampled beats that made Winehouse's "old soul" sound at once classic and contemporary: Nas's "Made You Look," the Harlem Underground Band's "Smokin Cheeba-Cheeba," a bit of horn section from Les Brown and his Orchestra's "You Won't Be Satisfied (Until You Break My Heart)," and more.

Amid the flood of attention Winehouse received for *Frank*, she made prophetic statements like "If I died tomorrow, I would still feel fulfilled" (after winning an Ivor Novello Award for "Stronger Than Me"), and how she couldn't handle enormous fame and would "go mad" if it came her way, but these are more likely signs of her ingenuousness. Offstage, she was bright and fun. Wildly creative with a sly sense of humor, she could outdrink and outsmoke anyone and loved going to pubs to play snooker and hear live music. She had a hard time writing songs in the wake of her success and instead spent a lot of time going out. The music scene in her adopted neighborhood of Camden was exploding in the early and mid-aughts with bands like the Kills, the Libertines, and Babyshambles. It was here that she met Blake Fielder-Civil, the boyfriend, future husband, and

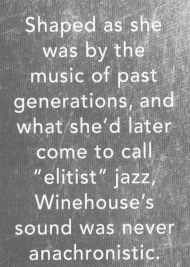

Shaped as she was by the music of past generations, and what she'd later come to call "elitist" jazz, Winehouse's sound was never anachronistic.

INFLUENCES: Billie Holiday, Carole King, the Shangri-Las, the Ronettes, Dinah Washington, Macy Gray, Sarah Vaughan, Salt-N-Pepa

INFLUENCED: Adele, Lily Allen, Janelle Monáe, Lady Gaga, Halsey, Florence Welch, Bruno Mars

DEEP CUTS: "When My Eyes" / "Trilby" / "You Sent Me Flying"

future ex. She turned their initial big breakup into her 2006 album, *Back to Black*.

Back to Black was suffused with the '60s girl-group sound that Winehouse had immersed herself in for inspiration. As a longtime fan of confessional singer/songwriter Carole King, it was a logical progression; King had written songs for the Shirelles, the Crystals, and numerous others. Winehouse expressed her love of the era, including the Shangri-Las and the Velvelettes, whose song "He Was Really Saying Something" was also a hit for the UK girl group Bananarama in 1982. Winehouse integrated the '60s style into her look as well. Her eyeliner became more exaggerated, she

adopted the beehive hairdo, and she wore vintage-inspired miniskirts and dresses. She found a musical soulmate in Mark Ronson, a British-born, New York–based deejay-turned-album-producer who was reinventing '60s soul music for the new millennium. Hiring New York soul revivalists the Dap-Kings to back her up, Winehouse's anguish over her busted love affair and struggles with addiction went platinum.

Winehouse owned the fiftieth Grammy Awards in absentia, with five wins for *Back to Black*. Unable to secure a visa from the US State Department until it was too late to travel to Los Angeles, she and the Dap-Kings were scheduled to perform live on the show via satellite from Riverside Studios in London. In the months leading up to the awards, she'd been hospitalized for a suspected overdose and arrested in Norway for marijuana possession. She appeared brittle and had canceled a number of concerts. Fielder-Civil, her husband at the time, was in jail, arrested for trying to bribe the pub owner he'd previously been charged with pummeling. Prior to the awards, Winehouse was seen smoking crack cocaine on video and had entered drug rehab. Anxious fans around the world speculated: Would she be able to sing? Would she even be able to stand?

The performance, back-to-back versions of "I'm No Good" and "Rehab," was thrilling. Winehouse looked healthy and sounded strong. Her victories seemed to bolster her even further. With the camera trained on her as she heard Tony Bennett, one of her idols, announce her win for Record of the Year, her face filled with astonishment and gratitude, and she threw her arms around her band and then her parents, who were in attendance. Aretha Franklin was the MusiCares Person of the Year, but it was Winehouse's night.

She'd go on to duet with Bennett and work on a project with QuestLove, but Winehouse's subsequent downward spiral was tragic, and very public. Her funeral was July 26, 2011, at Edgwarebury Cemetery in North London, ten miles from where she was born. The pain on the faces of her friends and family was visible. The men wore yarmulkes in keeping with the Winehouse family's Jewish tradition. Friend Kelly Osbourne wore her hair in a beehive in tribute.

It's heartbreaking to imagine what she would have done with the rest of her life, and not just as an artist. Winehouse was extravagantly charitable, donating money, music, time, and haute couture to numerous organizations, including the Global Fund's Born HIV Free initiative, the Prince's Trust, Save the Music Foundation, Nordoff Robbins Music Therapy, and Hear the World, as well as advocating for awareness of breast cancer and climate change, and many other causes. She deserves to be remembered, not as she was in the throes of addiction but rather as vibrant and generous, and as a brilliant singer who had only begun exploring her innate talent.

> It's heartbreaking to imagine what she would have done with the rest of her life, and not just as an artist.

PAGE 174: Amy Winehouse performing at South by Southwest in Austin, Texas, 2007. OPPOSITE: Performing at Coachella for the first time in 2007. ABOVE: Modeling her Fred Perry clothing line, 2010.

AMY LEE

BORN: Amy Lynn Lee / December 13, 1981 / Riverside, California

If the career curse of winning the Best New Artist Grammy was ever a thing, Evanescence used up every last bit of it. Nominated five times for their 2003 album, *Fallen*, the band won two statues, including one for Best New Artist. Goth-looking, ice-voiced singer Amy Lee, with pale skin, light blue eyes, and long black hair, seemed like she could deflect all of the bad mojo associated with that particular award. Born in the Inland Empire, Lee had grown up tough from frequently moving around the country, whenever her radio deejay father got a new gig. At thirteen, she'd landed in Arkansas, where she met guitarist and songwriter Ben Moody at camp and co-founded Evanescence.

Just before the Grammy nominations were announced, Lee and Moody had an acrimonious split. The rest of the original band was gone as well, and within a couple of years it had turned over again, and again with rancor. Lee became embroiled in lawsuits with her management, and then with her record label, Wind-Up, known for Christian-oriented hard-rock acts like Creed. Metalheads found Evanescence not "metal" enough, and Christian rock fans disavowed them when Lee proclaimed that her music was not intended to be religious. The band went on multiple hiatuses that lasted years.

Fallen, however, became an unlikely classic, selling millions. Lee, with her piano balladry and ethereal mezzo-soprano, broke through the male stranglehold on hard rock, dominated at the time by nu metal and then metalcore. She challenged the look and sound of women in pop music in that era as well, taking aim at them in the song "Everybody's Fool." Often clad in black, tulle, and body glitter, she presaged the early-aughts goth renaissance brought on by the teen vampire romance novel *Twilight*. *Fallen* is full of dark imagery, mining despair, death, suicide, and spirituality. Lee wrote from personal experiences, unhappy relationships, and losing her three-year-old sister when she was six (a brother, who had severe epilepsy all his life, died at age twenty-four in 2018). The album is like warm blood spreading across a cold marble floor, with the stark contrast of Lee's reflective moments and the abrasive crunch of guitars, and heavy beats giving way to a foreboding choir. Her three-octave voice, with its glacial tone, soars through the album's big symphonic arrangements.

With song titles like "My Immortal" and Lee's love of making cinematic music, it's remarkable that none of their songs ended up on any of the *Twilight* films. But "Bring Me to Life" was included on the 2003 *Daredevil* soundtrack, also released by their label, which helped catapult Evanescence to success. Fellow Wind-Up artist Paul McCoy of 12 Stones was prominently featured rapping and singing on the choruses, ostensibly added by folks at their label who felt the band wouldn't get radio airplay with just a "girl"

> The album is like warm blood spreading across a cold marble floor.

INFLUENCES: Shirley Manson, Björk, Tori Amos, Annie Lennox, Pat Benatar, Lita Ford, Heart, Janis Joplin, Alanis Morissette

INFLUENCED: Halestorm, the Pretty Reckless, Paramore

DEEP CUTS: "Give Unto Me" (with Evanescence) / "Listen to the Rain" (with Evanescence) / "The End of the Book"

singer. At the time, Lee demurred—that wasn't what she had in mind—but it was a hit, and it won them a second Grammy for Best Hard Rock Performance.

Despite the legal troubles, personnel turnover, and long gaps between albums, Evanescence released three more Top 10 albums. In 2017, they re-recorded a number of songs for their fourth album, *Synthesis*, replacing some of the harder elements with strings and timpani, including a version of "Bring Me to Life" without McCoy's parts. For Lee, it was not only vindication, but also the realization of years of hearing the song in her head a certain way. Intrigued with sound-building and in-studio creativity, she approached new projects differently than she had with the band. Lee collaborated with composer/cellist Dave Eggar on the moody, atmospheric *Aftermath*, the soundtrack to the indie film *War Story*, starring Catherine Keener and Ben Kingsley. She also made an album of mostly-original children's music, *Dream Too Much*, inspired by her young son with husband Josh Hartzler. Lee now lives in Brooklyn, extolling virtues of ordinary life like running "mom" errands and riding the subway, following her muse wherever it takes her.

PAGE 178: Amy Lee singing with Evanescence, 2004.
PAGE 179: Evanescence's debut and still-definitive album, *Fallen* (2003). LEFT: Performing in Prague, 2012.
ABOVE: In full gothic bloom, 2003.

KAREN O

BORN: Karen Lee Orzolek / November 22, 1978 / Busan, South Korea

After all the formidable female musicians who emerged in the '90s, from riot grrrl to Sheryl Crow to Missy Elliott, after all the articles written, sometimes the same ones repeatedly, about the rise of "women in rock" or "angry women in rock," after Lilith Tours and Daisy Rock guitars and Strong Women in Music actions, and so much promise that rock 'n' roll future belonged to women, the early aughts found its first female rock star feeling utterly alone.

Karen O and her band the Yeah Yeah Yeahs, formed in 2000, had generated enough buzz to incite a record-label bidding war that landed them on Interscope with a fat advance. She even had a sort of girl squad, "Karennabes," women who copied her torn fishnets, red lipstick, and single glove identifiers and clustered at the front of the stage and interacted with her at gigs. The Yeah Yeah Yeahs, along with their New York cohort the Strokes and Interpol, and Detroit's White Stripes, were being hailed as the saviors of rock, reviving rebellion, attitude, and style just months after boy band *NSYNC had sold a record-setting 2.4 million CDs in one week. O stood out as the lone female frontperson, an anomaly in this male-dominated scene.

To be fair, O was always an anomaly. Half Korean and half Polish, she attended a pricey prep school in her hometown of Englewood, New Jersey, and she dealt with feeling different by being either very quiet or boisterous. Through her older brother, she heard artists such as Aretha Franklin and Grace Slick. Too young to fully comprehend the lyrics, something in her latched on to their insubordinate message nonetheless. Already a punk-rock outcast by her early teens, O hung out with Deadheads in high school, getting into the music mostly to feel the sublime relief of fitting in somewhere and not being judged for a while. But with Manhattan just fifteen miles away, she also spent many underage nights seeing bands like the Jon Spencer Blues Explosion, Jonathan Fire*Eater, and Sonic Youth play at downtown clubs. At Oberlin College, where she met future YYY's drummer music-major Brian Chase, she found herself still at odds with a campus full of oddballs. Transferring to New York University and eventually moving to an apartment on Avenue A, she bonded with guitarist Nick Zinner amid the graffiti and stench of the Mars Bar, a cramped dive at the corner of First Street and Second Avenue known for its colorful characters and revolting restroom.

With Zinner and Chase, O built the Yeah Yeah Yeahs out of suburban misfit PTSD, Oberlin art-punk, and East Village grime. They peeled garage rock to the truss and played it with a galvanizing beat, all to transmit O's psychosexual lyrics. They were stripped-down dance-art-punk the way ESG, the Bronx-based sister act, were stripped-down dance-art-funk two decades earlier. O's voice snakes over and under the noise, shifting from guttural and hissing to evocative and soul-baring. She yelps and yowls through *Fever to Tell*, their 2003 debut, with the spitting spirit of Chrissie Hynde's "Precious" on the striding "Tick," and the handclaps and yaps of "Black Tongue." About two-thirds into the album, O delivers the aching "Maps" about

> She even had a sort of girl squad, "Karennabes," women who copied her torn fishnets, red lipstick, and single glove identifiers.

INFLUENCES: Debbie Harry, PJ Harvey, Siouxsie Sioux, Shirley Manson

INFLUENCED: Deap Vally, Angel Olsen

DEEP CUTS: "Machine" (with the Yeah Yeah Yeahs) / "Rich" (with the Yeah Yeah Yeahs) / "Singalong"

then-boyfriend, Liars's Angus Andrew, which was so devastating that Beyoncé borrowed it on *Lemonade*'s "Hold Up."

O's persona was at the center of the band's appeal, subverting expectations of beauty and behavior. Determined that being arty could coexist with being "girlie," her look dragged both notions through Alphabet City's gritty streets. Her friend and partner-in-style-crime, costume designer and artist Christian Joy, created preposterous outfits—odd colors and shapes, bodysuits painted with skeleton bones, gowns festooned with plastic toys or Sharpie doodles, weird headdresses, everything covered in string, tinsel, or Muppet fur, and makeup to match. No matter if O looked like a space alien, circus performer on acid, or demented escapee from Fraggle Rock, she turned the grotesque into glamour. Her stage antics matched her capricious appearance. Jumping, posturing, crouching, and bounding up again, she doused herself with beer or water, or even olive oil at the beginning of her performing career, shaking off and spitting the excess into the air, only to gulp down the microphone as a chaser.

With O as the focal point, the Yeah Yeah Yeahs' ascension was swift. Their debut was nominated for a Best Alternative Music Album Grammy, as were the two that followed. But O's approach to success was measured. With such an extroverted and ambitious stage persona and her unique voice, she could have had any kind of career she wanted, yet she appeared to put on the brakes. A video for the song "Zero" (from 2009's *It's a Blitz!*) seems to articulate her conflicted feelings about stardom. She's backstage, prepping to go onstage, applying black eyeliner, slipping into her studded leather jacket and walking through the

halls of a venue. When the curtain opens, however, there's no audience before her. She's alone on a street, and she dances her way to a bodega, where she meets up with her band to finish playing the song.

Instead of risking the flameout experienced by her peers, O parceled her imagination into divergent projects. She wrote most of the soundtrack to *Where the Wild Things Are*, a live-action adaptation of the Maurice Sendak children's book, directed by her ex-boyfriend Spike Jonze. She earned an Oscar nomination for "The Moon Song," which she wrote for Jonze's film *Her*. She created a sort of opera/performance art piece, *Stop the Virgens*, and wrote Google Doodle's first original song on pioneering female journalist Nellie Bly. She recorded a slackened, hypnotic spin of Animotion's "Obsession" for Starz's ballet series *Flesh and Bone*, and a minimalist, atmospheric version of "Mammas Don't Let Your Babies Grow Up to be Cowboys" for the Chipotle Cultivate Foundation in support of family farms.

In 2014, she released *Crush Songs*, her first solo album, a set of lo-fi recordings she'd done years earlier that she called "voyeuristic." A year later, O had a baby boy, Django, with her husband, music video director Barnaby Clay. And in 2017, the Yeah Yeah Yeahs' debut received a deluxe, expanded reissue. O may have shied away from fame but can't avoid infamy; for many punk-rocking millennials, *Fever to Tell* is their *Raw Power*, and she's their Iggy Pop.

PAGE 182: Karen O with the Yeah Yeah Yeahs in San Pedro, California, 2017. OPPOSITE, TOP: Karen O with Nick Zinner, performing in South Korea, 2006. OPPOSITE, BOTTOM: The Yeah Yeah Yeahs self-financed their debut album, *Fever to Tell* (2003). BELOW: The Yeah Yeah Yeahs playing in Berlin, 2003.

O's voice snakes over and under the noise, shifting from guttural and hissing to evocative and soul-baring.

GRACE POTTER

BORN: June 20, 1983 / Waitsfield, Vermont

Trying to work around the "girl with a guitar" cliché, Grace Potter took up piano as a child. She thought it looked cooler to stand behind a keyboard and sing. Eventually, she succumbed to the lure of the six-string. She couldn't have foreseen that nearly two decades later, Gibson would create her own signature model Flying V, the futuristic looking ax that had long been played by resplendent rock stars from Jimi Hendrix to Lenny Kravitz.

Potter shares not only their guitar, but also their swagger. In concert, she's in constant motion, whether she's slowly grooving or scooting and strutting across the stage in high heels and mini-dresses, or short-shorts and barefoot, layers of beads and amulets, fringe, feathers, sparkle booties, always something glittering, even if she has to glue it on herself. She switches off between Hammond B3 and electric guitar, or piano and acoustic guitar, often mid-song, sometimes playing two instruments at the same time. She'll sit on, climb on, or drape her body over the big wooden keyboard cabinet, extend her leg up on the monitor, and whip her long blond hair around while squeezing chords out of her Flying V. Some performers look like they're acting when they attempt such rock posturing, but Potter's physicality is just part of the music.

Potter has said she never expected a music career because playing came so naturally to her, but she was bound for a creative life of some sort growing up in a family of artists in central Vermont's Mad River Valley. Her parents opened a wood shop in the early '70s, selling signs, furniture, and everything in between. Her mom became regionally well known for her "Peggy Potter Bowls," crafted out of solid maple, painted in vibrant colors, and sealed so they could be used to serve food. From a young age, Potter absorbed the idea of wood as form and function, visible in her approach to musical instruments, particularly onstage. Her sister, Charlotte, is a glass blower who also curates the "Tent of the Weird" at the annual Grand North Point Music Festival that Potter founded in 2011. The town's only other famous modern resident is Bill Parker, who invented the psychedelic-looking plasma lamp. Potter sometimes jokes that the only things to do growing up in Vermont were to see the band Phish and drop acid, but she loves the state and lured her band there after meeting them as a student at her parents' alma matter, St. Lawrence University, in 2003.

With her college boyfriend, drummer Matt Burr, she formed Grace Potter and the Nocturnals, a loose aggregation of southern rock and New England jam-band boogie with glimmers of pop and blue-eyed soul. Potter's voice, rangy with a little rasp on the edges, lush and resonant enough to carry the entire melody of a song, unadorned by harmonies or effects, has enough muscle to

> In concert, she's in constant motion, whether she's slowly grooving or scooting and strutting across the stage.

INFLUENCES: Sheryl Crow, Janis Joplin, Bonnie Raitt, Christine McVie, Stevie Nicks, Susan Tedeschi, Heart, Grace Slick, Jennifer Hartswick

INFLUENCED: Hurray for the Riff Raff, Jaime Wyatt, Haim, Rubblebucket, Larkin Poe

DEEP CUTS: "Stop the Bus" (with the Nocturnals) **/** "Go Down Low" (with the Nocturnals) **/** "The Miner"

fire notes across the growing sea of fans who packed into venues to hear her play. After releasing two independent albums and scoring a handful of local awards, and a 2006 Jammy for "Best New Groove," they signed with Hollywood Records and made *This Is Somewhere*. The songs were driven by the churning rhythm of a baby band on the open road, already caught up in the cycle of touring, beginning to feel the strain of fractured relationships and delayed adulthood, yet still young enough to experience the extemporaneous thrills of the lifestyle.

Becoming a staple on the outdoor festival circuit, they grew a significant base of rock and jam-band fans, but Potter was already starting to evolve. She recorded and then shelved her own album with producer T Bone Burnett, instead releasing a self-titled album with the Nocturnals in 2010 that was more glam and less jam. They had a hit with "Paris (Ooh La La)," a sexy strut

befitting Steven Tyler or Heart that some "Potter-heads," as the GPN fans called themselves, didn't follow. After releasing *The Lion the Beast the Beat*, Potter began to write and record as a solo artist, though members of her Nocturnals family continued to record and perform with her. She also ended her fifteen-year relationship and four-year marriage with Burr, moved from Vermont to the groovy enclave of Los Angeles's Topanga Canyon, and had a child, Sagan, with her new producer Eric Dodd, aka Eric Valentine.

Potter's 2015 solo debut, *Midnight*, was cathartic for her, going deeper into the pop and funk of her '80s childhood and shirking her tie-dyed tether to the scene that both nurtured her and kept her in a creative rut. She auditioned a new, bigger band, with three keyboardists and two drummers, naming them the Magical Midnight Road Show and loading them into her newly acquired tour bus that once belonged to Lil Wayne. Her "new" direction, though, had long been part of her music—the early ballads that might have been big hits if she'd sold them to a pop star, her Grammy-nominated duet with Kenny Chesney ("You and Tequila"), even the GPN cover of Blondie's "Heart of Glass," slowed down to the way it was originally written. They're all steps in Potter's cosmic journey.

> Potter's voice is rangy with a little rasp on the edges, lush and resonant enough to carry the entire melody of a song.

PAGE 186: Grace Potter playing with her signature Gibson Flying V guitar. OPPOSITE: Playing at San Francisco, 2008. LEFT: Backstage before a show at New York's Irving Plaza, 2012.

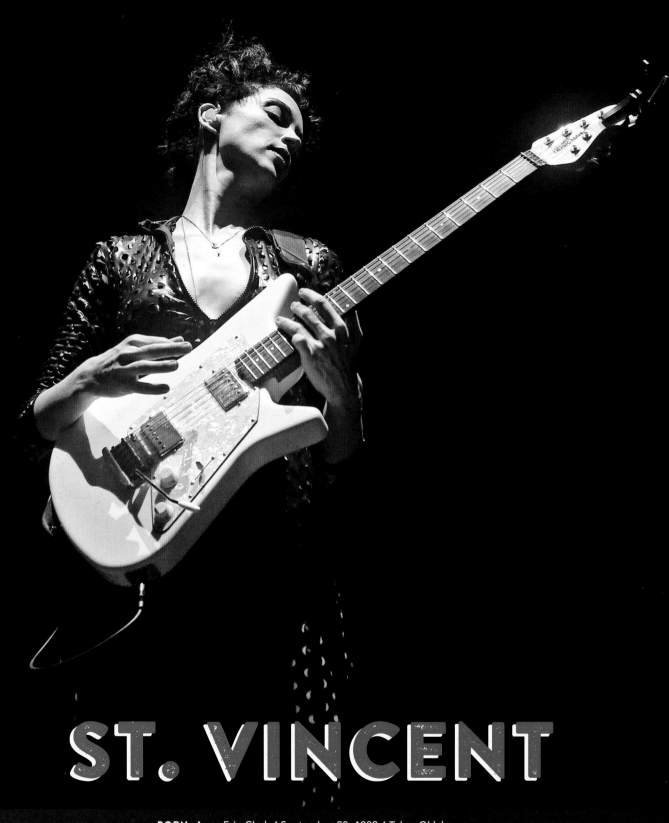

ST. VINCENT

BORN: Anne Erin Clark / September 28, 1982 / Tulsa, Oklahoma

Before Annie Clark played guitar, she dreamed of guitar. Growing up in suburban Dallas amid a blended family of eight siblings, she'd draw pictures of guitars, over and over, until her mother finally relented and bought her one.

Two decades later, under the *nome d'arte* St. Vincent, Clark started drawing guitars again, this time to design her own signature Ernie Ball Music Man STV. Debuted in 2016, its modernist style is a reflection of her angular and uniquely wired form. Its specifications are inspired by her needs as a player, from releasing five electro-art-pop albums (plus one with former Talking Head and artistic kindred spirit David Byrne) to the way she re-creates her songs on stage.

Having spent much of the last decade on tour, Clark made her ax lightweight enough to hang on her small frame night after night, even though she chose mahogany and an all-rosewood neck to give chords and notes extra resonance. She designed the body with a cutaway so her fingers could access every note on the neck. An able shredder, she's nonetheless more interested in the sounds and textures she can extract from her instrument, running it through numerous pedals and programs. Fond of bending notes with a whammy bar—the metal arm attached to the bridge—she chose locking tuners to keep the strings in tune, no matter how hard she presses or pulls. She added more sound possibilities with a unique wiring configuration to connect the three mini-humbuckers pickups (so called because they literally "buck" the ambient "hum" of the electronics) to a five-way switch.

As complex as her music is, Clark is just as focused on visual presentation, creating guises and garb for each song cycle. She made her guitar body slim in the middle to elongate the appearance of her torso, accentuating her waistline and whatever she's wearing on any given tour. She hand-mixed the original color, "St. Vincent Blue"—a metal-flake sapphire. The custom inlay in the neck (the same two intersected circles on the cover of her fourth album), is the *vesica piscis* symbol from sacred geometry, which connects the ancient and modern world, spirituality and design, math and the human body.

Music connects these realms as well, and Clark's awareness of that underlies her ambitious, wildly inventive compositions. She draws from literature, film, design, fashion, and a broad array of musical influences, everything cannily reinvented and densely arranged. There's a hint of magic realism in her work, both musically and visually, which allows her to mine art and culture without ever coming close to pastiche or pandering. Something is always just a little off-kilter, whether it's the slight arrhythmia of her torqued, Robert Fripp-y guitar note bursts, her sonic and lyric leaps, or her perfectly made-up face with lips and eyes smudged in an unexpected direction. She is engaging you, making you both listen and look harder.

> As complex as her music is, Clark is just as focused on visual presentation.

INFLUENCES: PJ Harvey, Poison Ivy, Grace Jones, Debbie Harry, Björk, Laurie Anderson, Kate Bush, David Bowie

INFLUENCED: Grimes, Lucy Dacus, Emilie & Ogden

DEEP CUTS: "Emotional Rescue" / "Bad Believer" / "Teenage Talk"

The element of surprise is one of her sharpest tools. It is in her music, from her 2007 debut album *Marry Me*, deconstructed singer/songwriter fare with intermittent gusts of guitar back-masking, surging piano key strikes, drums crashing like nighttime ocean waves; to the mechanized rhythms of her '80s-inculcated, Grammy-winning eponymous 2014 release; to 2017's *Masseduction*, on which she interpolates her most accessible work (and first Top 10 album) with repeated F-bombs. Surprise also features in her various personae. *St. Vincent*'s was a "near-future cult leader," as she put it, her hair shaped into a lavender-gray fright wig and matching utilitarian tunic. *Masseduction*'s brightly colored, vinyl-and-rubber-clad pop-dominatrix turned the power theme personal (she'd come off of two high-profile relationships, first with actor Kristen Stewart, then with model Cara Delevingne—the latter sang backing vocals on the tragic/comic "Pills," and even Clark's reveal that some of album was about her private life was uncharacteristic for the taciturn songwriter). She veers from the expected in her interactions with the audience, especially during the *St. Vincent* tour, when she was working through some extra-heavy emotional machinations. She'd stage-dive and crowd-surf while singing into the mic, or wade into the audience playing her guitar on the shoulders of concert security. Her stunts reached daredevil level when she'd climb on theater balconies or scale festival scaffolding

> The element
> of surprise
> is one of her
> sharpest tools.

in a miniskirt and heels, dangling by her arms while frantic venue staff lingered beneath her.

Introduced to the life by her uncle Tuck Andress, the acoustic shredding half of New Age jazz duo Tuck & Patti, Clark has called touring her "blood sport." After a stint as Tuck & Patti's teenaged tour manager, she studied music at Boston's Berklee College but dropped out after nearly three years. She went back on the road as a member of sprawling choral-rock Polyphonic Spree and, in butterfly wings, backing indie singer/songwriter Sufjan Stevens before unleashing St. Vincent.

Ever evolving, her "Fear the Future" tour for *Masseduction* was a one-woman multimedia experience—no backing band, though the backing tracks were big enough to make reviewers wonder if a band was in fact behind the curtain. Clark appeared to be accompanied only by a series of large images and GIFs projected behind her, including the distinguishing tight shots of her inscrutable face. Rather than an opening act, she screened *The Birthday Party*, a short film she made for the all-female directed horror anthology *XX*, followed by a chronological set of early material and then the new album in its entirety. Even the tour announcement was an art project, a "fake news" conference and a series of shorts made with musician/actor/author (and ex) Carrie Brownstein in which St. Vincent was asked ridiculous interview questions ("What's it like to play in heels?"), offering pre-fab replies and a manicure that spelled out "FUCK OFFF." With every new endeavor, Clark continues to challenge rock precepts, what it means to be a guitar hero, and even guitar itself.

> Her "Fear the Future" tour for *Masseduction* was a one-woman multimedia experience.

PAGE 190: St. Vincent playing in Camden, New Jersey, 2015. OPPOSITE: Performing in Saxapahaw, North Carolina, 2014. ABOVE, TOP: Crowd-surfing at the Way Out West festival in Gothenburg, Sweden. ABOVE, BOTTOM: St. Vincent's *Masseducation* (2018).

ST. VINCENT — 193

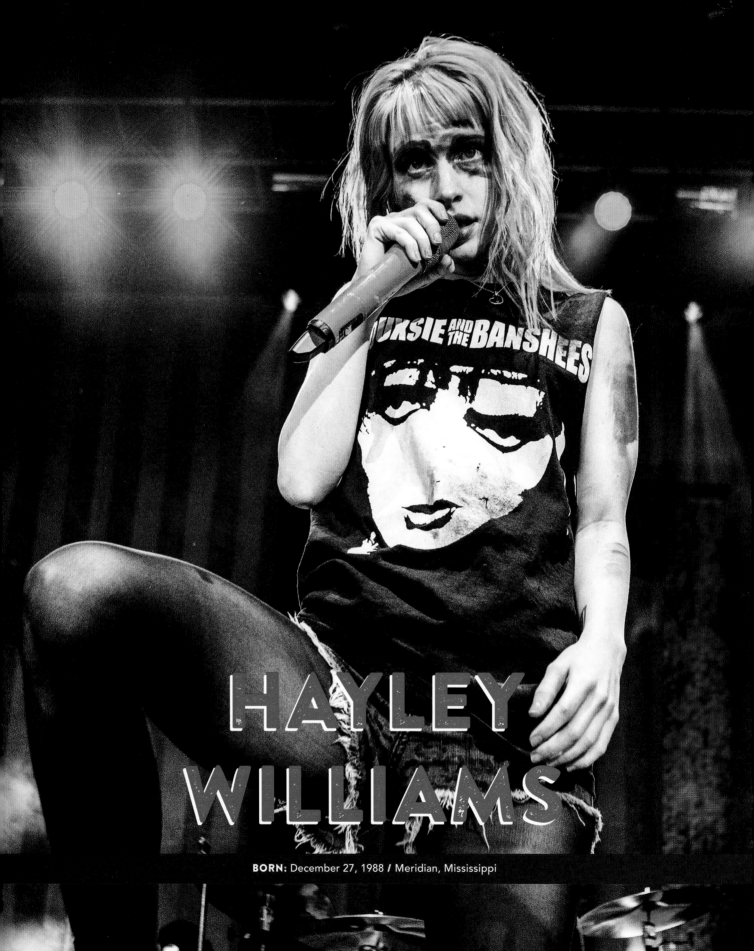

HAYLEY WILLIAMS

BORN: December 27, 1988 / Meridian, Mississippi

Fronted by the magnetic, fire-haired Hayley Williams, Paramore started in a Franklin, Tennessee, garage and became emo-pop exemplars, playing guitar-cranked, fourth-iteration punk, distilled into something clean and polished yet jammed with palpable teen angst. Williams's lissome, four-octave wallop cuts through the band's chunky power chords, her lyrics seething beneath a bright pop veneer. At just over five feet tall, often clad in T-shirts and shorts or miniskirts that reveal her leg tattoos, she skips and bounces around the stage, punching the air and headbanging. An occasional keyboardist, her main instrument is her remarkable voice. Edgy and resilient, it's an upward projectile—the higher she goes, the louder she gets.

After releasing four progressively maturing albums and as many Grammy nominations (with one win), Paramore turned toward the sounds of the decade in which most of the band members were born: the '80s. Their 2017 album *After Laughter* is filled with Williams's doleful insights on the foibles and fallout of fame, but the music chirps with synth-y, semi–New Wave, and Afrobeat inflections. Lyrically, it's as sad as the dissolution of Williams's decade-long relationship with ex-husband Chad Gilbert, frontman for New Found Glory. Musically, it's as happy as her newfound fixation with Talking Heads. The album landed on many "Best of" lists that year, but for fans who gave them rations of crap for changing musical direction, Williams had a pointed retort. "Old Pmore [sic] is on Youtube. Whenever you want!" she posted to Instagram. "But I still promise I will never ask you to be whoever you were 15 years ago."

> ## Williams's lissome, four-octave wallop cuts through the band's chunky power chords, her lyrics seething beneath a bright pop veneer.

At twenty-nine years old, Williams has been Paramore's singer for nearly half her life. Formed in 2004, the same year as Facebook, the band ascended alongside social media, making them first-gen entertainers to emerge and evolve under a new kind of fame and its correlating relentless spotlight. As of 2018, Paramore has more than 26 million "likes" on Facebook, has sold millions of albums, and has sold out London's Wembley Arena in ten minutes—all without a number-one song. Williams inspired a new wave of female rock artists, but Paramore's style-bending sound reaches beyond both genre and gender; '90s-born performers as disparate as country singer Tucker Beathard, son of a successful Nashville songwriter, and Philadelphia hip-hop artist Lil Uzi Vert, have namechecked Williams and the band as an influence.

Atlantic Records saw so much star potential in Williams that they signed her as a solo artist at fifteen. Singer Avril Lavigne had just ridden her skater-punk persona to the top of the pop charts and earned eight Grammy nods, fueling an industry feeding frenzy for alternative pop female artists. Despite Williams's powerful pipes and pop-star looks, she balked at the notion of being a solo act and made a case for writing and

INFLUENCES: Gwen Stefani, Debbie Harry, Cyndi Lauper, Alison Mosshart, Avril Lavigne, Brody Dalle

INFLUENCED: Chrissy Costanza, Lynn Gunn, Jenna McDougall, Sydney Sierota, Bethany Cosentino

DEEP CUTS: "Turn It Off" / "Temporary" / "Brighter"

performing with a band. Her deal with Atlantic was separate from the band's and would later be at the root of a revolving door of personnel. Seven musicians would join, quit, return, and quit again in the decade and a half that followed, but the changing lineup contributed to advancing their sound and their enduring success.

In 2004, Williams reconnected with bassist Jeremy Davis, with whom she'd played funk covers when she was thirteen. She knew the Farro brothers from a meetup for homeschooled kids, guitarist Josh and drummer Zac, who was still a tween when Paramore was born. The whole band was so young that their label hired Williams's mother to tour with the band so they could continue their homeschooling, and Williams's father drove their van. They joined the Warped Tour in 2005, playing the first year of the Shiragirl Stage, which had been created in response to a lack of female performers despite Warped's more than half female audience. A converted box truck, the small stage was hand-built, painted pink, and booked by performer Shira Yevin. By the time they'd released their 2007 breakthrough album, *Riot!*, however, they were a main attraction. Tweens and teens were turning up with their hair dyed in Williams's orange, yellow, and red hues.

Riot! gave Paramore their breakthrough hit, "Misery Business," a zealous mean-girl revenge fantasy. More than a decade later, Williams is still being pressed about her use of the word "whore" to demean a romantic rival in the song. The video, however, depicts her antagonist as a universal bully, a justification of Williams's satisfaction at humiliating her. Williams has said numerous times that she no longer relates to those particular lyrics that she wrote as a teenager, and though the band continues to play "Misery Business" live, she now introduces it on stage with a moment of reflection not only on her growth, but on her audience's as well.

Growing up with their fans is a big part of Paramore's success. In 2008, they recorded "Decode," the lead single for the soundtrack of *Twilight*, their generation's vastly influential vampire film (based on the Stephenie Meyer novel). In the decade that followed, their music

reflected a transition into adulthood, with its pressures, depression, and anxiety, all of which Williams has admitted to suffering. Each of their albums kept fans fascinated with kernels of the band's drama as members

clashed and left, a reflection of conflict, pain, and desire to move forward—and, on each, the writing and sound became more mature. Williams and Josh Farro were both songwriting and romantic partners, yet their acrimonious split launched a regrouped Paramore to the next level. Their 2013 self-titled album was more pop than punk, more Gwen Stefani and less Green Day. It also brought them their first Grammy for "Ain't It Fun." When Williams collected the award for Best Rock Song in 2015, she was the first woman to do so since Alanis Morissette took it home in 1999 (Alabama Shakes won it the following year, in 2016).

"Ain't It Fun" also finally replaced "Misery Business" as Paramore's defining work. In the lyrics, Williams, who wanted to be part of a band and who'd grown up

> Each of their albums kept fans fascinated with kernels of the band's drama as members clashed and left, a reflection of conflict, pain, and desire to move forward.

an only child, sarcastically touts the joys of "being all alone." For all the talk of how Williams soaks up the limelight—for her dozen or so recordings with other artists, including the hit "Airplanes" with rapper B.o.B., and EDM songwriter/deejay Zedd's "Stay the Night"; for her business ventures (in 2017 she made the *Forbes* "30 under 30" list), including a MAC cosmetics line and goodDYEyoung, her hair color company—Paramore, like Blondie before them, remains a group.

PAGE 194: Hayley Williams with Paramore, paying homage to Siouxsie Sioux at Camden, New Jersey, 2013. OPPOSITE: With Paramore in the Netherlands, 2013. ABOVE: With Paramore in Atlanta, 2017.

BRITTANY HOWARD

BORN: October 2, 1988 / Athens, Alabama

Being a five-foot, ten-inch biracial bespectacled music nerd made Brittany Howard a misfit in rural Alabama, but she's so proud of her home state that she sports a large tattoo of it on her upper arm. A northern, central red heart demarcates her hometown of Athens, just twenty miles from the Tennessee border and an hour's drive east of the Southern soul-recording mecca of Muscle Shoals.

Onstage, Howard often channels another female Southern guitar-slinger, the godmother of rock 'n' roll, Sister Rosetta Tharpe (who she inducted into the Rock and Roll Hall of Fame in 2018). The mighty soul singing. The Gibson SG guitar, with its distinctive body carved into "batwings" at the top. The vehement string-bending. The cape, worn over a long dress. Going fishing as a break from her relentless tour schedule, one of Tharpe's favorite pastimes. Even the way Howard sometimes throws her head back from the microphone and sings toward the sky.

But while Tharpe left her native Arkansas for Chicago as a child, Howard's family remained in Alabama, living at the end of a long gravel road several miles outside of downtown Athens. Without much around them, she and older sister Jaime learned to entertain themselves, and music became a central part of that. They played piano together, wrote songs and poems, and drew pictures, even as Jaime's eyesight failed from a retinoblastoma. She succumbed to cancer at thirteen. Howard was nine and nearly blind in one eye from the same syndrome. Her parents divorced shortly thereafter.

Losing her sister and playmate motivated Howard to keep making music. Having a female teacher at school who played guitar encouraged her to take up the instrument; and after seeing future Alabama Shakes guitarist Heath Fogg's band perform, she decided she wanted to do that, too.

An intuitive player, Howard taught herself guitar by cluing in to what guitarists did on records, paying mind to sounds rather than virtuosity, and to songs rather than scales. At fourteen, hearing Pink Floyd set her off exploring classic rock like Led Zeppelin and

> Howard taught herself guitar by cluing in to what guitarists did on records, paying mind to sounds rather than virtuosity, and to songs rather than scales.

Black Sabbath, but it also opened her mind to rock's creative possibilities. Befriending fellow music fan and high school student Zac Cockrell, the two began to put together what would become the Shakes, and then the Alabama Shakes. But first she'd land a job with the US Postal Service as a rural letter carrier. With no radio in the mail truck, Howard spent most of her working days dreaming of her band's next gig or conjuring up her next song.

Though she grew up somewhat heedless of the fertile musical ground in her vicinity, Howard's self-education led her to blues, soul, and rhythm-and-blues,

INFLUENCES: Sister Rosetta Tharpe, Tina Turner, Mavis Staples, Janis Joplin, Sharon Jones, Barbara Lynn

INFLUENCED: Thunderbitch, Bermuda Triangle, Deap Vally

DEEP CUTS: "Heavy Chevy" / "I Found You" / "Always Alright"

and also to more contemporary bands. Her eclectic taste found a way into the songs she wrote. If the Alabama Shakes' 2012 debut, *Boys & Girls*, sounded remarkably self-possessed for a first album, perhaps it's because it was years in the making, a combination of Howard's musical immersion and the band working out their material playing regional gigs.

Recorded in between day jobs and night gigs with money they'd stashed, the Shakes didn't even have a label when they went into the studio. But their interpretation of bluesy, soul-steeped rock on songs such as "Hold On" and "You Ain't Alone" began to garner national attention, and they were soon signed to ATO Records. In an era when real guitar and drums are inaudible in so much contemporary music, they were rock 'n' roll heroes right out of the gate. Howard's spare, clean riffing and succinct, reverb-drenched thwacks give the album a retro feel, while drummer Steve Johnson's heavy backbeat moves the songs at the sultry tempo of the American South. As a vocalist, Howard invokes blues moaners, rhythm-and-blues shouters, and lo-fi indie rockers. As a performer, she's stirring, her face contorting to emit every last bit of emotion, her jaw appearing almost unhinged as she delivers semi-autobiographical lyrics.

The album earned three Grammy nominations, and Howard took her nana Ruthie to the awards in Los Angeles. Alabama Shakes would spend a year in studio recording the follow-up, *Sound & Color*. Howard saw a chance to explore and experiment, and came up with a dozen songs that build upon the band's framework with surprising sonic expeditions. Over a compendium of atmospheric soul, funk swagger, and traces of psyche-delia, gospel, and fuzztone, she pushed her own voice

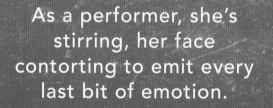

As a performer, she's stirring, her face contorting to emit every last bit of emotion.

both louder and softer, as close to a croon as someone with her depth of vocal power can do.

The creative gamble paid off. *Sound & Color* went to number one upon its release, earned six Grammy nominations, and took home three awards. Howard had gone from postal worker to playing with Prince and Paul McCartney, and from singing Led Zeppelin covers in bars to performing in front of Robert Plant, in less than four years. In that time, she also created an alter ego in the vein of David Bowie's Ziggy Stardust or Beyoncé's Sasha Fierce. Howard named her Thunderbitch, a ghost-faced, motorcycle-riding garage rocker in black shades, and always speaks of her in the third person.

With the success of the band, Howard, who had never traveled, finally got to see the rest of the country and much of the world, but she still keeps a house in Athens, and one in Nashville (home of her more recent side project, Bermuda Triangle, a gentle multi-harmony acoustic-driven trio with singer/songwriters Becca Mancari and Jesse Lafser). She often praises her hard-working neighbors and waxes optimistic about her country. While the United States remains tangled in its polemic red-state-versus-blue-state culture wars, Howard continues to remind the rest of the nation of the things she loves about the South, from her nana's recipe for cracklin' corn bread, to the classic American music she and the Alabama Shakes have managed to reinvent.

PAGE 198: Brittany Howard shreds with Alabama Shakes in Las Vegas, 2015. OPPOSITE: Playing in Santa Monica, California, 2014. ABOVE: With Alabama Shakes in Montreal, 2017.

ACKNOWLEDGMENTS

THANK YOU:

To my Sterling editors (literally and figuratively), Barbara Berger, Chris Barsanti, and Kayla Overbey; designers Elizabeth Mihaltse Lindy, Shannon Nicole Plunkett, and Lorie Pagnozzi; photo researchers Stacey Stambaugh and Linda Liang; and my agents, Janet Rosen and Sheree Bykofsky.

To the fierce women in my world who've offered so much inspiration, advice, friendship, sparkle, love, or a combination thereof: Doreen Cronin, Julia Gottesman, Abigail Gottesman, Genghis Mom, Carly Sommerstein, Jill Sternheimer, Holly Gleason, Jennifer Cohan, Monika Evstatieva, Gale Sparrow, Heather Linson, Liz Weiswasser, Julia Spivack, Heather Youmans at Fendar, Ellen Voie, Suzanne Glickman, Lynnea Villanova, Patrice Fehlen, Mary Illin', Laura Zarrow, Steph at SassyBelleWares, Cindy at Sienna Grace Jewelry, Stevie and Sandy at Jewels for Hope, and the Alliance for Women in Media.

To the dudes: Rob Santos and Tom Tierney at Sony Music; Jason Elzy at Rhino; Erik Philbrook at ASCAP; Jeremy Tepper; Adam Budofsky at Modern Drummer; Gordon Anderson at Real Gone; Jay Jannuzzi; Bob, Huck, and Danny (the Three Amigos); and Randy Ertman at Bliss Hammocks.

To the families, with love: the Ochses, Gottesmans, Zorns, Sullivans, Oxmans, Blacks, Spivacks, Lowingers, Oseasohns, Griffins, Siclaris, Weiswassers, Paris and Henry, Sam, Isidoro, and especially my dad, who gave me my first 45 rpm and who patiently waited outside many NYC music venues to ensure my safe passage home.

ABOUT THE AUTHOR

In her years as a radio talk-show host, deejay, and magazine writer, **MEREDITH OCHS** has interviewed more than a thousand celebrities. A record collector and guitarist since childhood, she naturally gravitates toward music-related work, but she also covers pop culture, travel, food, tech, health, and style, always finding the connections between domains.

Ochs earned a degree in political science, history, and international relations from the University of Massachusetts with the intention of joining the US Foreign Service. Instead, she landed a job at the *Howard Stern Show* on New York City's K-ROCK. More radio gigs followed, including NPR, where she is a longtime commentator. Her writing has appeared in books, such as the critically acclaimed *Woman Walk the Line*; and in publications including *Entertainment Weekly*, *Rolling Stone*, and *Salon.com*; and she was a contributing editor at *Guitar World*. She has worked as a photographer, touring musician, newscaster, culinary judge, and boat skipper. She has also traveled cross-country in a big rig, performed with her band on the show *Mountain Stage*, and received a Gracie Award for her work in radio.

BIBLIOGRAPHY

SISTER ROSETTA THARPE

American Masters. "Sister Rosetta Tharpe: The Godmother of Rock & Roll." PBS. Feb 22, 2013.

docludi2. "Rosetta Tharpe .. 1964 .. Didn't it Rain .. Blues and Gospel train." Filmed by ITV/Granada Television, Aug 19, 1964. YouTube video, 3:55. Posted Jun 8, 2017. https://bit.ly/2wTntwJ

Long, Chris. "Muddy Waters and Sister Rosetta Tharpe's 'mind-blowing' station show." *BBC News*. May 7, 2014. https://bbc.in/2jVYUWy

Simadis, Valerie. "Sister Rosetta Tharpe Takes You Down by the Riverside." *Please Kill Me*. Sept 28, 2017. https://bit.ly/2wDpEnW

Wald, Gayle. *Shout, Sister, Shout!* Boston: Beacon Press, 2008.

BIG MAMA THORNTON

American Folk Blues Festival, concert performance. Video: Eine Produktion des Südenwestfunks. 1965. https://bit.ly/2rDtKaB

Gunsmoke Blues, concert performance and interview. Eugene, Oregon. 1971. Hip-O Records (DVD). Aug 31, 2004.

Holden, Stephen. "Willie Mae Thornton, Influential Blues Singer." *New York Times*. July 28, 1984. https://nyti.ms/2IkVLtW

Kennedy, Rick, and Randy McNult. *Little Labels—Big Sound*. Bloomington, IN: Indiana University Press, 1999.

"Legends of Rhythm and Blues." In *Repercussions: A Celebration of African-Influenced Music*. Los Angeles. 1984. New York: Films Media Group. https://bit.ly/2rBmlb2

Mixed Bag, television performance. WGBH. 1970

Shearer, Cynthia. "The Thinning of Big Mama." *Oxford American* 95, Winter 2016. https://bit.ly/2L36St3

Spörke, Michael. *Big Mama Thornton*. Jefferson, NC: McFarland, 2014.

Thornton, Willie Mae "Big Mama." *Arhoolie Foundation*. By Chris Strachwitz. Oct 20, 1965. https://bit.ly/2IeM6F0

"Willie Mae 'Big Mama' Thornton." *Find a Grave*. Nov 10, 1998. https://bit.ly/2IdYaKP

WANDA JACKSON

Dauphin, Chuck. "At 79, Wanda Jackson Looks Back on Introducing 'Sex Appeal' to Rock 'n' Roll in the '50s." *Billboard*. Sep 21, 2017. https://bit.ly/2L0um22

Gold, Adam. "Wanda Jackson and Justin Townes Earle on Their 'Unfinished Business.'" *Rolling Stone*. Oct 10, 2012. https://rol.st/2wGIk6j

Jackson, Wanda, and Scott B. Bomar. *Every Night Is Saturday Night*. Chicago: BMG Books, 2017.

Schonfeld, Zach. "Wanda Jackson 'In the Studio.'" *Rolling Stone*. July 10, 2012. https://rol.st/2IiMvum.

Sullivan, James. "Wanda Jackson Remembers Elvis." *Rolling Stone*. Dec 9, 2005. https://rol.st/2L2ACX2

ARETHA FRANKLIN

Brown, Mick. "Deep Soul." *Telegraph*. Mar 7, 2014. https://bit.ly/1cYz9t7

Cassimy, Evrod. "Local 4's Evrod Cassimy celebrates Aretha Franklin's birthday in New York." WDIV Local 4 NBC TV. Mar 24, 2014. https://bit.ly/2IggZ0d

———. "Queen of Soul Aretha Franklin Tells All to Local 4." WDIV Local 4 NBC TV. Oct 31, 2014. https://bit.ly/2G6Z1ao

Darrisaw, Michelle. "Aretha Franklin Talks Father's Influence on Her Music Career." *Southern Living*. 2017. https://bit.ly/2wK8cy9

Franklin, Aretha. "Aretha Franklin on Adele, Taylor Swift and being a diva." *Wall Street Journal*. By Christopher John Farley. Nov 10, 2014.

M., Andrew. "Aretha Franklin on Oprah (1999)." Filmed by *The Oprah Winfrey Show*, Nov 26, 1999. YouTube video, 28:20. Posted Jan. 7, 2013. https://bit.ly/2IafWij

O'Dell, Cary. "'Respect'—Aretha Franklin (1967)." 2002. https://bit.ly/2KU9k52

TIME. "10 Questions with Aretha Franklin." Filmed by *TIME*. YouTube video, 4:23. Posted Mar 11, 2010. https://bit.ly/2jSAr4s

Weaver, Hilary. "Aretha Franklin Out-Divas All Other Retiring Divas." *Vanity Fair*. Aug 17, 2017. https://bit.ly/2rKkYaI

RONNIE SPECTOR

Anderson, Kristin. "Talking Style With Ronnie Spector, the Quintessential '60s Girl-Group Star." *Vogue*. Oct 20, 2016. https://bit.ly/2KpT1vL

Hoby, Hermione. "Ronnie Spector interview: 'The more Phil tried to destroy me, the stronger I got.'" *Telegraph*. Mar 6, 2014. https://bit.ly/2KpozC2

Hull, Keldine. "Ronnie Spector, Lead Singer of the Legendary Ronettes, on Her Life, Music, and Message of Love." *Inspirer*. Dec 29, 2017. https://bit.ly/2rIVb2F

Muller, Marissa G. "Ronnie Spector: The Original Icon." *Noisey*. Nov 12, 2013. https://bit.ly/2Kijmfq

Runtagh, Jordan. "Ronnie Spector's Victory Lap: The Original Rock Queen Talks New Music and Reviving the Ronettes." *People*. June 24, 2017. https://bit.ly/2KqdyjS

Spector, Ronnie, and Vince Waldron. *Be My Baby*. New York: Harmony Books, 1990.

———. "Exclusive: Ronnie Spector Pays Tribute to Amy Winehouse." *Rolling Stone*. July 27, 2011. https://rol.st/2rI5Qee

TINA TURNER

Arrington, Carl. "Tina Turner, the Woman Who Taught Mick Jagger to Dance, is on the Prowl Again." *People*. Dec 7, 1981. https://bit.ly/2KpJwNb

Bryant, Tom. "Tina Turner Comes Out of Retirement to Launch New Show and Reveals Why She Felt She Had to Do It." *Mirror*. Oct 17, 2017. https://bit.ly/2rCXaF4

CNN. "Why Tina Turner left the U.S. (1997 *Larry King Live* Interview)." Filmed by *Larry King Live*, Feb 21, 1997. YouTube video, 33:07. Posted May 20, 2016. https://bit.ly/1WHyjuN

Collins, Nancy. "Tina Turner: Queen of Rock & Roll." *Rolling Stone*. Oct 23, 1986. https://rol.st/2IGCiY5

Fan Argentina. "Tina Turner interview *The Jonathon Ross Show* 28102017." Filmed by *The Jonathon Ross Show*, Oct 28, 2017. YouTube video, 12:11. Posted Oct 28, 2017. https://bit.ly/2ISLnNm

Fong-Torres, Ben. "Tales of Ike and Tina Turner." *Rolling Stone*. Oct 14, 1971. https://rol.st/2L0tnyW

OWN. "Tina Turner Was Becoming Tired of Singing and Dancing | Oprah's Next Chapter | Oprah Winfrey Network." Filmed Aug 25, 2013. YouTube video, 3:33. Posted Aug 26, 2013. https://bit.ly/2rMDH5J

Turner, Tina, and Kurt Loder. *I, Tina*. New York: William Morrow and Company, 1986.

Winfrey, Oprah. "Oprah Talks to Tina Turner." O, *The Oprah Magazine*. May 2005. https://bit.ly/2qesyeg

JANIS JOPLIN

Arbus, Doon, and Richard Avedon. *The Sixties*. New York: Random House, 1999.

Berg, Amy. *Janis: Little Girl Blue*. Film. Directed by Amy Berg. Nov 27, 2015.

"Bessie Smith Grave, Unmarked Since '37, Finally Gets a Stone." *New York Times*. Aug 9, 1970. https://nyti.ms/2wzUKwA

Dick Cavett Show. "August 3, 1970." ABC TV. Jul 18, 1969.

———. "June 25, 1970." ABC TV. Jul 25, 1970.

———. "July 18, 1969." ABC TV. Aug 3, 1970.

Evans, Greg. "Straightening Up Janis Joplin." *Slate*. Dec 3, 2015. https://slate.me/1lzEq4c

"Goodbye, Janis Joplin." *Rolling Stone*. Oct 29, 1970. https://rol.st/2rJBR4M

Joplin, Janis. Last Will and Testament. Oct 9, 1970. https://bit.ly/2jUFhxP

Joplin, Laura. *Love, Janis*. New York: Villard, 1992.

Millar, Jeff. "Janis Joplin: Port Arthur and the Thomas Jefferson Class of '60 may never be the same again." *Houston Chronicle*. Jan 17, 2017. https://bit.ly/2KrmaXC

Schulman, Michael. "My Big Sister, Janis Joplin." *New Yorker*. Oct 29, 2013. https://bit.ly/2IoscYo

GRACE SLICK

artski101. "Grace Slick appearing with Jefferson Starship." Filmed Sep 29, 2001. YouTube video, 9:14. Posted Nov 1, 2015. https://bit.ly/2G99Zfm

Browne, David. "Grace Slick's Festival Memories: Fearing Orgies and Getting Lit." *Rolling Stone*. May 23, 2014. https://rol.st/2k0Stl9

Cagan, Andrea, and Grace Slick. *Somebody to Love?* New York: Grand Central Publishing, 1998.

Chonin, Neva. "Gracefully Outrageous / Rock's original high priestess simply refuses to mellow with age." *San Francisco Chronicle*. Sep 6, 1998. https://bit.ly/2KgVTem

Fong-Torres, Ben. "Grace Slick With Paul Kantner: The Rolling Stone Interview." *Rolling Stone*. Nov 12, 1970. https://rol.st/2IiNc6S

Gorney, Cynthia. "Grace Slick 1966-." *Washington Post*. May 30, 1978. https://wapo.st/2rKfs85

"Grace Slick." Area Arts. 2001. https://bit.ly/2KfmxnY

Myers, Marc. "How Jefferson Airplane's Grace Slick Wrote 'White Rabbit.'" *Wall Street Journal*. May 31, 2016. https://on.wsj.com/2ryNmv9

Slick, Grace. "Summer of Love: 40 Years Later / Grace Slick." With Joel Selvin. *San Francisco Chronicle*. May 20, 2007.

———. "Why I Decided To License Starship's Music To Chick-fil-A." *Forbes Showbiz*. Feb 21, 2017. https://bit.ly/2rDzEsh

Smith, Patrick. "Lost Star Cars: Grace Slick's Aston Martin DB6." *PHS Collector Car World*. Sep 2, 2012. https://bit.ly/2Gbyhp0

Stanley, Mickey. "Jefferson Airplane's Grace Slick on Aging Rock Stars and Life as a Painter." *Vanity Fair*. June 15, 2012. https://bit.ly/2rH8Rvm

Tamarkin, Jeff. *Got a Revolution!* Brooklyn, NY: Atria Books, 2005.

Tannenbaum, Rob. "An Oral History of 'We Built This City,' the Worst Song of All Time." *GQ*. Aug 31, 2016. https://bit.ly/2vR3ax4

"They Called Grace Slick of Jefferson Starship the Acid Queen, but Her Real Battle Is with the Bottle." *People*. Aug 28, 1978. https://bit.ly/2rLP3pJ

FANNY

"Fanny: Godmothers of Chick Rock." Fanny. Accessed May 18, 2017. https://bit.ly/2G9puEb

France, Pauline. "Front and Center: Co-Founder and Lead Guitarist of Fanny, June Millington." *The Women's International Music Network*. Nov 17, 2014. https://bit.ly/2IarO3P

Lewis, Randy. "Fanny Walked the Earth Reunites Trail-blazing Female Rock Band." *Los Angeles Times*. Feb 28, 2018. https://lat.ms/2IkFvcs

Tedx Talks. "Rocking the Boat: How Playing Like a Girl Can Change the World." Filmed by Tedx Talks, Nov 3, 2012. YouTube video, 9:14. Posted Nov 20, 2012. https://bit.ly/2jPDNF9

"The Institute for the Musical Arts." Institute for the Musical Arts. Accessed May 18, 2017. https://bit.ly/2rEy2O4

CAROLE KING

Bissell, Therese. "Carole King's Idaho Home." *Architectural Digest*. Dec1, 2009. https://bit.ly/2ILKDtG

Heller, Karen. "Carole King's Musical Odyssey." *Washington Post*. Dec 1, 2015. https://wapo.st/2jYh1er

King, Carole. "A Conversation with Carole King." By Mike Barnicle. John F. Kennedy Presidential Library and Museum. Washington, DC. Apr 12, 2012. https://bit.ly/2IyeF3H

———. *A Natural Woman*. New York: Grand Central Publishing, 2012.

———. @Carole_King. Twitter. https://twitter.com/Carole_King

Kreps, Daniel. "Carole King Revisits 1983 Song 'One Small Voice' After Women's March." *Rolling Stone*. Jan 27, 2017. https://rol.st/2IkNDxB

Mark, David. "A natural environmentalist." *Politico*. July 13, 2009. https://politi.co/2GibEzj

Perone, James E. *The Words and Music of Carole King (The Praeger Singer-Songwriter Collection)*. Santa Barbara, CA: Praeger, 2006.

Zongker, Brett. "Carole King Wins Library of Congress Gershwin Award." *Billboard*. Dec 13, 2012. https://bit.ly/2rJlZjk

MARIANNE FAITHFULL

Faithfull, Marianne, and David Dalton. *Faithfull*. New York: Little Brown & Co., 1994.

Linning, Stephanie. "From Sixties Wild Child to a Life of Solitude." *MailOnline*, Dec 11, 2017. https://dailym.ai/2wG11GW

Neustatter, Angela. "Marianne Faithfull: It wasn't just Mick Jagger who couldn't get satisfaction." *Telegraph*. Sep 9, 2013. https://bit.ly/2GkBnaz

Springer, Mike. "David Bowie Sings 'I Got You Babe' with Marianne Faithfull in His Last Performance As Ziggy Stardust." *Open Culture*, Apr 12, 2013. https://bit.ly/1gFqCjk

Bruin, Carl. *Marianne Faithfull 1972*. Sept 30, 1972. Published in *Sunday Mirror*, under "The Curse of being Marianne," Oct 1, 1972.

Todd, Bella. "Marianne Faithfull talks heroin, the Rolling Stones and '60s London." *Time Out London*. Feb 1, 2016. https://bit.ly/2IniIwF

Tyler, Andrew. "Marianne Faithfull: As Years Go By." *New Musical Express*. Feb 2, 1974. https://bit.ly/2IxVST9

Watts, Miv, and Hugh Stewart. *The Maverick Soul*. San Francisco: Hardie Grant Books, 2017.

SUZI QUATRO

Back2thedrive. "Suzi Quatro rare interview." Filmed 1996. YouTube video, 8:19. Posted Feb 11, 2009. https://bit.ly/2jS62TW

Bosso, Joe. "Suzi Quatro: Born Ready." *Bass Player*, Dec 29, 2017. https://bit.ly/2GjWAS0

Lynne, V. K. "Legendary: The Badass with The Bass, Suzi Quatro." *Guitar Girl*. Sep 18, 2017. https://bit.ly/2KhALVg

Quatro, Suzi. *Unzipped*. London: Hodder, 2008.

———. *This Is Your Life*. Thames Television International, Feb 22, 1999.

Quatrorock. "QUATROROCK presents the Pleasure Seekers 'Reach Out.'" Filmed 1968. YouTube video, 3:36. Posted Oct 30, 2010. https://bit.ly/2rIjTAz

Parker, Pat. "Suzi Unzipped." *Essex Life*. Aug 20, 2010. https://bit.ly/2INBC2Y

STEVIE NICKS AND CHRISTINE McVIE

Bienstock, Richard. "Christine McVie on Fleetwood Mac's 'Peculiar' 'Mirage' Sessions, New LP." *Rolling Stone*. Sep 26, 2016. https://rol.st/2rObU3S

Davis, Stephen. *Gold Dust Woman*. New York: St. Martin's Press, 2017.

Connelly, Christopher. "Christine McVie Keeps a Level Head After Two Decades in the Fastlane." *Rolling Stone*. July 7, 1984. https://rol.st/2Ir7XcD

Crowe, Cameron. "The True Life Confessions of Fleetwood Mac." *Rolling Stone*. Mar 24, 1977. https://rol.st/2wOFT1s

Edwards, Gavin. "Stevie Nicks Spills *American Horror* Story Secrets." *Rolling Stone*. Dec 3, 2013. https://rol.st/2rMwSQV

Fleetwood, Mick. *Love That Burns*. Guildford, Surrey: Genesis Publications, 2017.

Friedman, Ann. "Fleetwood Mac's Christine McVie is Ready to Rock. Again." *Elle*. Sep 2014. https://bit.ly/2IraIuu

Greene, Andy. "Q&A: Christine McVie Can't Wait for Fleetwood Mac World Tour." *Rolling Stone*. Mar 27, 2014. https://rol.st/2wIZ7Wo

———. "The Last Word: Stevie Nicks Talks Aging, Addiction, Fleetwood Mac's Future." *Rolling Stone*. Mar 15, 2017. https://rol.st/2rOz4ax

Marsh, Dave. "Big (Fleetwood) Mac: The 1978 Cover Story." *Rolling Stone*. Jan 12, 1978. https://rol.st/2L1XRk1

Moore, Ralph. "10 Questions for Christine McVie of Fleetwood Mac." *TheArtsDesk.com*, Sep 20, 2016. https://bit.ly/2KfD9Mo

Scaggs, Austin. "Stevie Nicks On Turning 60, Fleetwood Mac's New Tour." *Rolling Stone*. Mar 5, 2009. https://rol.st/2IpJbcG

Williamson, Nigel. "Fleetwood Mac: 'Everybody was pretty weirded out'—the story of *Rumours*." *Uncut*. May 2003. https://bit.ly/2rMBbf3

ANN AND NANCY WILSON

Porch, Scott. "Nancy Wilson on leading Heart with her sister: 'The guys in the band sometimes had a hard time with that.'" *Salon*. Aug 13, 2015. https://bit.ly/2k2zh6A

Reiff, Corbin. "Interview: Nancy Wilson – Goddess of Rhythm." *Premier Guitar*. July 2013. https://bit.ly/2rOE1A9

Shindler, Merrill. "Wilson Sisters Talk Heart to Heart." *Rolling Stone*. July 28, 1977. https://rol.st/2L5ypKs

"The 35th Annual Kennedy Center Honors." Directed by Louis J. Jorvitz. Written by George Stevens Jr., Michael Stevens, Lewis Friedman, and Sara Lukinson. CBS TV. 2012.

Wilson, Ann; Nancy Wilson; and Charles R. Cross. *Kicking & Dreaming: A Story of Heart, Soul, and Rock & Roll*. New York: It Books, 2012.

Wilson, Nancy. "Nancy Wilson (Lead Guitarist From Heart/Film Composer)." *The Believer*. Interview by Maura Kelly. Aug 2007.

LINDA RONSTADT

Barton, Laura. "Linda Ronstadt: 'I Don't Like Any of My Albums.'" *Guardian*. Sep 28, 2017. https://bit.ly/2jZwkmW

Holden, Stephen. "For Linda Ronstadt, the Past Continues to Inspire." *New York Times*. Sep 14, 1986. https://nyti.ms/2IlACUt

LibraryOfCongress. "Linda Ronstadt: 2013 National Book Festival." Filmed Sep 21, 2013. YouTube video, 46:58. Posted on Dec 12, 2013. https://bit.ly/2KTjva6

Maiscott, Mary Lyn. "Linda Ronstadt: I Know When Parkinson's Hit from Listening to My Own Singing." *Vanity Fair*. Oct 28, 2013. https://bit.ly/2k0CQde

Nash, Alanna. "Heart-to-Heart With Linda Ronstadt." *AARP*. Aug 26, 2013. https://bit.ly/2KwvcTo

Rich, Frank. "Stage: 'Pirates of Penzance' on Broadway." *New York Times*. Jan 9, 1981. https://nyti.ms/2IH5cHD

Ronstadt, Linda. *Simple Dreams*. New York: Simon & Schuster, 2013.

———. "In Memoir, Linda Ronstadt Describes Her *Simple Dreams*." *Fresh Air*. By Terry Gross. NPR, WHYY Philadelphia. Sep 17, 2013.

Tamarkin, Jeff. "Linda Ronstadt—A Rare Interview (Part One and Two)." *Best Classic Bands*. Apr 19, 2017. https://bit.ly/2G8wtxj

BONNIE RAITT

Bonnie's Pride and Joy. "Bonnie Raitt – The Woman Behind The Blues – VH1-1989." Filmed by VH1, 1989. YouTube video, 25:14. Posted Mar 27, 2016. https://bit.ly/2k9i5w8

Elie, Paul. "Bonnie Raitt and the Fugitive Emotions Evoked by Slide Guitar." *New Yorker*. Apr 9, 2016. https://bit.ly/2L78qCn

Giller, Don. "Bonnie Raitt, Sippie Wallace on Late Night, April 27, 1982." Filmed by *Late Night with David Letterman*, April 27, 1982. YouTube video, 16:12. Posted Oct 28, 2015. https://bit.ly/2IwytRZ

Lawrence, Dave. "Touring Hawai'i, Bonnie Raitt Shares Roots in Activism and Philanthropy on HPR's ATC." Hawai'i Public Radio. Mar 23, 2017. https://bit.ly/2rBBdHm

Raitt, Bonnie. *60 Minutes II*. CBS TV. Jan 13, 1999.

Washington, Denzel, and Daniel Paisner. "Manna From Heaven: Bonnie Raitt, Musician." In *A Hand to Guide Me*. New York: Meredith Books, 2006.

THE RUNAWAYS

Cherkis, Jason. "The Lost Girls." *Huffington Post*. July 10, 2015. https://bit.ly/2KffNq7

Currie, Cherie, and Tony O'Neill. *Neon Angel*. New York: It Books, 2010.

Ford, Lita. *Living Like a Runaway*. New York: Dey Street Books, 2016.

McDonnell, Evelyn. "Joan Jett." *Andy Warhol's Interview*, February 2010.

———. "The Runaways: Wild Thing." *LA Weekly*. Mar 18, 2010.

Newman, Melinda. "Cherie Currie sets the record straight on 'The Runaways.'" *Uproxx*. Jan 26, 2010. https://bit.ly/2k3GzqG

"The Runaways." Concert poster. *The Concert Database*. Mar 5, 1977. https://bit.ly/2IbpHwz

SIOUXSIE SIOUX

Bracewell, Michael. "Her Dark Materials." *Guardian*. Sep 23, 2005. https://bit.ly/2IAWLgR

Coon, Caroline. *1988: The New Wave Punk Rock Explosion*. New York: Hawthorn Books, 1977.

Hewitt, Ben. "Siouxsie Sioux at 60: More Than a Monochrome Goth-pop Priestess." *Guardian*. May 27, 2017. https://bit.ly/2r64GHR

Mathur, Paul, and Marc Paytress. *Siouxsie and the Banshees*. London: Sanctuary Publishing, 2003.

Savage, Jon. "High Priestess." *SPIN*, June 1986.

THE SLITS

Albertine, Viv. Clothes, Clothes, Clothes. Music, Music, Music. Boys, Boys, Boys. New York: Thomas Dunne Books, 2014.

———. *To Throw Away Unopened: A Memoir*. London: Faber Social, 2018.

Bright, Kimberly. "Ari Up on The Slits and Chris Spedding." *Trebuchet*, 2004. Posted to Trebuchet-Magazine.com on December 1, 2015. https://bit.ly/2wBj69h

Coon, Caroline. *1988: The New Wave Punk Rock Explosion*. New York: Hawthorn Books, 1977.

Garratt, Sheryl. "Viv Albertine on 'shy' Sid Vicious, IVF and life after punk." *Telegraph*. May 11, 2014. https://bit.ly/2IoacNP

Mar, Alex. "The Return of the Slits." *Rolling Stone*. Feb 1, 2005. https://rol.st/2wLhGsK

Parkhouse, Will. "I Do Not Believe In Love: Viv Albertine On Life Post The Slits." *Quietus*. Feb 25, 2010. https://bit.ly/2KY6sEz

Pollitt, Tessa. "Earthbeat: In the Beginning There Was Rhythm." Interview by Gregory Mario Whitfield. *3:AM*. 2003. https://bit.ly/2wzE3BB

Rawls, Alex. "Slits Tribute: Previously Unpublished Q&A with Ari Up." *SPIN*. Oct 22, 2010. https://bit.ly/2k1kEQL

The Culture Show. "Girls Will Be Girls." BBC Two. July 1, 2014.

Sullivan, Caroline. "How we made *Cut* (the Slits)." *Guardian*. June 24, 2013. https://bit.ly/2rRTwZ1

POISON IVY

Wallis, Kristy Marlana. "How We Met: Poison Ivy and Lux Interior." *Independent*. Interview by Nicholas Barber. May 9, 1998. https://ind.pn/2KeFC9Z

Breihan, Tom. "Cramps Frontman Lux Interior R.I.P." *Pitchfork*. Feb 4, 2009. https://bit.ly/2Gdj5rs

Burg, William. *Sacramento's K Street*. Stroud, England: The History Press, 2012.

Obrecht, Jas. "Oooh! Poison Ivy." *Guitar Player Magazine*, Aug 1990.

Porter, Dick. *Journey to the Centre of the Cramps*. London: Omnibus Press, 2015.

PATTI SMITH

Baltin, Steve. "Patti Smith, Michael Stipe, Flea Lead Pathway To Paris Concert For Climate Change." *Forbes*. Nov 1, 2017. https://bit.ly/2L7Ed67

"CBGB's Last Shows." *SPIN*. Oct 16, 2006. https://bit.ly/2GqxL6L

Hermes, Will. " Patti Smith Group and Television at CBGB." In web series "The 50 Greatest Concerts of the Last 50 Years." *Rolling Stone*. June 12, 2017. https://rol.st/2Is4kDo

Milzoff, Rebecca. "Influences: Patti Smith." *New York*. Dec 5, 2005. https://nym.ag/2k0Ot3T

Morgan, Eleanor. "Lenny Kaye on 'learning how to gallop' with Patti Smith." *Guardian*. Sep 9, 2011. https://bit.ly/2InDzzW

"Patti Smith & Lenny Kaye celebrating the 40th Anniversary of their 1st Poetry Project performance." *The Poetry Project*. Feb 15, 2011. https://bit.ly/2jTf2rR

Robinson, Lisa. "Rebel Nights." *Vanity Fair*, Nov 2002.

Smith, Patti. *Devotion (Why I Write)*. New Haven, CT: Yale University Press, 2017.

———. *Just Kids*. New York: Ecco, 2010.

———. *M Train*. New York: Knopf, 2015.

———. "Patti Smith And Robert Mapplethorpe: Kindred Spirits." *Fresh Air*. By Terry Gross. NPR, WHYY Philadelphia. Jan 19, 2010. https://n.pr/2rNgLSW

———. "Patti Smith's My First Gig: Desecrating A Church With Electric Guitar." *New Musical Express*. Jun 12, 2014. https://bit.ly/2IeiyYo

——— and Lenny Kaye. Untitled album, recorded at St. Mark's Church, New York City. Recorded Feb 10, 1971. Mer Records. Compact disc.

Thompson, Dave. *Dancing Barefoot*. Chicago: Chicago Review Press, 2016.

TINA WEYMOUTH

Boehm, Mike. "Ex-Heads Say They Got Byrned." *Los Angeles Times*. Sep 10, 1992. https://lat.ms/2wKvnbF

Clarke, John. "Rockers Chris Frantz and Tina Weymouth Talk Marriage." *Rolling Stone*. July 4, 2013. https://rol.st/2wVG6jF

Courogen, Carrie. "40 Years Later, Talking Heads' Most Valuable Member is Still its Most Under-Recognized." *Paper*, Sep 15, 2017. https://bit.ly/2jvhsj6

Handelman, David. "Are Four (Talking) Heads Better Than One?" *Rolling Stone*. Jan 15, 1987. https://rol.st/2rLBiaH

Isola, Gregory. "Tina Talks Heads, Tom Toms, and How to Succeed at Bass Without Really Trying." *Bass Player* (Internet Archive, Wayback Machine). Mar 1997. https://bit.ly/2IAtvHa

Frantz, Chris, and Tina Weymouth. "Tom Tom Club." Presentation at the Red Bull Music Academy Tokyo. Tokyo, Japan. Nov 2014. https://win.gs/2Ge6pVq

Spitz, Marc. "Tom Tom Club's 'Genius of Love,' a Hip-Hop Staple, Turns 30." *Vanity Fair*. Jan 10, 2011. https://bit.ly/2Gol3FQ

Weymouth, Tina, and Bobbi Brown. "Tina Weymouth writes a letter to her younger self." *i-D*, Vice Media. Jan 30, 2017. https://bit.ly/2hN1MXx

DEBBIE HARRY

Burston, Paul. "Lightning Strikes Twice." *Guardian*. Jan 22, 1999. https://bit.ly/2IqhzUV

"Debbie Harry." *Biography Channel*. A&E Television Network. 2003.

Harry, Debbie, and Ilana Kaplan. "Debbie Harry on moving to the East Village in 1965." *Time Out New York*. Sep 27, 2017. https://bit.ly/2IqhP6l

James, Jamie. "Platinum Blondie." *Rolling Stone*. June 28, 1979. https://rol.st/2rMq72g

Moody, Rick. "Debbie Harry." *Andy Warhol's Interview*. March 14, 2014. https://bit.ly/2L36GtQ

Stein, Chris. *Negative*. New York: Rizzoli, 2014.

Poe, Amos, dir. *TV Party*. January 8, 1979 episode. Brink Films; Sep 1, 2005. DVD.

CHRISSIE HYNDE

Durrant, Sabine. "Chrissie Hynde interview." *Telegraph*. June 15, 2009. https://bit.ly/2GoLMSE

Hollow, Christopher. "Hard rockin' Chrissie Hynde unleashes solo album: 'I'm way past writing my break-up album.'" *Sydney Morning Herald*. June 6, 2014. https://bit.ly/2wSuRbk

Hynde, Chrissie. *Reckless*. New York: Doubleday, 2015.

Obrecht, Jas. "James Honeyman-Scott: The Complete 1981 Pretenders Interview." *Guitar Player*. Apr 1981. https://bit.ly/2IPqBOZ

Rocca, Jane. "Chrissie Hynde: What I Know About Men." *Sydney Morning Herald*. Mar 4, 2015. https://bit.ly/2GplvDB

PAT BENATAR

Benatar, Pat, and Patsi Bale Cox. *Between a Heart and a Rock Place*. New York: William Morrow, 2010.

Betts, Stephen L. "Pat Benatar and Neil Giraldo: 'We're Like Johnny and June.'" *Rolling Stone*. May 21, 2015. https://rol.st/2INFYY3

Hazel, Allison. "Pat Benatar Supports Women's March With Original Song 'Shine.'" *Billboard*. Jan 20, 2017. https://bit.ly/2L5TJQb

Lunch, Lydia. "Lunch with Benatar." *SPIN*, September 1985.

Newman, Melinda "Pat Benatar Premieres Powerful 'Dancing Through the Wreckage' Video: Exclusive." *Billboard*. Sep 29, 2017. https://bit.ly/2IHX2yH

"Pat Benatar." *American Woman with Brooke Baldwin*. CNN Digital. Jan 3, 2018. https://cnn.it/2IbnLUR

"Pat Benatar for the Sunday Conversation." *Los Angeles Times*. June 27, 2010. https://lat.ms/2rM8DD1

Pond, Steve. "Pat Benatar: This Year's Model." *Rolling Stone*. Oct 16, 1980. https://rol.st/2k6wcCx

Rock 'n' Moms. TV. Produced by Pete Menzies. New York: WE tv, 2002. https://bit.ly/2k8YTOT

SXSW. "SXSW Interview: Pat Benatar & Neil Giraldo | SXSW Music 2016." Filmed by SXSW. YouTube video, 1:10:58. Posted Mar 17, 2016. https://bit.ly/2jUJq5c

EXENE CERVENKA

Darling, Nikki. "B-Side Stories: X, the Whisky A-Go-Go, a Tragic Night, and *Under the Big Black Sun*." *Los Angeles Weekly*. July 14, 2009. https://bit.ly/2GpHI4j

Doe, John, with Tom DeSavia. *Under the Big Black Sun*. Cambridge, MA: Da Capo Press, 2016.

Edwards, Gavin. "X's Exene Cervenka Cleans Out Her Closet." *Rolling Stone*. Feb 13, 2014. https://rol.st/2INHZ6z

Fossum, Melissa. "X's Exene Cervenka's Advice to Female Musicians: 'Don't Get Married.'" *Phoenix New Times*. Dec 6, 2011. https://bit.ly/2GsqKCI

Grow, Kory. "X Look Back on 40 Years of Punk Iconoclasm." *Rolling Stone*. Sep 5, 2017. https://rol.st/2IrIIa7

Lunch, Lydia, and Exene Cervenka. *Adulterers Anonymous*. New York: Grove Press, 1982.

Stevenson, Arielle. "Interview: Exene Cervenka talks about her Pinellas days, punk, and what it's like to play with X forty years later." *Creative Loafing*. May 10, 2017. https://bit.ly/2k43ZMD

KIM GORDON

Blistein, Jon. "Sonic Youth's Kim Gordon Explains Split From Thurston Moore." *Rolling Stone*. Apr 23, 2013. https://rol.st/2ImqDOK

Chicago Humanities Festival. "Kim Gordon: 'Girl in a Band.'" Filmed by Chicago Humanities Festival, Feb 26, 2015. YouTube video, 53:05. Posted Mar 2, 2015.

Dolan, Jon. "Unkool Thing: Notes on the Split of Sonic Youth's Kim Gordon and Thurston Moore." *Grantland*. Oct 17, 2011. https://bit.ly/2IdxzO6

Goodman, Lizzy. "Kim Gordon Sounds Off." *Elle*. May, 2013. https://bit.ly/2rKXouK

Gordon, Kim. *Girl in a Band*. New York: Dey Street Books, 2015.

Hyman, Dan. "Q&A: Kim Gordon on Her New Band Body/Head and Missing Sonic Youth." *Rolling Stone*. Sep 12, 2013. https://rol.st/2IoeDYW

Johnson, Rebecca. "The X-Girl Factor: How the Cult '90s Label Set the Standard for Skater-Girl Style." *Vogue*. July 1, 2016. https://bit.ly/2KtHED5

Moore, Booth. "'90s Style Icon Kim Gordon on Her New Fashion Collection With & Other Stories." *Hollywood Reporter*. Aug 30, 2017. https://bit.ly/2wM609k

O'Dair, Barbara. "Kim Gordon: The Godmother of Grunge on Feminism in Rock." *Rolling Stone*. Nov 13, 1997. https://rol.st/2rKHU9Y

Pelly, Jenn. "Unconventional Idol: Kim Gordon's *Girl in a Band*." *Pitchfork*. Feb 26, 2015. https://bit.ly/2IG9vD6

Ratliff, Ben. "A Lasting Experiment With Music." *New York Times*. Sep 6, 2013. https://nyti.ms/2IOcr0q

TheMusicComAu. "BIGSOUND 2016 Keynote: Kim Gordon." Filmed Sep 7, 2016. YouTube video, 1:03:18. Posted Sep 7, 2016. https://bit.ly/2IhwdOn

Thompson, Elizabeth, and Alexis Swerdloff. "An Oral History of X-Girl." *Paper*. Aug 20, 2012. https://bit.ly/2oBtuog

Weiner, Jonah. "Kim Gordon on Divorce, Art and Life After Sonic Youth." *Rolling Stone*. Feb 26, 2015. https://rol.st/2rL0sqK

THE GO-GO'S

Behind the Music. "The Go-Go's." VH1. Jan 21, 2012.

Carlisle, Belinda. *Lips Unsealed*. New York: Crown Archetype, 2010.

Connelly, Christopher. "The Go-Go's: A Year of Living Dangerously." *Rolling Stone*. July 5, 1984. https://rol.st/2k14k2p

Duersten, Matthew. "The Go-Go's Take Their Girlie Show from the Gutter to the Mall." *Los Angeles Magazine*. July 8, 2014. https://bit.ly/2L9pO9w

Eisenberg, Susan Dormady. "Belinda Carlisle Still Has 'The Beat' as She Riffs on Rock and Her Remedy for Menopause." *Huffington Post*. Jan 26, 2015. https://bit.ly/2KeI00n

Grow, Kory. "Belinda Carlisle on Go-Go's Punk History, Farewell Tour." *Rolling Stone*. Aug 2, 2016. https://rol.st/2IHzGJk

Ryan, Kyle. "The Go-Go's made history with *Beauty And The Beat*—and barely survived it." *AV Club*. Sep 17, 2013. https://bit.ly/2rNtncW

Sharp, Ken. "The Go-Go's Charlotte Caffey: The Beat Goes On (Interview)." *Rock Cellar*. July 7, 2014. https://bit.ly/2wFnmok

Tannenbaum, Rob. "The Go-Go's Recall the Debauched Days of Their Hit 'We Got the Beat' 35 Years Later: 'We Were a Five-Headed Monster.'" *Billboard*. May 20, 2016. https://bit.ly/2wPjiSq

Vine, Hannah. "First Look at Go-Go's Musical *Head Over Heels* in San Francisco." *Playbill*. Apr 17, 2018. https://bit.ly/2jRxWPH

CYNDI LAUPER

Cocks, Jay. "These Big Girls Don't Cry: Madonna and Cyndi Lauper are the hottest women in rock. Why?" *TIME*. Mar 4, 1985.

Cumming, Alan. "Cyndi Lauper." *Andy Warhol's Interview*, May 2009.

Dilbert, Ryan. "How Cyndi Lauper Was Essential in the Launch of WWE WrestleMania." *BleacherReport*. Mar 30, 2017. https://ble.ac/2rCPGT9

Jerome, Jim. "She Wants to Have Fun." *People*. Sep 17, 1984.

Lauper, Cyndi, and Jancee Dunn. *Cyndi Lauper*. New York: Atria Books, 2012.

Love, Gael. "New Again: Cyndi Lauper." *Andy Warhol's Interview*, June 2013. https://bit.ly/2GptGzN

McCormick, Neil. "Cyndi Lauper interview: 'I just want to be taken seriously.'" *Telegraph*. Apr. 24, 2016. https://bit.ly/2Im2SX0

ANNIE LENNOX

thisearismine. "Eurythmics on their beginnings." Filmed by *Late Night with David Letterman*, Mar 19, 1984. YouTube video, 10:30. Posted Aug 20, 2014. https://bit.ly/2GxkedM

Frank, Alex. "Annie Lennox on Her Hit Grammys Performance—Plus an Exclusive Clip of Her PBS Special." *Vogue*. Mar 4, 2015. https://bit.ly/2IrJJyM

Good Morning Britain. "Piers Morgan Discusses International Women's Day With Annie Lenox | Good Morning Britain." Filmed by *Good Morning Britain*, Aug 3, 2017. YouTube video, 7:54. Posted Mar 8, 2017. https://bit.ly/2rPbIT2

Kletnoy, Sergio. "Annie Lennox: 'Music Has No Color.'" *Elle*. Nov 3, 2014. https://bit.ly/2Iox16X

Kornhaber, Spencer. "Annie Lennox, the New Grammy Idol." *Atlantic*. Feb 9, 2015. https://theatln.tc/2rNv5uS

Larry King. "Annie Lennox on 'Larry King Now' – Full Episode in the U.S. on Ora. TV." Filmed by Larry King Now, Oct 20, 2014. YouTube video, 27:12. Posted Oct 21, 2014. https://bit.ly/2wYMhDA

Lennox, Annie. "Annie's Message." *TheCircle*. Accessed May 16, 2017. https://bit.ly/2rF6wjt

Stevens, Mark. "Annie Lennox Extreme Close Up interview Part 1." Filmed by E! TV, 1992. YouTube video, 21:55. Posted Sep 8, 2017. https://bit.ly/2k7Dndr

professorenol. "Annie Lennox In Conversation With Jo Whiley." Recorded by BBC Radio 2, March 6, 2018. YouTube video, 29:17. Posted Mar 6, 2018. https://bit.ly/2wT48LQ

Mewborn, Brant. "Eurythmics Unmasked." *Rolling Stone*. Oct 24, 1985. https://rol.st/2Kvsiy5

Neese, Joseph. "Annie Lennox: 'AIDS Isn't Over . . .We Still Have a Long Way to Go.'" *NBC News*. Nov 30, 2016. https://nbcnews.to/2IbRSeW

Omnibus. "Greetings from the Gutter." Episode 20. BBC, May 2, 1995.

Simpson, Dave. "Eurythmics: how we made 'Sweet Dreams (Are Made of This).'" *Guardian*. Dec 11, 2017. https://bit.ly/2C5OgUK

Sutherland, Bryony, and Lucy Ellis. *Annie Lennox – The Biography*. London: Omnibus Press, 2001.

THE BANGLES

Behind the Music. "The Bangles." Season 3, episode 40. VH1. July 30, 2000.

Blackman, Guy. "Bangles shake again." *The Age*. Nov 6, 2005. https://bit.ly/2IetJjO

Hann, Michael. "The Paisley Underground: Los Angeles's 1980s psychedelic explosion." *Guardian*. May 16, 2013. https://bit.ly/2IFOB75

McCartney, Kelly. "The Origin of The Bangles." *Cuepoint*. June 5, 2015. https://bit.ly/2IgErKM

Orlean, Susan. "The Bangles: California Girls." *Rolling Stone*. Mar 26, 1987. https://rol.st/2l9mNJ2

Steele, Michael. Interview by Liz Kershaw. BBC Radio 6 Music. Mar 2003.

MELISSA ETHERIDGE

Azzopardi, Chris. "Q&A: Melissa Etheridge On Letting Go, Moving On & The Song 'I Didn't Wanna Do.'" *PrideSource*. Nov 4, 2014. https://bit.ly/2Iasu93 https://bit.ly/2Iasu93

Bloom, Steve. "Melissa Etheridge on Her Marijuana Arrest: 'I Feel Like a Rock Star Now' (Exclusive)." *Variety*. Oct 16, 2017. https://bit.ly/2KXRtKE

Dunn, Jancee. "Melissa Etheridge Takes the Long Hard Road from the Heartland to Hollywood." *Rolling Stone*. June 1, 1995. https://rol.st/2KvUpwS

———. "Melissa Etheridge's Secret." *Rolling Stone*. Feb 3, 2000. https://rol.st/2Krh11J

"Melissa Etheridge's Battle with Cancer." *People*. Oct 21, 2004. https://bit.ly/2IrC87K

Philbrook, Erik. "A Fearless Career: Melissa Etheridge Celebrates 25 Years of Success." *ASCAP Foundation*. Aug 2010. https://bit.ly/2jSOo28

"Rebels & Pioneers: Melissa Etheridge." *Advocate*, 35th Anniversary Issue. November 2002.

Ryder, Taryn. "Melissa Etheridge: 'I'd Much Rather Have a Smoke With My Grown Kids Than a Drink.'" *Yahoo Entertainment*. Apr 17, 2017. https://yhoo.it/2oOWBIy

"The 47th Annual Grammy Awards." Directed by Walter C. Miller. Written by Karen Anderson, Ken Ehrlich, Matt Johnson, and David Wild. CBS TV. Feb 13, 2005.

KIM DEAL

Aaron, Charles. "Kim Deal: The Breeders Leader Gets Pissed." *SPIN*, July 1995. Posted to SPIN.com Feb 11, 2014. https://bit.ly/2ImaybM

Cobain, Kurt. "Top 50 by Nirvana." Journal entry, circa 1993. Posted by Thomas Kennedy. *Internet Archive Wayback Machine*. May 9, 2013. https://bit.ly/2IFocX3

"Dayton Heroes The Breeders Still Battling." *Studio Sessions*, NPR. July 18, 2008. https://n.pr/2GsP9b2

Nicholson, Rebecca. "The Breeders on Kicking Drugs, Kurt Cobain and Life After Pixies." *Guardian*. Oct 7, 2017. https://bit.ly/2xvEjwo

Schoemer, Karen. "A Breed Apart." *Rolling Stone*. May 19, 1994. https://rol.st/2Iox8k2

Serota, Maggie. "Kim Deal Is Back, And She Doesn't Want To Talk About The Pixies." *Refinery29*. Dec 18, 2014. https://r29.co/2Iz2Om2

Spitz, Marc. "Life to the Pixies." *SPIN*, September 2004. Posted to SPIN.com, June 16, 2013. https://bit.ly/2jTehyL

L7

Dickinson, Chris. "L7—Bricks Are Heavy." *Chicago Reader*. Oct 15, 1992. https://bit.ly/2rPUOCZ

Hung, Melissa. "Bored? Tired? . . ." *Houston Press*. Nov 11, 1999. https://bit.ly/2IoI29m

Lawrence, Matthew. "A Short History of Women Throwing Their Tampons at You." *Hornet*. Oct 19, 2015. https://bit.ly/2jSjR4D

Lecaro, Lina. "L7 Thrash Hard, Take Tinder Selfie at Wild First Show Back." *Rolling Stone*. May 29, 2015. https://rol.st/2Gujh5Q

Murphy, Tom. "Donita Sparks of L7 on Why the Band Reunited." *Westword*. Aug 28, 2015. https://bit.ly/2rG0zTq

Powell, Alison. "Fast and Frightening." *SPIN*, April 1992.

Reynolds, Simon and Press, Joy. *The Sex Revolts*. Cambridge: Harvard University Press, 1996.

Tehabsim, Anna. "Turning Points: L7's Donita Sparks." *Crack*. 2015. https://bit.ly/2rDhYNv

Wolfe, Allison. "Allison Wolfe and Donita Sparks Talk Bloody Tampons, Pantsuits and More." *I'm In The Band*. Podcast audio. Aug 15, 2017. https://bit.ly/2uG6f4m

KATHLEEN HANNA

Bennett, Kim Taylor. "Kathleen Hanna on Tokenism, Therapy, and Where Riot Grrrl Went Wrong." *Noisey*. Oct 21, 2016. https://bit.ly/2rDg67c

Cooper, Leonie. "Bikini Kill's message of female empowerment is more important now than ever." *New Musical Express*. Nov 9, 2017. https://bit.ly/2rSCVTI

Hanna, Kathleen. *The Punk Singer*. IFC Films, 2013.

Marcus, Sara. *Girls to the Front*. New York: Harper Perennial, 2010.

Minsker, Evan and Wicks, Amanda. "Bikini Kill Reunite for the First Time in 20 Years." *Pitchfork*. Nov 5, 2017. https://bit.ly/2wBNDUI

Smith, Rachel. "Revolution Girl Style, 20 Years Later." *NPR Music*. Sep 22, 2011. https://n.pr/2KiJOFB

The Riot Grrrl Collection. Fales Library, New York University. https://bit.ly/2rPJLum

COURTNEY LOVE

Brite, Poppy Z. *Courtney Love*. New York: Simon & Schuster, 1997.

Conniff, Tamara. "Lived Through This." *Billboard*, Oct 28, 2006.

France, Lisa Respers. "Courtney Love on Raising Frances Bean." CNN, June 7, 2017.

Fricke, David. "Courtney Love: Life Without Kurt." *Rolling Stone*, Dec 15, 1994.

Hillburn, Robert. "The Trials of Love." *Los Angeles Times*, Apr 10, 1994.

Love, Courtney. *Behind The Music*. VH1 TV, June 21, 2010.

— — —. "Courtney Love Does the Math." *Salon.com*. June 14, 2000. https://bit.ly/2GbIKB1

— — —. *Dirty Blonde*. London: Faber & Faber, 2006.

Rich, Katey. "Why Courtney Love Hasn't Written About Kurt Cobain in Her Memoir Yet." *Vanity Fair*, Sep 18, 2017.

"Sugar Baby Doll: the best or worst 'supergroup' that never happened?" *Dangerous Minds*. July 14, 2016. https://bit.ly/2Ibfnoe

Yapp, Will. *The Return of Courtney Love*. Dec 2006, More4 TV.

PJ HARVEY

Bailie, Stuart. "Dead Lambs And Dark Sounds." *New Musical Express*, 1993. Posted to NME.com, Aug 3, 2015. https://bit.ly/2jRMcIg

Freeman, John. "Queen Sized Polly: PJ Harvey's *Rid Of Me* Revisited." *Quietus*. May 21, 2013. https://bit.ly/2d1wbvE

Hasted, Nick. "Inside the Hidden Heart of PJ Harvey." *Independent*. Mar 27, 2009. https://ind.pn/2GsDuJs

Kot, Greg. "My Music Has Not Been Easy Listening. That Stops People." *Chicago Tribune*. Dec 18, 2000.

"Local Rock Star PJ Harvey Talks to the News." *Bridport & Lyme Regis News*. Jan 26, 2011. https://bit.ly/2rMT0LO

Lynskey, Dorian. "PJ Harvey: 'I feel things deeply. I get angry, I shout at the TV, I feel sick.'" *Guardian*. Apr 23, 2011. https://bit.ly/1sgpQ5q

Martinez, Christina. "Polly's Phonic Spree." *Bust*, Fall 2004.

Reynolds, Simon. "PJ Harvey: 'I'm always looking for extremes.'" *Melody Maker*, 1993. Posted to Guardian.com, July 9, 2014. https://bit.ly/2rEKIEU

Topping, Alexandra. "PJ Harvey Wins Mercury Music Prize for the Second Time." *Guardian*. Sep 6, 2011. https://bit.ly/2LcHl0y

White, Megan. "PJ Harvey makes new album in a glass box for you all to see." *Huck*. Feb 4, 2015. https://bit.ly/1KoubY0

SHERYL CROW

Gannon, Louise. "How Sheryl Crow Took on the Klan, White House, Depression and Cancer." *Daily Mail*. June 23, 2008. https://dailym.ai/2rOSdZS

Kauss, Katie. "Sheryl Crow Launches a Clothing Line for HSN, Still Isn't Over That 'Famous Actress' Who Stole Her Favorite Leather Jacket." *People*. Feb 23, 2017. https://bit.ly/2wRFefP

McLean, Craig. "Sheryl Crow interview: 'I've attracted people who are very . . . challenged.'" *Telegraph*. Jan 14, 2014. https://bit.ly/2GsUPBL

Stern, Howard. "How Sheryl Crow Went from Fired Waitress to Michael Jackson's Backup Singer to Grammy-Winning Superstar." *The Howard Stern Show*, Sirius XM, New York City, Apr 18, 2017. https://bit.ly/2Ke2bf2

Weller, Sheila. "At Home with Superstar Sheryl Crow." *Good Housekeeping*. July 11, 2014. https://bit.ly/2IsYhyc

Willman, Chris. "Sheryl Crow on Loving Her Age, Fearing Real-Life 'House of Cards' and Being a Country Misfit." *Variety*. May 1, 2017. https://bit.ly/2Laruj7

ALANIS MORISSETTE

Alanis Morissette (blog). http://alanis.com/blog/

Brown, August. "Ready for Alanis Morissette's 'Jagged Little Pill' as a Musical? It's Happening." *Los Angeles Times*. May 30, 2017. https://lat.ms/2IMV7ce

Chiu, Melody. "Alanis Morissette Reveals Battle with Crippling Postpartum Depression That Took Hold Seconds After Daughter's Birth." *People*. Sep 6, 2017. https://bit.ly/2rPrBI8

France, Kim. "Ray of Light." *SPIN*, April 1998. Posted to SPIN.com, Mar 3, 2016. https://bit.ly/2wSnH7a

Hannaham, James. "Alanis in Wonderland." *SPIN*, November 1995.

Curb Your Enthusiasm. "The Terrorist Attack." Season 3, episode 5. Directed by Robert B. Weide. HBO. Oct 13, 2002.

Morissette, Alanis. "Feminism Needs a Revolution." *TIME*. Mar 8, 2016. https://ti.me/2k5NW0L

Sullivan, Kate. "Well-Rounded Little Pill." *SPIN*, March 2002.

GWEN STEFANI

Anderson, Stacey. "Gwen Stefani 'All Tied Up' at L.A.M.B. Fashion Week Show." *Village Voice*. Feb 12, 2010.

Mizoguchi, Karen. "Gwen Stefani Talks How No Doubt's Hit 'Just A Girl' Came to Be." *People*. Mar 3, 2017. https://bit.ly/2rPm05p

Niven, Lisa. "On Beauty: Gwen Stefani." *Vogue*. Dec 4, 2017. https://bit.ly/2L8Gf60

Van Meter, Jonathan. "Gwen Stefani: The First Lady of Rock." *Vogue*. Apr 2004. Posted to Vogue.com, Apr 1, 2008. https://bit.ly/2IpFibV

Vineyard, Jennifer. "Gwen Stefani says Acting is a Lot Harder Than Singing." *MTV News*. Dec 2, 2004. https://on.mtv.com/2Kykwnf

SHIRLEY MANSON

Bacher, Danielle. "Shirley Manson Revisits Childhood Sexual Trauma as She Moves Forward with New Garbage Album." *Billboard*. June 4, 2016. https://bit.ly/2IuNxPZ

Domanick, Andrea. "Welcome to Girlschool, the Festival and Community Bringing Equality Center Stage." *Noisey*. Feb 2, 2018. https://bit.ly/2EDBjDA

Evans, Dayna. "The Return of a Grunge Goddess." *New York*, May 29, 2017 . Posted to TheCut.com, June 6, 2017. https://bit.ly/2sOhClk

Garbage. *This Is the Noise That Keeps Me Awake*. New York: Akashic Books, 2017.

Michelson, Noah. "Shirley Manson Has A Lot To Say About Women In Music (And She's Not Afraid To Say Any Of It)." *Huffpost Personal*. Feb 8, 2018. https://bit.ly/2ICRNQL

"Shirley Manson – Charity Work, Events and Causes." *Look to the Stars*. Accessed May 17, 2018. https://bit.ly/2jSwU5S

SLEATER-KINNEY

Brownstein, Carrie. *Hunger Makes Me a Modern Girl*. New York: Riverhead Books, 2015.

Buchanan, Daisy. "Sleater-Kinney: Bring on the return of riot grrrl!" *Independent*. Jan 10, 2015. https://ind.pn/2GqCy8d

Goldman, Marlene. "Hot-Rockin' Beats." *Rolling Stone*. Feb 19, 1999.

Marcus, Greil. "Sleater-Kinney: America's Best Rock Band." *TIME*, July 9, 2001.

Maron, Marc. "Carrie Brownstein." *WTF with Marc Maron*. Podcast audio. Apr 1, 2012. https://bit.ly/2GaTsYA

Nevins, Jake. "Carrie Brownstein: 'It's OK to Make Art for the Sake of Making People Laugh.'" *Guardian*. Jan 18, 2018. https://bit.ly/2L8GT3L

"Riot Grrrl Redux." *Evergreen*, Fall 2011. Posted to Evergreen.edu, accessed May 21, 2018. https://bit.ly/2GxqEtc

Siemers, Erik. "The End of 'Portlandia': Inside the scrappy cable show's career-launching legacy." *Portland Business Journal*. Sep 8, 2017. https://bit.ly/2wRzoeb

Stiernberg, Bonnie. "Carrie Brownstein: Fill in the Blank." *Paste*. Jan 6, 2015. https://bit.ly/2rPCHh4

Talbot, Margaret. "Stumptown Girl." *New Yorker*. Jan 2, 2012

Vozick-Levinson, Simon. "Carrie Brownstein's Life After Punk." *Rolling Stone*. Mar 20, 2014. https://rol.st/2k3GdQG

Weiner, Jonah. "Sleater-Kinney: Return of the Roar." *Rolling Stone*. Jan 20, 2015. https://rol.st/2IrvU7N

SUSAN TEDESCHI

Knopper, Steve. "How Susan Tedeschi and Derek Trucks fell in love over Chicago blues records." *Chicago Tribune*. Jan 18, 2018. https://trib.in/2rpDXKj

Spera, Keith. "For guitarist Derek Trucks, his band with Susan Tedeschi is literally family." *NOLA.com/The Times-Picayune*. Oct 17, 2013. https://bit.ly/2rFsToS

Tortorici, Frank. "Blues Singer Susan Tedeschi is Grammys' Odd Woman Out." *MTV News*. Jan 14, 2000. https://on.mtv.com/2KhgE9M

AMY WINEHOUSE

Amy. Directed by Asif Kapadia. New York: A24, 2015.

"Amy Winehouse Denied Entry to U.S." *The Lede* (blog). *New York Times*. Feb 7, 2008. https://nyti.ms/2rOpFAC

"Amy Winehouse smoking crack." Filmed Jan 18, 2008. Originally posted by the *Sun*, Jan 22, 2018. https://bit.ly/2rDjlf8

Hughes, Hilary. "Here's the 'Back to Black' Story that hit the Amy Winehouse documentary's cutting room floor." *Village Voice*. July 17, 2015. https://bit.ly/2wP6MSR

Carroll, Jim. "Amy Winehouse, Act Two – 'This time, I know what is going on.'" *Irish Times*. Dec 1, 2006. https://bit.ly/2rQj33X

MacInnes, Paul. "Amy Winehouse arrested for drug possession in Norway." *Guardian*. Oct 19, 2007. https://bit.ly/2IpBabY

Marrs, John. "Amy Winehouse Unpublished Interview from 2004 — 'I Never Want To Remember Anything Bad in My Life.'" *Huffington Post UK*. July 18, 2014. https://bit.ly/2rCzwt0

Simpson, Dave. "Dietrich with a Nose-Stud." *Guardian*. Oct 28, 2003. https://bit.ly/2IxtL6c

"The 50th Annual Grammy Awards." Directed by Walter C. Miller and Paul Miller. Written by Ken Ehrlich and David Wild. CBS TV. Feb 10, 2008.

AMY LEE

Baker, Trevor. "Female rock stars not wanted in the UK. Apparently." *Guardian*. Nov 22, 2007. https://bit.ly/2GqGRQV

Eliscu, Jenny. "Q&A: Amy Lee." *Rolling Stone*. Mar 10, 2004. https://rol.st/2wN2lIs

Goodman, William. "Exclusive: Amy Lee on the New Evanescence Album." *SPIN*. Mar 5, 2010. https://bit.ly/2Gm2WQN

Kaufman, Gil. "Evanescence Fall from Grace." *Rolling Stone*. Apr 15, 2003. https://rol.st/2IIGpmz

Morris, Catherine. "Evanescence's Amy Lee: I had to step away from being a rockstar." *LouderSound.com*. Nov 13, 2017. https://bit.ly/2LbZDiK

Titus, Christa. "Evanescence, *Fallen*: Classic Track-By-Track." *Billboard*. Mar 4, 2013. https://bit.ly/2KxdsHg

———. "Amy Lee on Being a Woman in Music: 'I Have Fought So Many Fights.'" *Billboard*. Nov 30, 2017. https://bit.ly/2GsZfc7

KAREN O

Battan, Carrie. "Yeah Yeah Yeahs." *Pitchfork*. Jan 14, 2013. https://bit.ly/2IQKpBp

Fitzmaurice, Larry. "5-10-15-20: Karen O." *Pitchfork*. Sep 11, 2014. https://bit.ly/2Kyyq8V

Goodman, Lizzy. *Meet Me in the Bathroom*. New York: Dey Street Books, 2017.

Hahn, Rachel. "Karen O Is Back With a Jaw-Dropping Performance Look." *Vogue*. Nov 8, 2017. https://bit.ly/2ItHlHV

Leonard, Marion. "The Riot Grrrl Network: Grrrl Power in Indie Rock." In *Gender in the Music Industry*. Abingdon, England: Routledge, 2007.

O, Karen. "Karen O: Soundtrack of my Life." *Guardian*. Aug 29, 2014. https://bit.ly/2LcXHX0

Perpetua, Matthew. "Karen O to Premiere 'Psycho-Opera' in Brooklyn." *Rolling Stone*. Aug 25, 2011. https://rol.st/2k7SdRp

Shteamer, Hank. "New York Kids: Julian Casablancas and Karen O interview each other." *Time Out New York*. Sep 23, 2014. https://bit.ly/2KyOnvB

GRACE POTTER

Gleason, Holly. "Grace Potter: Anything But Nocturnal." *Paste*. Aug 11, 2015. https://bit.ly/2rR6Ook

Hallenbeck, Brent. "Grace Potter on divorce, life and this weekend's Grand Point North Festival." *Burlington Free Press*. Sep 11, 2017.

Haller, Val. "If You Like Heart's Hard Rock . . ." *New York Times*. Oct 16, 2012. https://nyti.ms/2Ity2Ym

Harward, Randy. "Grace Potter Talks First Guitars, Nightmare Gigs and Her Beloved Flying V." *Guitar World*. July 27, 2016. https://bit.ly/2k76MEs

Niesel, Jeff. "Singer Grace Potter Ditches the 'Safety Blanket' of a Band and Issues Solo Debut." *Cleveland Scene.* Sep 29, 2015. https://bit.ly/2L9XnZp

Mettler, Mike. "Grace Potter takes a sonic road trip (but leaves the vinyl behind) on *Midnight.*" *Digital Trends.* Dec 11, 2015. https://bit.ly/2wzMxZt

"WEDDING: Grace Potter and Matthew Burr." *FishersIsland.net.* May 11, 2013. https://bit.ly/2IkuKXH

ST. VINCENT

Angle, Brad. "St. Vincent Talks New Album and Why She Wore a 'Bikini' on Her *Guitar World* Cover." *Guitar World*, February 2017. Posted to GuitarWorld.com, December 22, 2016. https://bit.ly/2KB5InP

Kot, Greg. "St. Vincent renews her music with 'technology detox.'" *Chicago Tribune.* Sep 29, 2011. https://trib.in/2IOVS4k

Lamont, Tom. "St Vincent: 'I'm in deep nun mode.'" *Guardian.* Aug 19, 2017. https://bit.ly/2ifhkmY

Monroe, Jazz. "Watch St. Vincent and Carrie Brownstein's Surreal Short Film Series." *Pitchfork.* Sep 4, 2017. https://bit.ly/2rFPwtH

Paumgarten, Nick. "Singer of Secrets." *New Yorker*, Aug 28, 2017. Posted to NewYorker.com, Aug 28, 2017, under title "St. Vincent's Cheeky, Sexy Rock." https://bit.ly/2gyz7kU

Snapes, Laura. "St. Vincent Is Telling You Everything." *BuzzFeed.* Sep 10, 2017. https://bzfd.it/2IuZll6

Wood, Mikael. "St. Vincent's new album is brilliant. But what about her concert to unveil it?" *Los Angeles Times.* Oct 8, 2017. https://lat.ms/2z8Q7H1

HAYLEY WILLIAMS

Connick, Tom. "Paramore's Hayley Williams responds to criticism of 'anti-feminist' 'Misery Business' lyrics." *New Musical Express.* July 31, 2017. https://bit.ly/2rRtWTS

Coscarelli, Joe. "Paramore Bounces Back with Old Faces and a New Sound." *New York Times.* Apr 19, 2017. https://nyti.ms/2oMEW3T

Dodson, Claire P. "Paramore's Hayley Williams On The Personal, The Political, and Getting 'Riled Up.'" *Fast Company.* Jan 9, 2018. https://bit.ly/2D0trxt

Frank, Alex. "Adult Emotions." *The Fader*, Summer Music Issue, July/Aug 2017.

"Hayley Williams on the Changing Perception of Women in Rock: 'It's Amazing to See.'" *The Rock Sound*, Summer 2016. Posted to RockSound.tv, July 22, 2016. https://bit.ly/2IboSni

Hogan, Marc. "Hayley Williams on Love, Haters, and 'Paramore's Soap Opera.'" *SPIN.* Mar 13, 2013. https://bit.ly/2k2zKFx

Idika, Nicky. "Why is Warped Tour Still a Bit Sh*t When it Comes to Women?" *PopBuzz.* July 11, 2016. https://bit.ly/2KWU731

Muller, Marissa G. "Paramore's Hayley Williams Talks Slaying Sexism, Her Oddest Tour Rider." *Rolling Stone.* Oct 11, 2013. https://rol.st/2GsOCpv

Sherman, Maria. "Hayley Williams is a Feminist, Says 'Misery Business' is Behind Her." *Fuse.* June 1, 2015. https://on.fuse.tv/2rEUnft

Wolfson, Sam. "Paramore: 'I've wanted to quit this band so many times.'" *Guardian.* Apr 22, 2017. https://bit.ly/2rTtkvZ

BRITTANY HOWARD

Charlton, Lauretta. "Alabama Shakes: 'There's No Way to Be Original.'" *Vulture.* June 12, 2015. https://bit.ly/2rDocvW

Felsenthal, Julia. "Alabama Shakes' Brittany Howard Makes Music That's All About the Music—And We Love Her for It." *Vogue.* Dec 12, 2015. https://bit.ly/2Ldgodu

Haney, Melissa L. "Meet Brittany Howard Of Alabama Shakes—The Coolest Woman in Music and Your New Fashion Inspiration." *Bustle.* Apr 29, 2015. https://bit.ly/2rEW38x

Howard, Brittany. "How Alabama Shakes Singer Brittany Howard Lives Her Best Life." By Arianna Davis. *O, The Oprah Magazine*, July 2013. Accessed on Oprah.com, May 18, 2018. https://bit.ly/2LbJ5HD

McGuinn, Jim. "What Bands Do on Their Days Off, or How I Ended Up Going Fishing with Alabama Shakes' Brittany Howard." *The Current.* June 1, 2015. https://bit.ly/2KWdMAw

Mervis, Scott. "Alabama Shakes Needed Break After Sudden Success." *Times Daily.* May 12, 2014. https://bit.ly/2GwHJDE

Peisner, David. "Muscle Shoals Revival: Alabama Shakes Take Off." *Rolling Stone.* Jan 24, 2012. https://rol.st/2Guqcfi

Reyna, Fabi. "Brittany Howard on Collaboration, Gear, and Making Up Your Own Chord Shapes." *She Shreds*, Nov 2016. Posted to SheShredsMag.com, Mar 29, 2017. https://bit.ly/2rQgYFF

Rodgers, D. Patrick. "Brittany Howard's Thunderbitch Unleashes Raw and Radical Debut Record." *Nashville Scene.* Aug 31, 2015. https://bit.ly/2Iz5wof

Rothbaum, Noah. "Eating on the Road With the Alabama Shakes." *Daily Beast.* May 30, 2017. https://thebea.st/2L1Kdxc

Russell, Kate. "BackTalk: Brittany Howard Of The Alabama Shakes." *Offbeat.* Mar 1, 2013. https://bit.ly/2rRBF4n

Vozick-Levinson, Simon. "Alabama Shakes' Brittany Howard on Jamming with Prince, Her Secret Identity." *Rolling Stone.* Dec 1, 2015. https://rol.st/2Gurkzy

INDEX

Note: Page numbers in **bold** indicate biographical sketches. Page references to photos indicate caption location.

PHOTO CREDITS